ANNA: 1

Ashutosh is one of Hindi journalism's best-known faces. He is currently managing editor at IBN7 and was an important member of the original Aaj Tak team, which revolutionized TV news.

ANNA

13 Days That Awakened India

Ashutosh

HarperCollins *Publishers* India
a joint venture with

THE
INDIA
TODAY
GROUP

New Delhi

First published in India in 2012 by
HarperCollins *Publishers* India
a joint venture with
The India Today Group

Copyright © Ashutosh 2012

ISBN: 978-93-5029-215-0

2 4 6 8 10 9 7 5 3 1

Ashutosh asserts the moral right to be identified as
the author of this work.

The views and opinions expressed in this book are the author's own
and the facts are as reported by him, and the publishers are not in any way
liable for the same.

HarperCollins *Publishers*
A-53, Sector 57, Noida 201301, India
77-85 Fulham Palace Road, London W6 8JB, United Kingdom
Hazelton Lanes, 55 Avenue Road, Suite 2900, Toronto, Ontario M5R 3L2
and 1995 Markham Road, Scarborough, Ontario M1B 5M8, Canada
25 Ryde Road, Pymble, Sydney, NSW 2073, Australia
31 View Road, Glenfield, Auckland 10, New Zealand
10 East 53rd Street, New York NY 10022, USA

Typeset in 10/12 Sabon Roman at
SÜRYA

Printed and bound at
Thomson Press (India) Ltd.

CONTENTS

FOREWORD BY ASHIS NANDY   vii

INTRODUCTION BY YOGENDRA YADAV   xiii

ANNA — THE UNKNOWN   1

CORRUPTION — THE CURSE   10

THE AWAKENING   19

THE NEW MAHATMA   26

THE EMPIRE FIGHTS BACK   43

THE FARCE THAT WAS RAMDEV   52

SONIA'S ABSENCE AND THE CONGRESS ARROGANCE   61

ANNA DETAINED   68

ANNA DEFIANT. PEOPLE FURIOUS   79

ANNA AT RAMLILA GROUNDS   92

OVERWHELMING SUPPORT   103

ANNA, RSS AND MUSLIMS   115

SIBAL UNWANTED   125

POWER STRUGGLE AND HIDDEN AGENDAS   137

DEADLOCK ENDS   148

RAHUL GANDHI – STAGE FRIGHT?   160

JUDGEMENT DAY   171

ANNA BREAKS HIS FAST   184

AFTER THE ANSHAN   202

EPILOGUE   215

ACKNOWLEDGEMENTS   225

FOREWORD

The Not–So–Strange Case of Anna Hazare

Who is Anna Hazare, where does he come from, and on what does he perch his political self? These questions are interrelated, but they are not the same.

Anna, we all know, comes from a small village in western India. He has even managed to put that village on the map of India. Many now know it by name. This is not as trivial a detail as it at first seems. The great protagonists of the Indian village, whether in competitive politics or in major non-party political movements identified with the interests of rural India have mostly come from cities. From Mohandas Karamchand Gandhi and Jayaprakash Narayan to their more modest followers such as Medha Patkar and Vandana Shiva it is the same story. It is only in recent decades that such protagonists have begun to actually come from villages. It is a bit like India's national game, cricket. Only in the last two decades has a section of the national team begun to come from where more than two-thirds of the nation live.

Hazare's background has created problems for us, not unlike the ones created by UP's present chief minister. While she comes from the underside of Indian society, Hazare comes from the periphery. They share a style and a language of politics that offend the mainstream, into which they, some feel, have gate-crashed. To a majority of well-educated ideologues, these actors in our public life look terribly unmanageable, unbelievably crude and inconsistent. They seem to lack correct ideology, vision and manners. Due to political exigencies, they sometimes become likeable to our newspaper-reading, television-watching public. This is considered forgivable as long as the spell lasts only for short stretches of time or when taken in homeopathic doses, otherwise not. Digvijay Singh's response to Anna is a good example. Singh is an accomplished politician; he does not hold office by virtue of being a technocrat, successful professional or retired civilian. Nor does he depend on the courtesy of leaders who have sizeable political bases. He has an independent support base. If he falters and stumbles when confronting Anna, we can imagine the plight of the amateur politicians who have entered politics with a different set of qualities, who have graduated to politics as first-class-first students or debating stars from prestigious colleges and see the public sphere as an arena where to display their virtuoso intellectual skills in front of an admiring audience.

The other question I have raised at the beginning is more important. What is the source of Anna's political strength? The answer to that is more complicated because Anna means different things to different sections of Indians. Ultimately, we are forced to admit that he is a creation of his admirers and detractors. Like all charismatic leaders, he is a projection of our yearnings and there could have been as many Annas as his fans and detractors.

Fortunately, his own rather limited personal and intellectual resources have reduced the range of choices in this matter. But that cannot wipe out the fact that India needed someone like him and it got him. Many in India were waiting impatiently for a figure like him to take up a cause that moved them but also made them feel dreadfully inefficacious and impotent. To deploy a cliché, if there was no Anna, they would have invented one so that they could, at the same time, pontificate on the subject of corruption and criticize his simple-mindedness, immaturity and double-faced choices.

Yet, corruption in India now touches not only the super rich and the *haute bourgeoisie*, but also the urban slum dwellers and the landless agricultural labourers. They too have the right to look at the problem their own way, using their own categories, however ill-formed and harebrained these categories might look to middle-class intellectuals. Only the politically myopic and the ideologically blinkered, with disdain for human subjectivities, will try to supply a purely socio-political and institutional explanation of Anna's rise and his esoteric, often self-defeating political style. The mix of inconsistency, naiveté, and oversimplification in his public utterances has been an inescapable part of Indian politics for nearly three decades. It supplies crucial clues to the protolanguage of India's new politics.

However, there is an apparent contradiction here. Anna seems to share – with many movements in areas such as environment, peace, human rights and alternative sciences in India – an open hostility to politicians. Opinion polls have repeatedly shown over the last two decades that the politicians occupy, along with the police and bureaucrats, the three least preferred occupations. This is not unique to India. The discomfort with and distrust of politics and politicians is gradually becoming a normal part of democratic politics in many parts of the world. Democratic politics requires politicians but we are also learning the hard way that democracies have to live with robust scepticism and suspicion of politics and politicians in the electorate.

As part of the same package, there is also the growing belief that elections are not won only through healthy competition and past political performance, but also through money power, cleverly made deals and opportunistic social coalitions. Some party systems have institutionalized these beliefs; they openly prefer candidates who can mobilize larger war booties. They see a large war chest as a measure of popularity and 'winnability'.

In India, however, this has gone further. Not only is it now mandatory for the losing parties to blame winners of vote-buying and poll-rigging, many have come to believe, despite all empirical evidence, that one can win elections by offering the poorer voters money, alcohol and fake promises. Anna openly shares these beliefs. Not much exposed to professional politics and political analyses, he picks up clues from popular beliefs and stereotypes and has turned them into an odd, rickety but nonetheless effective critical apparatus that has touched millions. Indeed, the more he falls back on that apparatus, the more he seems to be in touch with the people. Sophisticate journalists and political analysts might find his categories prejudiced, stereotypical and gossipy but these ideas are working among a large section of the people, waiting with a clear touch of despair, for some respite from omnipresent corruption and nepotism. (These ideas perhaps have also been strengthened by his long association with the army, as a relatively modest functionary. The culture of our army *does* encourage some undervaluation of civilian life as more wily, hard-eyed and corrupt.)

The more inane anti-political comments of Hazare come from his life experiences. He may not be the quintessential citizen of late twentieth-century India, but he *is* identifiably a product of his times and his life experiences. He has entered public life with much of his biases and easy judgements intact. That is his strength and, I must add, his weakness. He represents the anguish and the anxiety of ordinary citizens over the omnipresence and routinization of corruption and nepotism, but he perhaps lacks the robust scepticism, shrewdness and war-weary instinct for survival that has made the Indian voter what he or she is. He is unaware that the legitimacy of the democratic system in India is high precisely because, at the bottom and peripheries of the society and for millions of Indians at the receiving end of the system, the right to vote is an imperfect but powerful means protecting their political efficacy and ensuring social mobility. Democratic politics, with all its imperfections, has changed the fate of entire communities and it still remains the most potent pace-setting force in our society.

Perhaps I am not being fair to Anna Hazare. If he is that limited in his understanding of the vicissitudes of democratic politics, why is he spending so much of time and energy at his age not to lead a proper non-party movement but to get a particular law passed by a democratically elected Parliament? Why is he forcing the same politicians he considers ugly carpetbaggers to push his project through? Perhaps his instincts tell him what his analytic skills do not. In this respect, too, he is true to his time and location.

On the other hand, Indian democracy too knows how to use him. It has, if you forgive the anthropomorphism, used him to bring the issue of corruption centre-stage, despite the discomfort of parliamentarians and mainline parties with the idea of a powerful Lokpal or, for that matter, any form of an ombudsman outside their control. Ordinary citizens were given a glimpse of that discomfort by television channels when Lalu Prasad Yadav spoke against the Lokpal Bill in Parliament. The glee and the sense of relief at the honest-to-god stand of the former chief minister of Bihar was writ large on the face every parliamentarian irrespective of his or her party. Yet, despite all this, there is little chance of killing the bill altogether. Anna may have won, even by losing.

Indian democracy has also taught Anna, an unruly student of democratic politics if ever there was one, another lesson on the art of politics. In Indian politics it is always better to survive to fight another day than dream of a heroic victory with all your enemies lying prostrate at your feet. Just when his team had begun to proclaim from the housetops how easy it would have been for the Congress, with its stable parliamentary majority, to push through a proper Lokpal Bill, sections of the Opposition have conspired to show the knight on a white charger what most of his admirers outside his charmed circle knew all along. Corruption is a highly successful joint venture that conforms to an alternative, invisible set of rules faithfully and obediently. Indian politics not merely has its distinctive culture but also, as its underside, an unacknowledged, shadowy anti-culture.

The idea of a Lokpal Bill has been gathering dust in Parliament for forty years without giving any party sleepless nights. Within the period, not only the Indian National Congress, but the Bharatiya Janata Party, the many-splendored Janata Party of the post-Emergency days, and three other short-lived coalition governments ruled India. One of these coalitions even came to power using specifically the issue of corruption. None took the problem seriously; they all were complicit with the theft and they have had full cooperation from even some of our iconic business tycoons and financial institutions. It will not be a hyperbole to claim that the vivacity and energy of Indian democracy is now heavily dependent on large-scale, organized larceny and conmanship.

A politically less naive set of political reformers could have sensed the presence of ornate institutional structures and the strong psychological defences that protect the present culture of corruption and underwrite a resilient culture of impunity as part of everyday politics. A more alert set of reformers would have at least suspected that corruption is now an organized, well-entrenched principle of Indian democracy in its full glory. You cannot expect Indian democracy to retain its liveliness or vivacity without some scope for corruption. I sometimes suspect that to insist on zero corruption in India is to ensure the creation of a police state. India is not Singapore.

Perhaps, this is not a bad way to end this foreword and invite the reader to turn to this important book. Ashutosh is much younger than me and more optimistic. In his version of the story, Anna appears as a more likeable and well-crafted reformer fighting cynical, thin-lipped politicians calculating their gains and losses like so many chartered accountants. It is a patently honest account that, even within the hard realities of everyday politics, finds space for political ethics. If he seems less critical than he should be, it is because Ashutosh paradoxically rises above his profession to hold up Anna Hazare and his movement as a mirror to the tacit possibilities that are still open within our public life.

December 2011   ASHIS NANDY
                                        Centre for the Study of
                                    Developing Societies, Delhi

INTRODUCTION

Anna Hazare's fast and the huge groundswell of support it received represent a critical moment in our recent history. Anyone who lived through those momentous days at Ramlila Maidan will find it hard to disagree with this. There was an unmistakable sense of a profound transition, of witnessing the birth of a new yet unnamed energy. For a moment, rigid structures and sharp dividing lines turned labile. At the same time, anyone who has cared to reflect thereafter will find it equally hard to explain what it was all about. What exactly was critical about this movement?

When we stand so close to events that we analyse, there is a danger of slipping into hyperbole. Passionate admirers compared Anna to Gandhi or Jayaprakash Narayan. They called his movement the second freedom struggle. When Anna broke his fast, it was widely described as a historic moment, the beginning of the end of corruption in our country. The critics were no less passionate and over the top. They described Anna as fascist, his movement as anti-political and its confrontation with the government as blackmail of peoples' representatives by unelected and unelectable agitators. These passions have not died down. Anna and his movement are very much a living reality. The Lokpal Bill is still pending before Parliament. We may not have achieved the distance necessary to answer the question posed above.

The lack of an appropriate framework compounds this

difficulty. Underlying the partisan political dispute around Anna, there was a wider and deeper intellectual disagreement about how to assess a movement of this kind. To begin with, there was the factual dispute of whether the movement enjoyed popular support and if so among which sections. As always in political disputes, there were questions about the past and present linkages of the movement leaders to political parties and their affiliates. The factual dispute extended to a larger difference on cause–effect relationship: what was the role played by media in the making of the Anna phenomenon? This empirical and causal dispute was, of course, linked to a deeper difference at the normative and conceptual levels. What exactly are the norms of citizens' intervention in a parliamentary democracy? How does parliamentary supremacy square with popular sovereignty? And, finally, what are the appropriate conceptual tools with which to understand a movement like this one? What is 'civil society' in the Indian context and what role does it play? What is 'popular' or 'political'? Placing this movement in perspective presupposes an answer to all these questions.

Perhaps we can begin to move towards a sober answer by noting what was not critical about this movement. The people who gathered at Ramlila Maidan were unusually diverse and self-mobilized, but their sheer number was not unprecedented for the capital city. The issue of corruption in body politic was hardly novel. The element of innovation in the speeches, the slogans and the symbolism at the Ramlila Maidan were moderate at best. There was something fresh about coming out with a piece of legislation to take on the establishment, but the Jan Lokpal Bill invited as many questions as it answered. Besides, very few of Anna's followers had a clear sense of the exact provisions of the bill. Anna Hazare was a charismatic presence during those days, something new for the television-watching national public. But it is only fair to note that Anna Hazare has been around for a long time and has not been associated with this kind of charisma in the past. His colleagues, or 'Team Anna', did comprise many new faces and activists of extraordinary courage, integrity and imagination. Yet, such a combination is not unknown in the rich world of social movements in India.

Going by conventional political wisdom, this movement did not stand much of a chance. 'Anti-corruption' is a generic and vague issue that did not appeal to any one class. Jan Lokpal Bill was too technical a plank for a popular agitation. Nationalist language and symbols were out of place in an allegedly post-nationalist age. Invoking Gandhi was hardly a smart move in an age of sectional politics, if not a political liability. Besides, this movement did not have an organization or a cadre, nor a coherent political strategy. If any 'seasoned' political observer (including the present author, I must confess) was asked to assess the prospects of such an agitation, say at the beginning of 2011, the answer would have surely been dismal.

Yet, the movement succeeded, and how. When history does not take the turn that one expected, there is a temptation to deny, to suspect foul play or to hold a grudge against history. Most of the early critics of the Anna movement appear to have given in to one of these temptations. Hence the refusal to acknowledge the widespread popularity of the movement, despite overwhelming evidence of big self-mobilized crowds in big cities, smaller mobilizations in small towns and a fair degree of interest and some action in villages. The same appears to be the case with allegations about its being confined to the middle class or upper castes. No doubt, the movement shared its social profile with most other popular movements in the country that draw disproportionately from the better-off and more articulate sections of society. But to describe these as 'middle class' is to stretch the term to cover half of India's population.

This unlikely success of the movement led observers to believe that this was either a fluke or a grand conspiracy. Hence the frequent resort to blaming the RSS. It is natural that anyone opposed to the ruling establishment would wish to take advantage of such an opportunity; it would be surprising if the RSS did not do so. Yet, there is little evidence to suggest that the RSS guided or controlled the movement. The principal blame – or credit, depending on the vantage point – went to the media. The movement was presented as nothing but a media creation. Now, there is no doubt that media, especially 24x7 television, enabled the movement to cross the vital threshold of visibility and viability, sometimes at the cost of professionalism. Yet, once this threshold was crossed, the enthusiasm of the media and that of the public at large reinforced each other; the media could not have sustained such an all-out coverage in the absence of public response. In this sense, the media's response too should be seen as a part of public opinion.

As we gain some distance and perspective on the movement, one can hope that we will move beyond these early reactions and begin to entertain a troublesome thought: history did not obey us because there was something wrong in our reading of history. Perhaps there was something fundamentally wrong, not with history and its agents, but with its privileged interpreters. That is perhaps why the 'wise' got it wrong and those unencumbered by theories of social transformation managed to do something that was considered impossible. Perhaps the movement was not such a fluke after all. Perhaps a small band of energetic and focused activists managed to intuitively grasp something for which theorists do not have a name yet.

This perhaps is what makes the Anna movement a critical moment in the history of the present. In defying conventional wisdom and pre-existing lines of divisions, it marked a shift in the nature of public sphere in contemporary India and in the form of what we call politics. Though the gaze of the cameras was on Ramlila Maidan, the real theatre was outside the grounds and the capital. The movement signalled and perhaps constituted a new 'public' that was not connected by physical proximity and social bonds. Although Anna appeared the fountainhead of this public energy, he was as much a creation of his followers. Anna Hazare was just the pretext for everyone discovering an Anna within himself or herself. The movement was for a Jan Lokpal Bill, yet very few seemed to know about or care for the legal nuances. The movement was about holding an irresponsible and arrogant political establishment to account. Corruption was, no doubt, the central issue; anger against blatant corruption gave rise to the movement in the first place. Yet, the historic significance of the movement may not lie in what it did or did not do to fight against corruption in public life. It is too early to arrive at a judgement on that score, but the historical record of struggles against corruption has sobering lessons. But we do know that this movement enabled a large number of Indians, mostly young Indians, to make a transition from being mere subjects to being citizens. In the long run, the movement may prove critical in what it did to the nature and quality of democracy in India.

If there is any merit in thinking of the Anna Hazare movement as a 'critical' moment which invites us to rethink the framework through which we look at our present and future, we need to record its history meticulously for future generations. Unfortunately, this is one of the most neglected aspects of our intellectual life. Writing the history of the present often falls between two academic stools. Historians do not have the material they insist upon; political scientists do not have the method or the training. This gap needs to be filled by those who look at larger questions of our time from outside the disciplinary orthodoxies.

I am delighted that Ashutosh has accepted this challenge. He is widely respected in the journalistic community for his professional integrity as well as for his personal and intellectual courage. His passionate involvement and deep knowledge in reporting the Ramlila Maidan days were a source of inspiration and envy for many, including myself. As someone with intimate knowledge of Camp Anna and its critics, Ashutosh enjoys just the right vantage point to write about this movement. We should be grateful that he has taken time out of his editorial responsibilities to write this first draft of history. As the first of the many histories of the Anna movement that will no doubt follow, this well-timed and well-researched book will remain, I am sure, essential reading for any future historian of Indian democracy.

December 2011
YOGENDRA YADAV
Centre for the Study of
Developing Societies, Delhi

ANNA — THE UNKNOWN

'He has been discharged.'

'What?'

'Yes, he has been discharged. PTI has just flashed the news.'

'What are you saying? Where is the reporter? Where is Vikrant? Ask them to check. You guys don't keep track of anything,' I shouted at everyone in the newsroom. 'Find out and find out fast.'

Anna Hazare had been discharged from Medanta Hospital. You could feel the charge in our newsroom. But how was this possible? Just a few hours ago, Dr Trehan had told the press that Anna would take another four to five days to be fully fit. So what had happened? Had someone pulled a fast one on us?

'Please check, yaar,' I roared at the assignment desk. 'Ask Alok to check with the police. They must have an idea. They are sure to know where he is going.'

Meanwhile, Punit had called the assignment desk and confirmed the news. 'Yes, it is true. He has left the hospital. The police have also confirmed it.'

Alok showed me an SMS that a source had sent him. 'He has left for Delhi,' the SMS read.

But what had happened to Team Anna? Why couldn't we reach them? Arvind (Kejriwal) was not answering his phone. Manish's (Sisodia) phone was out of reach. Prashant (Bhushan) said he had no idea, he was at home. What was going on? Anyway, within minutes, the news was out on every channel.

1

'He had left the hospital by 7.15 p.m. through the back door, away from the television cameras,' the security in-charge of the hospital was heard saying. An enterprising gentleman had a few pictures of Anna getting into a car and we immediately put those on air. Now the big question was, where was he going? Was he going to Supreme Apartments in Mayur Vihar? Or to Kiran Bedi's house in Uday Park? These were the two places he stayed at whenever he was in Delhi.

'Please send reporters to both places. We can't afford to miss the visuals. Rush. Move both the OBs as well. It's a big story, you idiots.'

But why did he move out of the hospital? What was the hurry? And why isn't anybody from Team Anna picking up the damn phone? Too many questions and no answers.

Suddenly Rajdeep (Sardesai) called. 'He is going to the airport. He is catching the flight to Pune. He wants to be in Ralegan Siddhi, his native place, on Ganesh Chaturthi.' His Marathi connections had worked, I guessed.

I had no reason not to believe him. I still said, 'Check again, and also flash this information with a question mark: is he going to Ralegan?' Assignment was now in hyper-action mode. There is a flight to Pune at 9.10 p.m. I looked at the watch. It was 7.45 p.m. 'Let's put somebody on the same flight. Ask Punit to leave Medanta immediately and reach the airport. Somebody book his tickets.'

Now it was a race against time. We only had half an hour to organize things. Luckily there were still a few seats left on the flight. Two tickets were booked, one for the reporter and another for the cameraman. Would Punit reach the airport on time? I was keeping my fingers crossed. Everybody in the newsroom was praying. Still, there was no confirmation from Team Anna.

'Send two reporters and an OB to Ralegan from Mumbai. We have to plan big,' said somebody at the output desk.

'Yes,' was my immediate response.

'Punit has reached.'

'Great.'

Could he trace Anna at the airport? By now, the information had started coming in thick and fast. Contact had also been established with Team Anna. Now we were very sure that he was taking the 9.15 p.m. flight that would land in Pune around 11.10 p.m. He was to drive down to Ralegan straight from the Pune airport. But why, I wondered, were all the Team Anna phones out of reach?

The flight was ten minutes late. Punit was on the job. He boarded the flight, but Anna was not there. My heart sank. Had we been fooled? Time was running out and I felt desperate. Even on the plane, nobody had a clue that Anna would be travelling with them. The assignment desk was constantly in touch with Punit on the phone. He sounded nervous. '*Kuchh gadbad hai kya?*'(Is something wrong?) Poor fellow. It was his first outstation assignment.

It was almost 9 p.m. Anna should be on the flight anytime now. The prime time bulletin was about to go on air. Should we open the bulletin with Anna? We were in two minds. We had planned another story for prime time. No, we should start with Anna, I decided. These are the defining moments of television journalism, when editors have to use their judgement to take split-second decisions. We shall go ahead with the story of Anna's discharge from the hospital. 'Have Punit live on the phone, put two reporters live on air as well, one in Delhi reporting how Anna has left for the airport and another in Mumbai to inform viewers about Anna's plan and his eagerness to be with his own people in Ralegan Siddhi.'

Meanwhile, Punit's updates were all about Anna's absence on the plane. Had Anna escaped us? Had he taken an earlier flight? Punit got more nervous and the newsroom got more jittery.

Suddenly, I could feel the excitement from the other end of the phone. Yes, Anna was boarding the plane. He and his secretary boarded the flight. He looked tired. All the passengers were very excited. Anna was booked for seat number 19. But a front seat passenger got up and requested him to take his seat as it had more leg room. Anna accepted. Amidst all this, the captain announced Anna's arrival and welcomed him on behalf of the crew members and passengers. Before Anna could settle down, a few passengers shouted: '*Anna tum sangharsh karo, hum tumhare saath hain.*' (Anna fight on, we are with you.) Punit was on the phone, relaying the scene live. There was a lot of commotion on the plane as everyone tried to get a glimpse of Anna. As passengers shouted '*Vande Mataram*', Anna smiled, greeted everyone and settled down in the front seat. The gentleman who was the original occupant of that seat was greatly thrilled. Punit was busy with his live commentary and the cameraman was also busy capturing these historic moments. Punit handed over his cellphone to a passenger and the anchor in the studio asked him how he was feeling. 'Great man. I am lucky to see him now, I have seen him only on TV so far.' Viewers could hear the excitement in his voice. Another passenger was a bit calmer. He seemed well educated, in his mid-thirties and could only say, 'I have not seen God, but I have seen Anna.' The camera was rolling and everything was being recorded. I could not believe this. The flight was about to take off. Punit had to switch off his phone as per aviation norms. But that mild-mannered man's words kept replaying in my mind, 'I have not seen God, but I have seen Anna.' And to think that just four months ago almost no one outside of Maharashtra had heard of Anna!

I still remember my editorial meeting of 4 April 2011. Anna was arriving in Delhi that morning.

'What are we planning?' I asked. 'How are we going to cover this?'

Senior editors seemed to have no interest. 'Anna is holding a press conference, we will send a reporter.'

I was a little upset. 'He is seventy-four years old and sitting on a fast unto death. If something happens to him, the government could be in jeopardy. Manmohan Singh will have to resign. Don't take it lightly. Send somebody immediately, get a short interview done, and find out his plan. What are his issues?' At that point, even I knew very little about him.

Anna's given name is Keshav Baburao Hazare. An ex-army man, he hasn't studied beyond VII standard. He fought in the war against Pakistan in 1965. Apparently, he was shot while driving his truck across the war zone. 'He was lucky to survive,' was the popular saying in his village, Ralegan Siddhi, in Ahmednagar, Maharashtra. Once he retired from the army, he took up social service as a mission and decided to change the face of his village. Ralegan Siddhi had two major problems – one, there were thirty-four liquor shops in the village and its vicinity, and two, there was an acute scarcity of water. He organized the people of Ralegan Siddhi and transformed the village without any outside support. Ralegan Siddhi is now considered Maharashtra's model village. There is not a single liquor shop and the per capita income is at par with Delhi. Now there is enough water in the village to grow a water-absorbent crop like onion in abundance. People no longer remember Anna by his given name. He is Anna, elder brother. It is said that, for the last thirty-five years, he has not gone home though all his relatives live nearby. He has never married and lives in the village temple. 'I live in a small room, I have a *khat* to sleep on and a plate to eat from. *Mere jeevan me ek bhi daag nahi hai* (My life is pristine, without a single stain),' he had proudly declared in one of his speeches. 'I have dedicated my entire life to the betterment of society. *Tyag jeevan ka mool mantra hai* (Sacrifice is the core of life).' Anna's clean-up drive was in no way restricted to his village alone. Six ministers had to resign due to his various *anshans* (hunger strikes) and the Government of Maharashtra has created a department exclusively for him – the *Anna Prakoshth*, under the direct supervision of a principal secretary. At regular intervals the government reaches out to him. Every government in Maharashtra wants to keep him in good humour.

So when I heard that he was coming to Delhi for a fast unto death, I could sense trouble for the Central government.

Meanwhile my research team came back with some information about his plans. I was told that, on 26 February 2011, he had made his intentions very clear in a press conference, warning that if the prime minister did not decide to include members of the civil society in the drafting of the bill to curb corruption in public life, he would sit on a fast unto death.

This bill was to establish a Lokpal to keep an eye on corruption. Anna was mighty upset that the prime minister had not responded to the many letters that had been sent to his office in this regard. Anna's ultimatum had the desired result. On 3 March, Manmohan Singh invited him for a discussion. On 7 March, Anna and other members of the civil society met the PM. The very next day, Manmohan Singh constituted a committee to look into the matter. This did little to help matters. Civil society members were not happy with the committee's attitude and made it known that on 28 March Anna would go ahead with his fast.

The Manmohan Singh government was already in deep trouble. The man who had been credited with freeing the Indian economy from the morass of the quota-permit raj, who had successfully implemented the economic vision of the then prime minister Narasimha Rao and revolutionized the sick Indian economy, the man who is considered to be the cleanest politician the country has ever had, was now being accused of presiding over the most corrupt government post independence. In his first innings as prime minister, the country saw an unprecedented growth of nine per cent. India became a model for the rest of the world for the way it handled the recession. US President Barack Obama said, 'The whole world listens very carefully when Manmohan Singh speaks.' India was touted as the next big phenomenon in world economy and it was predicted that by 2050 India would emerge as the third biggest economy in the world after the United States and China. Now the same Manmohan Singh, the darling of the urban middle class, was trying to save himself and his government from the demons of corruption.

Looking back, it all started with one tweet from Lalit Modi, which questioned the holding pattern of the Kochi team in the Indian Premier League (IPL) and obliquely referred to the name of then minister of state for foreign affairs, Shashi Tharoor, as a beneficiary through Sunanda Pushkar, his girlfriend of the time, now wife. This resulting furore and revelations ended in Tharoor's resignation from the cabinet and Modi's flight from the country to avoid being hounded by investigating agencies. Modi was then the uncrowned king of the IPL and the golden boy of Indian cricket. He was spoken of as the genius who revolutionized world cricket, bringing the excitement back to cricket with his idea for a Twenty20 league and his robust marketing. Tharoor, former undersecretary general of the United Nations, who unsuccessfully contested for the post of secretary general of the UN, losing to Ban Ki Moon, was tipped to be the next big personality in Indian politics, and a potential foreign minister. He is relatively young, well read, urbane and handsome – a challenge to the stereotypical image of the Indian politician. But one tweet finished his career, and subsequently Modi's, as the media lapped up the controversy and kick-started an aggressive campaign, forcing the Manmohan Singh government to seek Tharoor's resignation.

This was the turning point in TV news coverage. TV had tasted blood and there was no looking back. TV news channels, specially the Hindi channels, which were synonymous with *bhoot-pret*s and mumbo-jumbo, and stories of snakes and rebirths, had little credibility. With its newly acquired confidence, TV turned its heat on the Central government. Scams began to surface one after the other, whether it was the Commonwealth Games (CWG) or the Adarsh Society scam, the 2G scam, or Spectrum allocation. The allegation of volume of money swindled was mind-boggling. If the Commonwealth Games scam was alleged to the tune of Rs 70,000 crores, the 2G broke all records with Rs 176,000 crores. Spectrum allocation figures touched Rs 200,000 crores. Suresh Kalmadi, Ashok Chavan and A. Raja became the new symbols of this new large-scale corruption. Raja and Kalmadi had to go to jail, as did Karunanidhi's daughter Kanimozhi. Chavan was sacked as chief minister of Maharashtra. Many top officials had to languish in jails. Ex-army and navy chiefs' names also appeared in relation to various scams. With a new Chief Justice, the Supreme Court had acquired renewed strength and power. Constitutional agencies like the Comptroller and Auditor General (CAG) too had become freshly assertive.

At first, nobody questioned Manmohan Singh. Everybody agreed that he was an honest man with impeccable credibility but as the campaign in the media snowballed and parties in the Opposition began reacting with increased belligerence, fingers were slowly raised at him as well. Questions were asked as to how he could let the CWG scam happen when the prime minister's office (PMO) was monitoring the whole thing. Why did he not stop Raja from doing what he did? Nobody accused him of complicity, but the impression gaining ground was that he was a weak prime minister who had no control over his cabinet, that he was guilty of inaction. He could be removed, was the talk in the corridors of power.

So Team Anna's declaration of a fast unto death at Jantar Mantar added to Manmohan Singh's woes. But it was not considered a big enough threat as the media was preoccupied with other, more important things, like the cricket World Cup and India's post victory euphoria. The government was also relaxed as no untoward incident had happened during the night of the victory, despite the madness on the roads. (It is rumoured that Sachin Tendulkar and Mahendra Singh Dhoni were slightly disappointed that there was no victory procession.) Overall, there was a very positive mood across the country. Cricket had helped people to forget momentarily the monster of corruption and *Mehengai Daiyan*. In the midst of the celebration and the resurgent nationalism it engendered, the announcement on 28 March was lost. People also did not take much notice when on 4 April Anna confirmed his resolve to go ahead with his fast in a press conference at the Press Club of

India. Civil society members confirmed to me that they also had no high hopes of the *anshan*. They were expecting, at the most, a thousand people to gather at Jantar Mantar and were solely relying on the strength of the Right to Information (RTI) activists.

To begin with, Anna was not very excited about the idea of sitting on a dharna in Delhi. He was not sure about people's response to his *anshan*. When this proposal was mooted, he had suggested to his followers that he could easily organize a decent crowd of a few hundred in Maharashtra. Delhi was new ground. He was hardly known outside Maharashtra and had never sat on dharna outside the state. But when Arvind explained to him the rationale that corruption was an all-India issue and that it was important to attract national attention to this issue, he reluctantly agreed. He had never failed with his protests until now and Anna did not want to lose this latest battle. It was a risk for him. Team Anna, though was relying on the fact that more than 20,000 people had assembled at Ramlila Maidan (as per Delhi Police assessment) when members of the civil society had organized their first rally on 30 January, but that was not Anna's show. Baba Ramdev was the main draw for the crowd. On that occasion, not more than 5,000 people were expected, so a 20,000 strong crowd was a major boost. Manish Sisodia, a core committee member of Team Anna, later confessed that it was the unexpected turnout at the Ramlila rally that gave them the confidence to build a movement against corruption. They were of the opinion that if they could mobilize properly, people would turn up in large numbers to protest. But even they had no idea about just how big all this would turn out to be.

CORRUPTION — THE CURSE

The news room was abuzz with curiosity and scepticism. Samajwadi Party leader Amar Singh, best known for cavorting with Bollywood stars, was to appear before the judge in a cash-for-vote case in the trial court. Everybody was guessing – bail or jail? Public confidence in the judiciary was at a high, but we journalists are of a different mettle altogether. We don't look at things straight. We are trained to read between the lines. So nobody was sure if Amar Singh would meet the same fate as Suresh Kalmadi or A. Raja. 'He is too smart a politician, he has contacts in all the right places; most well-networked leader,' was the general refrain in the newsroom. Meanwhile, I had to leave to interview Arvind for the prime time bulletin. As I was coming back, news started trickling in that Amar Singh might be in a soup. I was still not convinced. I reached office. The 3 p.m. editorial meeting was on and, as I was a little late, I was quickly briefed about the stories planned for the second half of the day. Suddenly Kiran screamed '*Amar Singh ko jail ho gayee hai*' (Amar Singh has been sentenced to a prison term) and rushed to the assignment desk. It took us a few moments for that to sink in, and then the rest of us ran out too to see those eagerly awaited visuals: Amar Singh being shoved into a police van to be taken to Tihar Jail.

Amar Singh had tried his best to hoodwink the trial court. He made a last-ditch effort. 'I am living on borrowed kidneys and need round-the-clock medical surveillance,' he told Special

10

Judge Sangeeta Dhingra Sehgal. But she remanded him to judicial custody till 19 September. What looked impossible a few months ago was a reality now. I could sense jubilation in the media and also a sense of relief that it had finally been proven that nobody was above the law. '*Achha hua*' (great going) was written all over the faces around me. I was not surprised at all. Amar Singh symbolized all that that was wrong with Indian politics. Even after fifteen years, it is fresh in my memory how my previous editor S.P. Singh (of Aaj Tak) had scolded me when I – then a rookie reporter – had come back with Amar Singh's byte. Amar Singh had recently joined Mulayam Singh Yadav's Samajwadi Party. S.P. Singh shouted at me, '*Kis dalaal ki byte lekar aa gaye ho, tumko koi politician nahi mila Mulayam ki party mein?*' (Did you not find any politician in Mulayam's party that you have brought me a byte of this middleman?) It was getting late but SP, as he was referred to, refused to use his byte in the story. I had no other option but to go back and get a reaction on camera from Ram Gopal Yadav. SP was an editor of a different era. A few years later, Amar Singh was all over the place and it was impossible to think of Indian politics without him.

In SP's eyes Amar Singh was not a politician. Anna's *anshan* and the popular support that he garnered was a reaction to that kind of politics, a politics that refused to be responsive to, and representative of, people's will and aspirations. Politics became a fixer's game, cut off from the roots. Instead of nurturing the constituency and serving people in order to win elections, politicians just bribed their constituency and their colleagues. Crores were spent; voters were lured with liquor bottles. Amar Singh never contested elections, but was the most powerful leader in the Samajwadi Party, second only to Mulayam Singh Yadav. Seasoned campaigners like Beni Prasad Verma, Azam Khan and Raj Babbar had to leave the party. Old horses like Janeshwar Mishra were sidelined so that their presence was meaningless in party matters. Amar Singh used to boast that he could fix anybody either by hook or by crook. He even dared to intimidate the higher judiciary. Supreme Court judges were not spared. Audio and video tapes were very effectively used to silence his adversaries. A recent example is the audio tape of a conversation between Shanti Bhushan and Mulayam Singh Yadav, which was alleged to be the handiwork of Amar Singh. His own taped conversation, which is in the public domain, exposes a sad picture of Indian politics. He told me once that the chair I was sitting in was customized to conduct sting operations! The minute someone sat down, the recording would begin. For him, buying and selling MPs and MLAs was a matter of great pride. So I was not surprised when his name figured in the cash-for-vote sting operation which finally proved to be his nemesis. But I must admit he was always candid about these things. He never tried to hide his true colours; if anything, he would freely boast about it in private. But on record he used to say, 'Media will continue to project me as a power broker though I am the National General Secretary of the Samajwadi Party.' (*Hindustan Times*, 7 May 2011)

But to blame only Amar Singh for the malaise in the Indian democracy would be to ignore the larger picture. He was a product of the system that we created in the last six decades. Yes, it does go back that far. Mahatma Gandhi – unhappy with the conduct of Congress ministers – proposed disbanding the Congress as a political party after independence. He was of the opinion that the Congress had outlived its utility as a political party now that independence had been achieved. C. Rajagopalachari, an eminent leader of the freedom struggle, wrote in his book, *How to Save Indian Democracy from Money Power*, 'Gandhiji wished to spiritualize politics.' In his opinion, Gandhiji was of the firm view that we are not capable of keeping politics and morality separate (N. Vittal, *Corruption in India*, p. 52). Gandhiji wanted to rebuild politics based on a true and reliable foundation: individual honesty. The individual honesty to which Gandhiji referred started disappearing from both private as well as public lives. This process was slower during the first two decades after independence. But the political and the national character of India changed dramatically with the emergence of Mrs Indira Gandhi. Due to her inherent insecurity, Mrs Gandhi did not let any person or institution grow beyond a point. Pranay Gupte quotes Romesh Thapar (Mrs Gandhi's friend and advisor) in his book *Mother India: A Political Biography of Indira Gandhi*, 'When she died, she left nothing, she left nothing behind of any redeeming value.' According to Gupte, Thapar told him that Mrs Gandhi 'tried to destroy our Parliament, our judiciary, our press, and she tried to undermine the states, particularly the states ruled by the Opposition parties' (p. 376). Gupte further quotes Thapar, 'If you looked at the scene even before the assassination, you could see that Indian states were highly disturbed over the concentration of power in Delhi' (p. 377).

It was this concentration of power which created an atmosphere where men with honesty and character were not welcome and were slowly pushed to the margins by a political class which was thriving only due to Mrs Gandhi's patronage. Political workers were replaced by political *chamchas* and these political *chamchas* subordinated all the structures of power. They were out to make money and found the bureaucracy willing too. The JP movement, like Anna's *anshan*, was a reaction to this systemic failure of the Indian democracy. Bipan Chandra writes in his book *India After Independence 1947–2000*, 'the government's capacity to redress the situation was seriously impaired by the growing corruption in most areas of life and the widespread belief that the higher levels of the ruling party and administration were involved in it' (p. 247). He adds, 'The whiff of corruption touched even Indira Gandhi when her inexperienced younger son, Sanjay Gandhi, was given a licence to manufacture 50,000 Maruti cars a year.'

Like Anna's call for the second freedom struggle from the dais of Ramlila Maidan, JP (as Jayaprakash Narayan was called) had also given a call for Total Revolution. Chandra defines this as 'a struggle against the very system which has compelled almost everybody to go corrupt' (p. 248). Sanjay Gandhi epitomized that system. He had no respect for democracy, he was dictatorial by nature, treated senior leaders and ministers like they were his servants, and was contemptuous of all kind of institutions – for him, the public was there to be ruled over. But the roots of Indian democracy were not yet so weak that mother and son could trample over them without consequences. Indian democracy could rejoice when, despite her dictatorial tendencies and corrupt political practices, Mrs Gandhi had to revoke the Emergency and call for elections, which she lost badly, leading to the formation of the first non-Congress government at the Centre. The Janata Party government, however, did not survive long due to its own contradictions and the electorate was so severely disappointed that it went back to the same Mrs Gandhi who only a few years ago had denied them their basic civil rights. If the Janata Party government had survived, the nature of the political class might have been different today. But this failure had given a new lease of life to the forces created by Mrs Gandhi and Sanjay Gandhi. The process continued and the possibility of reform within the system died prematurely.

Rajiv Gandhi was a breath of fresh air. The whole nation was optimistic about an impression that was reinforced by his famous statement in Mumbai that only fifteen paise reached the poor out of every rupee sent by the Central government. I was very young then. But even I had begun to dream afresh. He was called Mr Clean. But the system proved to be more powerful than the good intentions of a young prime minister. I had a rare opportunity to interact with Rajiv Gandhi when he was out of power, just before his death, and I can say with confidence that he had become much wiser then. He was conscious of his mistakes and was determined not to repeat them. He knew how he was misled by his selfish friends and petty politicians. He was no Sanjay Gandhi and was not a clone of Mrs Gandhi either. I felt he genuinely wanted to do the best for the country. He had a dream. But, unfortunately, he did not live to correct his mistakes and while he will be remembered as the man who unleashed the technological revolution in the country, he will also go down in history as the man who could not defend himself in the face of allegations that he was involved in the Bofors scandal. When Bofors hit India, I was a student. V.P. Singh turned Bofors into a very effective campaign against corruption in high places. People believed him. He became the new Mr Clean. The urban middle class was as crazy about him then as it is about Anna today. People were shouting '*Raja nahi fakeer hai, desh ki takdeer hai*' (He is not a king but a monk, he is the destiny of our country) all over India. His campaign against corruption was as effective as the JP movement. If in 1977 Mrs Gandhi lost her election badly, so did her son in 1989. For both, the mother and the son, corruption was the nemesis. But despite the decisive defeats of two prime ministers, the monster called corruption grew stronger and stronger because those who replaced them were worse than their predecessors.

So I was not surprised when, in the 1990s, lawyer Mr Ram Jethmalani accused the then prime minister Narasimha Rao of accepting one crore rupees from a scamster like Harshad Mehta. Narasimha Rao was a wily politician. He was running a minority government and his rivals, like Arjun Singh and Sharad Pawar, were always baying for his blood. It was the most turbulent phase in Indian politics. Communal and casteist forces were never so powerful. At stake was the idea of India. Rao had no charisma. Machiavellian politics was his only option. For the first time in the Indian parliamentary system, he experimented with the low tactics that were rampant at the state level. The Jharkhand Mukti Morcha (JMM) episode became a classic example of how to save a minority government by bribing members of Parliament (MPs). Although the bribery was proved in court, the Supreme Court decided not to interfere with the inner functioning of the Parliament. Therefore, Team Anna was not wrong in demanding that MPs be made accountable for their deeds. If history remembers Narasimha Rao as the prime minister who scripted a new chapter through economic liberalization, history will also not forget him as the person who got the who's who of Indian politics tangled in the Hawala scandal. Though the Hawala investigation reached a dead end, to date nobody knows what really happened. Was the Central Bureau of Investigation (CBI) used for political purposes to serve a political end? I never found a satisfactory answer and that is also the reason why I support Team Anna when they demand that the CBI should be freed from governmental control. As a fallout of the the Hawala case, and following the judgment of the Supreme Court in the Vineet Narain case, the Central Vigilance Commission (CVC) was created to monitor the functioning of the CBI. But is the CBI truly beyond the control of the political masters?

If the Vajpayee government had a Bangaru Laxman and a Dileep Singh Judeo, Manmohan Singh can boast of A. Raja, Suresh Kalmadi and Ashok Chavan. If the Vajpayee government had *Tehelka* and the petrol pump scam, Manmohan Singh has 2G and CWG. They might have flags of different colours, but the fact is that the political class in this country has the same colour. With every subsequent government, corruption becomes more and more entrenched. And this system has become so powerful that even clean and spotless prime ministers like Atal Bihari Vajpayee and Manmohan Singh appear helpless. Coalition politics has sharpened this process further – the political class indulges in unprecedented corruption as a weak Centre becomes a mute spectator to political blackmails for the survival of the government. A. Raja at the Centre and the Reddy brothers in Karnataka are classic examples. Someone like Amar Singh was so powerful because he knew that even one MP could destabilize the government and, at the same time, the crafty use of money could save it too. The 1998 Vajpayee government will always be remembered as the government that lost the majority in Parliament by just one MP.

Anna did not commit the mistake that JP and V.P. Singh did.

Like a good student, he had learnt his lessons from history. He declared that he was not here to change the government, as demanded by JP and V.P. Singh, but to change the system because if this government has a master's degree in corruption then the next would have a doctorate in it. The collective outpouring of people's emotions in the Ramlila Maidan and on the roads was an angry outburst against years of disgusting politics. All the while that I was at the Ramlila Maidan, hundreds of people came to me, registering their revolt against the political class. '*Ye sab chor hain*' (All of them are thieves). '*Ye sirf apna pet aur apni tijori bharna jante hain*' (They are only concerned about themselves and want to amass wealth for their families). '*Sab dalaal hain, desh bech denge*' (All of them are wheeler-dealers, they will sell this country). '*Bhrasht neta aur bhrasht afsar is desh ko ghun ki tarah kha rahe hain*' (The collusion of corrupt leaders and officers are eating this country like termite). This feeling intensified in the last one-and-a-half years with the daily exposé of scams in the media. Arvind, the architect of Anna's *anshan*, told me that the everyday front-page news about the Commonwealth Games scam had forced him to think about finding a permanent solution to this national disease.

It is in this spirit that on 8 August a few prominent citizens of this country got together at the India International Centre and discussed the matter, hoping to find a solution. Santosh Hegde, Shekhar Singh, Prashant Bhushan, Nikhil Dey, Shanti Bhushan, J.M. Lyngdoh, etc., tried to prepare a draft paper. The Lokpal Bill was seen as one such solution. This initiative gained further momentum on 19 September, when the National Council for People's Right to Information (NCPRI), led by Aruna Roy, discussed forming a subcommittee to deal with corruption and the proposed whistle-blower bill, which was considered weak. Arvind was the chairperson of this committee. Prashant Bhushan, Nikhil Dey, P.M. Bhatt and Shekhar Singh were the other members. Santosh Hegde was also consulted. And thus the first draft of the Jan Lokpal Bill was born.

This draft was sent to Nikhil Dey who was the convenor of the draft committee. Arvind wanted to push the draft fast and put pressure on the government to adopt it as Lokpal bill but Aruna Roy and her followers were not in hurry. They wanted to take up the matter with the government after the assembly elections in five states – West Bengal, Kerala, Assam, Tamil Nadu and Puducherry – which was scheduled in April–May. Arvind did not want to wait so he split with them and found his own team. Arvind was convinced that a movement was needed, collaboration with government would not work.

The idea was that corruption was too deep-rooted and needed a systemic remedy to break the dangerous nexus of politicians and bureaucracy. In their opinion, the Right to Information (RTI) Act was a great effort to expose corruption at all levels, but did not provide a solution to the problem. When queries were raised through the RTI, the bureaucracy was forced to act, but there was no guarantee that this would bring about systematic reform. The victims had the information they wanted, but what was to be done with the information? What was the next step? That was begging an answer. RTI activists like Arvind and Manish were often very frustrated. In the Jan Lokpal Bill, they found an answer.

THE AWAKENING

Arvind was in touch with Anna. He got to know that Anna had taken a vow of silence, *maunvrat*, and he would be breaking his silence on 10 February. Anna was also upset with the government's attitude. According to a senior member of the team, Anna had written a letter to the prime minister in the first week of December 2010 but had got no response. In his letter, he had talked about the rampant corruption in the government and stressed that a strong law was needed to eradicate this menace. Anna, in his letter, also proposed that the Lokpal Bill could be an effective instrument to fight corruption. He waited for an acknowledgement and when he did not receive any, he decided that he would sit on dharna. After Anna broke his silence, he spoke at length with Arvind and hinted that *anshan* was the only way out. That was Anna's own instinctive decision. But before he could embark on this new crusade, he wanted to consult his team and followers in Maharashtra, his original *karmabhoomi*. He has a well-oiled machine of supporters and he has also appointed his own coordinators in every block of every district in Maharashtra to fight corruption. On 12 February he called a meeting of the block coordinators. In the meeting, the issue was discussed threadbare. For Anna it was a big decision, because this time he needed to step outside his comfort zone and grab national attention – ignite the national imagination against the national phenomenon that is corruption and to look for a national solution to this problem.

Until then he had taken on only individual cases of corruption. In Maharashtra he had a strong following. He was born and brought up in the Marathi culture. He was well versed with the nuances of governance and administration there. He was aware that he knew very little of the world outside the state and that he himself was not well known outside it. Moreover, his interaction with what would go on to become Team Anna had also been very limited till then. He hardly knew them. He had had occasional meetings with Arvind in the past. But the bigger question was, could he trust them? Could he trust a new team of strangers, in a strange territory? He was confident of himself, but could he place the same confidence in these new set of people? What was the guarantee that they would be equally strong-willed and would not leave him midway or be lured or intimidated by the might of the government? This was no ordinary government. Till then Anna had fought the state government, but fighting the Central government was a different ball game altogether. He had dealt with the likes of Sharad Pawar, Vilas Rao Deshmukh, Narain Rane, Manohar Joshi, Gopinath Munde. All of them are only regional heavyweights except Sharad Pawar, who has a presence in the Centre too. But in Delhi he had to face the top political brains and the mightiest of politicians and ministers. Sonia Gandhi, Manmohan Singh, Pranab Mukherjee, P. Chidambaram, Kapil Sibal, as well as his old foe Sharad Pawar, and a host of others. And all of his comrades-to-be spoke different languages and came from different cultures. So it was not an easy decision for Anna. At stake was his hard-earned reputation built over almost forty years.

Anna is not a professional politician in the strict sense of the word. He is a man driven by his own passion and a sense of his own righteousness. He carefully listened to his well-wishers in the meeting and then decided to go for the kill. On 12 February 2011 he called Arvind and agreed to work with them. Now there was no looking back. In the last week of February, Anna wrote another letter to the prime minister reminding him about the last letter and requesting a response. According to Arvind, 'Anna was very critical of the government's effort to make a weak Lokpal Bill and demanded that members of the civil society should be incorporated in the drafting of a strong bill.' Anna's second letter warned the government that if his demands were not met, he would be left with no other option but to sit in a dharna. This had the desired result. The prime minister proposed to meet them on 7 March. A team comprising Arvind, Swami Agnivesh, Kiran Bedi, Prashant Bhushan, Manish and Anna went for the meeting on the designated date. According to a senior member of the team, 'The attitude of the government was not very positive.' The prime minister suggested that they meet the group of ministers with their suggestions because, institutionally, that is the body empowered to make suggestions to the cabinet on the shape of a bill that is to go before the Parliament. He also made it clear that this would take time as assembly elections in West Bengal, Tamil Nadu, Assam and Kerala were due. After the elections he promised to expedite the matter. Team Anna smelt a rat. In their opinion, it was an attempt on the part of the government to checkmate them and dilute the bill. Anna was convinced that they were not being taken seriously and the time had come to deliver a strong message to the government.

It was now time for Team Anna to sit down and decide the date, strategize and fine-tune the preparations for the battle. The first of April was the date proposed for the *anshan* and Jantar Mantar was chosen as the location. Later, they postponed the date to 5 April for two reasons. One, 1 April being All Fools' Day, there was a possibility that people might think the whole thing was a prank. Two, the Cricket World Cup final was scheduled for 2 April. If India won, nobody would take note of their *anshan* and the entire effort could go waste. In hindsight, the postponement was a smart move as Team India did indeed win the World Cup and the euphoria which it created on the streets across India also helped Team Anna at a subliminal level. The swelling, aspirational middle class of

India wants to be noted and recognized. The World Cup victory was a great boost to their new confidence and pride. An exuberant exhibitionism was evident, like painting the tricolour on the face, wearing tricolour T-shirts and caps, waving national flags in stadia, hosting flags on their houses and cars – all manifestations of this newly acquired muscular sense of nationalism. It was for this reason that, after the victory, Mumbai was choked for hours in the dead of night. You could see Aamir Khan and the who's who of Mumbai in the stadium, getting excited and depressed with every turn of the match. It is no coincidence that Aamir Khan was there, many days later, on the dais, when Anna was to make the declaration about breaking his fast. The entire Ramlila Maidan was flooded with national flags. In fact, I have never seen so many tricolours in a political rally or any *morcha*. So very subtly something got transferred from the Wankhede Stadium to the Ramlila Maidan.

But that was to happen in the future; at the moment I was discussing earlier, Team Anna's main concern was how to make their presence felt. They were not sure of success at all. They had a strategy to mobilize people in both the physical as well as the virtual spaces. Shivendra, the tech-savvy member of India Against Corruption, had opened up an altogether new world for them. Shivendra told me that the 30 January rally and the response generated towards it through Facebook was a great morale booster. In that rally Anna was not an active participant though he had supported the cause. Anna's participation was a new element for mobilization, particularly in the virtual space. He immediately got cracking. This time he added Twitter too. His brief was very clear – to connect 300 cities. Shivendra's earlier experience came in handy this time round. By now, he had a strong social media community that was a willing cadre for the issue. The idea was to expand this community. Earlier, Shivendra had posted anti-corruption messages on the 'India against Corruption' page, for example, 'Is there anyone in Pune who will fight against corruption?' and invited reactions. Those who reacted were later contacted on the phone. Efforts were made to motivate them to be volunteers in this campaign but not without proper screening so as to avoid unscrupulous elements who could give them a bad name later. The focus was on quality, not on quantity. Volunteers included a senior software engineer at Infosys, a professor from Allahabad University, a vice-president in GE Company, etc. A few of them immediately loved the idea and promised to do what they could. When they were requested to add ten more for the protest, they added fifty. But there were also a few who preferred to be active on Facebook and refused to play the game offline. Those who became volunteers were assigned different tasks. A few had shown leadership qualities and were willing to go an extra mile to take the concept further; depending upon their capabilities they were asked to organize fasts, rallies, marches and assemblies. But all of them had to work within the basic parameters of the philosophy of the agitation. A guideline was prepared for such volunteers. The dos and the don'ts were circulated. It was part of the bigger strategy that no provocative slogans would be allowed. Slogans and speeches had to be secular in nature. No donations would be accepted. Funds would be organized from their own contributions. And at all costs the movement has to be peaceful, non-violent and inclusive.

A young woman volunteer offered to explore and widen the scope on Twitter. This girl from Mumbai wanted to be part of the movement, but on the condition that her name would not be disclosed at all, which was respected. There were a few who were already running anti-corruption and anti-graft campaigns on the web in their individual capacity, like 'Youth for Better India' in Hyderabad. Such websites were also integrated in the scheme of things. This had a multiplier effect. A friend in Mumbai advised Arvind that SMS could be of great use. In his opinion it would be slightly expensive but very effective. Immediately, a plan was made to connect with one crore people through SMS. Anti-corruption messages were sent to people with a request that if they felt that corruption should be eradicated, they should send it to another ten people. In no

time, a chain was created. Another innovation was done with
missed calls. Missed calls are free of cost. A message was
spread through the virtual media and other sources that those
who wanted to be associated with the anti-corruption campaign
could make a missed call to the given number. In Delhi, 50,000
people gave missed calls. The same experiment was carried out
in other small and big cities. When the request was made for
the first time, only thirteen people turned up to volunteer.
When the second call was given, 800 people showed up – a
clear indication of how well their outreach was working.

This time, with the advantage of past experience, senior
members of Team Anna took a special interest; messages to be
sent on the Facebook, Twitter and SMS were decided after a lot
of consultation and discussion. It was decided that the message
should be emotional, direct and simple, and should connect
with the common man. Messages like '*Meri paanch saal ki beti
upwas rakhegi, kya aap bhrashtachar se ladne ke liye itna bhi
nahi kar sakte?*' (My five-year-old daughter is fasting; can't
you do just this much to fight corruption?), '*Chauhattar saal
ka buzurg hamare liye anshan par baithega, aap kya karenge?*'
(A seventy-four-year-old man is willing to sit on a fast for us;
what will you do?) became instant hits.

Other than virtual space, the physical space was also
important. The protest needed physical presence and committed
workers at Jantar Mantar. According to Manish, he toured
forty to fifty colleges in the NCR. He met students, interacted
with them, tried to explain the rationale behind the *anshan* –
why the Jan Lokpal Bill was needed and why the government's
Lokpal Bill was incapable of addressing the issue of corruption
in its entirety. Their traditional association with RTI activists
had proved to be a boon for the 30 January rally in Delhi, so
they were contacted again. The RTI network was more than
willing to jump onto the bandwagon.

Preparations were in full swing. Anna was to reach Delhi on
4 April. On 3 April, a very emotional appeal was made through
different media. Various messages were sent out; for example:

You go to malls, can't you go to the airport with a tricolour to receive Anna? Everyone was to assemble at a designated place and proceed to the airport from there. According to Manish, he was not expecting more than a dozen cars. But the number was beyond their expectations. The appeal had worked. About sixty cars with national flags reached the airport. This was a day when a few Delhi-bound cricketers were coming back after the World Cup victory, almost at the same time. A lot of media, especially TV, was already there. Rather amused, Manish told me that, for some reason, they had not considered inviting the media to the airport. Cricketers came and went, but the journalists, photographers and cameramen stayed back. According to him, the presence of such a big fleet of cars must have given the media the impression that an important person was coming. When Anna came out of the airport, the media beseiged him.

They had planned only a small welcome for Anna but, as fate would have it, his arrival turned into a big media event. Manish also told me that originally the plan was to take Anna to Kiran Bedi's residence without much ado. But the entire plan went haywire and the journey became a rally. 'It took us two hours to reach Uday Park where he had to stay, which normally takes half an hour,' Manish said, flushed with happiness as he filled me in. Television reporters had all along been busy shooting visuals. Anna was the big thing on television throughout the day. It was a great beginning. Anna and Arvind slept over at Kiran Bedi's house.

Before sitting on a fast unto death, Anna wanted to visit Rajghat. He arrived to find a massive crowd there. His journey from Rajghat to Jantar Mantar via India Gate took him more than two hours. Team Anna was not expecting more than 2,000 people, but when Anna reached Jantar Mantar, the crowd was in its thousands. Already the unexpected was happening. Team Anna was more than thrilled. They had won half the battle. But they were still not sure of how the Government of India would react. Was India ready to escalate the fight? That was the million-dollar question.

THE NEW MAHATMA

W ael Ghonim was an unknown entity before 25 January 2011. Other than a few friends and acquaintances, nobody knew him. The thirty-year-old executive, a West Asia and North Africa region marketing manager at Google was just a name. He had an account on Facebook. But within three months, the same Wael Ghonim became the face of *Time* magazine. Ghonim topped the list of 100 most influential people, ahead of economist Joseph Stiglitz, Facebook founder Mark Zuckerberg, Wikileaks founder Julian Assange and the German Chancellor Angela Merkel. You can well ask what he did in these three months. He became the agent of change against the dictatorship of Hosni Mubarak in Egypt. He was the hero who triggered a revolution in Egypt. Mohamed El Baradei, the Egyptian Opposition leader, wrote in *Time*, 'He gave hope to a generation that remained apolitical due to loss of hope that things could change in a society permeated for decades with a culture of fear.' El Baradei wrote that Ghonim was convinced that the regime would listen only when citizens exercised their right to peaceful demonstration and civil disobedience; so he helped initiate a call for a peaceful revolution. Before 4 April, Anna was also an unknown face for Delhi but he gave hope to a generation of people condemned as apolitical. He also became an agent of change, a kind of revolution that a few months ago was unthinkable.

Before Ghonim, there was Mohamed Bouazizi, a twenty-six-year-old who sold vegetables to sustain his family in Sidi Bouzid, a small city in Tunisia in the Middle East. He was a poor man, who earned approximately $7 a day. On 17 December 2010, a policewoman misbehaved with him, slapped him, spat on his face and confiscated his vegetable cart. The poor man could not bear the insult and went to the local authorities for justice, but the corrupt system gave him no time of day. When he lost all hope, Bouazizi decided to protest in a different way. He went back to the headquarters of the local administration, doused himself with petrol and set himself on fire. Bouazizi's immolation triggered a wave of protests which finally engulfed all of Tunisia, and led to the ousting of President Zine El Abidine Ben Ali in January 2011. Ben Ali had been the president of Tunisia for more than twenty years. This momentous event came to be termed the Jasmine Revolution. One man's sacrifice changed the socio-political landscape of North Africa and West Asia. Within days, the region's dictators were shivering in their pants as an awakened mass revolted in almost the entire Arab world. In no time, protests broke out in Bahrain, Syria, Yemen, Algeria, Morocco, Libya, Jordan and Mauritania. People were angry about high unemployment, inflation, corruption and just lack of basic freedom. Faceless and voiceless people in the Arab world had suddenly discovered their faces and voices.

It was a similar mass of faceless and voiceless people who were waiting for a Wael Ghonim or a Mohamed Bouazizi to prick their conscience in India too. Anna was incidental. It could have been anybody with a strong moral fibre. So on the morning of 5 April, when Anna reached Jantar Mantar, these faceless, voiceless common men and women were ready to lend their voices to protest against the corrupt political establishment. The revolution had been in the making for long and on that day it started unfolding. I am not sure if people at Jantar Mantar and on the streets in different cities throughout India were inspired by their brothers and sisters in Tahrir Square, Cairo, Egypt, but there must certainly have been some mystical connect.

Just as people in Tahrir Square were proclaiming '*We Are All Khaled Saeed*' (an Egyptian businessman who was beaten to death by the police in June 2010 for posting a video clip on the Internet of policemen sharing the spoils of a drug bust), here too, everyone became Anna, shouting, '*Main bhi Anna, tu bhi Anna, everyone is Anna.*'

That morning at Jantar Mantar, a not-so-big stage had been constructed on the footpath, with a picture of Mother India in the background and an old man was sitting on the dais with a few young protesters. There was hardly any known face. Everyone seemed to be an NGO activist. There were many TV crews, with their OB vans stationed nearby. Roads were closed to normal traffic on both sides of the road. Across the road, at an old south Indian dhaba, people were enjoying dosas and idlis. This dhaba is famous for dishing out some of the best south Indian dishes at very low prices. Whenever I happen to pass by, I always stuff myself to the gills here. At one point in the late 1990s, I used to be a regular customer here but with time, and my office moving to Noida, I hadn't been back in a while. There was another reason to be nostalgic about this place. Behind the stage is a historic building. I still remember the day when in this very building, S.R. Bommai, former chief mnister of Karnataka, on behalf of the Janata Dal, informed the press that the BJP had withdrawn its support to the V.P. Singh government. In the late 1980s, this place used to house the headquarters of the Janata Dal and it was a major centre for the anti-Bofors movement as well. But much before this, till 1969, it was the headquarters of the Congress. When the Congress split into Congress (I) and Congress (O), this office went to the Congress (O) and, subsequently, with the merger of the Congress (O) into the Janata Party, it became the latter's headquarters. Janata Dal became virtually another name for the Janata Party in the 1980s after many splits and mergers. In the late 1980s, I visited this place a number of times as a student and later as a cub reporter. And ever since the Boat Club lawns were closed to protesters, Jantar Mantar became an alternative venue for the defenders of democracy.

Anna and his fast unto death were definitely the news of that day. He had roused the media's curiosity. The media followed him closely. Anna reached Rajghat around 9 a.m. By 10.15 a.m. he was at India Gate and from there he took approximately one hour to reach Jantar Mantar in an open jeep. Jantar Mantar was not chock-full yet; reporters were still standing close to the dais and photographers could pick the spot and angle they wanted. By evening, they had been pushed to the other side of the road. Before he began the fast around noon, Anna made a brief speech. He said this fast was against corruption and that his agitation would be peaceful and non-violent. He also informed the crowd that his fight was for a strong Jan Lokpal Bill, to which end he wanted the government to include members of the civil society in the bill drafting committee. In his opinion, the government's proposed Lokpal Bill was weak and ineffectual. Anna suggested that people's participation in law-making was the need of the hour. It is because legislation has been in the hands of a few that it did not reflect the common man's aspirations. Parliament was no longer truly representational, he said and corrupt politicians were undermining the entire democratic system. As the day progressed, people started coming in and news from other cities also poured in. We all were taken aback by the news pouring in: in cities across the country, people on their own were assembling at specific places in a show of support. Mumbai in particular was very responsive. Azad Maidan turned into an agitator's paradise. The ground was full of men and women from all walks of life. Even kids were sitting on a fast and shouting slogans. Jantar Mantar, meanwhile, was witnessing a different scene, a scene that defined the nature of the movement and became the reason why politicians so strongly resented the Anna movement.

Within hours of the commencement of Anna's *anshan*, Sharad Yadav, president of Janata Dal (U) and a product of the JP movement, reached there. He picked up the mike to give a speech. As he started speaking, the assembled protesters started heckling him, and finally he had to stop midway and make a hasty retreat from the venue. Some time later, Uma Bharti, who has recently rejoined the Bharatiya Janata Party (BJP), and Ram Jethmalani, a senior lawyer and an MP, also met the same fate. They were not even allowed to approach the dais. Even the mere sight of politicians was inciting the crowd to anger. The protestors made it clear to the organizers that, since this agitation was against corrupt politicians, they should not be allowed to use the platform for their dirty games. The message was loud and clear: *politicians were not welcome.* And that's how the movement acquired its anti-politics tag.

Later Anna apologized to Uma Bharti publicly. He explained that everybody was welcome to join the agitation at Jantar Mantar but would not be allowed on the dais so as to avoid the platform from being misused. But Anna's critics pointed to this incident and claimed that this protest was an attempt to discredit the political establishment, was dangerous in nature and amounted to discrediting Indian democracy and the parliamentary system. Even in my newsroom, I had several arguments with my colleagues. According to them, who was Anna and who were these members of civil society? Who had elected them that they could dictate terms? The MPs and MLAs were chosen by the people and could claim to have the people's mandate. They were at least answerable to somebody, not like these people who were sitting at Jantar Mantar. Anna's answer was simple. He said that the MPs and the MLAs were servants of the people. They had been elected to serve them but, once elected, they tended to forget their duties and behaved like masters. In his own words: *'Janta asli malik hai, aur neta naukar. Lekin ye naukar log apne ko malik maan baithe hain.'* About the parliamentary system he said that the Parliament was not supreme, people were supreme: *'Jan sabha is bigger than Lok Sabha.'* What he was saying was elegant in its simplicity – the common man can always question his leaders and if they don't listen, he can always protest. By that logic he did not discredit the system; in fact, it was an attempt to correct the system.

There were a few who raised a much deeper question. Pratap Bhanu Mehta, a leading intellectual and president of the Centre for Policy Research, asked if a fast of this nature should be allowed. He wrote, as reported by Livemint (website of the business newspaper, *The Mint*, 7 April 2011) that the protest raised several issues, 'Whether or not a fast unto death is a right way to do it in a constitutional democracy?' He added, 'The presumption would be that these kinds of tactics should be used only in really extreme circumstances and I don't think these are those circumstances.' Those words were also echoed by Gautam Adhikari, ex-editor of the *Times of India* (10 September 2011), after Anna's second fast. He wrote, 'Fasts and hartals were instruments used by that great leader (Gandhiji) against an imperial system. Should they remain primary methods of protests in a constitutionally democratic republic?' These two gentlemen, along with several others, were raising a fundamental question about a citizen's right to protest – a right ordained by the Indian constitution. This was in tune with court orders that put severe restrictions on individual liberty, a few even banning strikes in the name of public order and discipline in the past.

Adhikari also raised a deeper philosophical argument. He wrote, 'Should not we as a nation now move on in our political style from Gandhi's ideas to something more appropriate for our time and global circumstances?' I am reminded of Rabindranath Tagore's words when he spoke to his students about Bapu's fast unto death on the question of marking scheduled castes as a separate electorate. He said, 'A shadow is darkening today over India like a shadow cast by an eclipsed sun. The people of a whole country are suffering from a poignant pain of anxiety . . . Mahatmaji, who through his life of dedication has made India his own truth, has commenced his vow of extreme self-sacrifice' (Louis Fischer, *The life of Mahatma Gandhi*, p. 389). Mehta and intellectuals like him live in a privileged environment where they don't have to face corruption on a daily basis and don't feel 'the darkening shadow', but the common man, the *aam admi*, has to fight every step of the way. He fights when his son or daughter is born and also when he has to get their death certificate. For Mehta, these might not be extreme circumstances, but for the common man they are.

Anna's answer was that you could fast only against a system or person or persons who will listen to you, not against those who are immune to your endeavour, which is to say dictators and emperors. According to him, even Gandhiji suggested this. In his opinion his method was purely democratic, legitimate and Gandhian. During his speeches Anna kept telling his followers, 'Don't use violence because the State is too powerful and will crush you in no time.' According to him, non-violence was the only method that a common man had. 'Gandhiji had an artist's genius for reaching the heartstrings of the inner man,' Fischer writes in his book (p. 401). According to him, Gandhiji had a compelling need to communicate with the hearts of men. Anna's fast was also an attempt to communicate with the masses as well as with a democratic government.

As questions were raised in a section of the press, the electronic media found an opportunity in this agitation and backed Anna with a vengeance. TV did cover the first day of the *anshan*, but as time passed, everybody realized that something unusual was happening across the country. By evening, all news channels had changed their agenda and Anna, and only Anna, was the news. To begin with, every channel had deputed a junior or middle-level reporter, but the next day senior reporters were given the task and many more reporters were sent into the field. Every channel got busy with special planning. New templates were designed and viewers were pleasantly surprised to see new kinds of graphics. Senior anchors were deputed during the day also. It was now the time for the government to take note of the media's unprecedented carpet bombing-style coverage. In my own memory, no agitation had been given so much importance or so much air time. Such coverage was reserved for 26/11 or the Mumbai blasts kind of situations.

The fact is that it had the desired result. The evening of 6 April witnessed one of the biggest candlelight processions at India Gate in Anna's support. This was a different crowd. It had not been brought there by any political party, neither had they been paid to be there nor were they coerced to make their presence felt. People had come of their own accord. Most of them were young and literate professionals. All of them found a cause in Anna's *anshan*. They also decided to be stakeholders in the fight against corruption. It was a very vocal crowd. They wanted to be heard. Similar pictures were coming in from other parts of India. Mumbai's Azad Maidan became the pilgrimage point for a new generation. A young school-going child's voice is permanently etched in my mind. She had proudly said, '*Maine Gandhiji ke bare me padha hai, aj main apne yug ke Gandhi ko dekhne ayee hun*' (I have read about Gandhiji and today I have come to see the Gandhi of our era). I could sense that she was not alone in thinking this. Towards the evening, the anti-corruption chorus acquired such a dimension that cabinet minster Sharad Pawar resigned from the panel of the group of ministers constituted to discuss the issue of corruption. During the day, leaders of the movement had mocked the government and questioned how it could fight corruption when the allegedly corrupt Sharad Pawar was one of the members of the panel. Pawar comes from Maharashtra and he was one of the first to feel the intensity of the anger and power unleashed by Anna. As Anand Mahindra, a leading businessman, very succinctly put it, 'This is a movement whose heart and voice can't be ignored.' The Congress party's official spokesperson Jayanti Natarajan said, 'We respect Anna and are committed to support him in his crusade against corruption.' Manish Tiwari had a different take even then. He said, 'Everyone is free to go on a hunger strike.'

Anna's *anshan* gained even more momentum as it entered its third day at Jantar Mantar. By then, more than 300 cities had witnessed all kinds of protests. The movement comprised the young and the aged, men and women, school kids and professionals, engineers and doctors, small and big businessmen, everyone. It was spreading like wildfire from big cities to small cities. If Delhi, Mumbai, Kolkata, Hyderabad, Lucknow, Ahmedabad, Bangalore and Chandigarh emerged as the nerve centres of this movement, small cities like Mathura, Jammu, Jaipur, Kanpur, Kharagpur, Bhopal, Patiala, Ayodhya, Sangroor, Ambala, Jalandhar, Jalgaon, Ahmednagar, etc., were its arteries. In Mumbai, Medha Patkar was holding the fort at Azad Maidan and, in Bhopal, RTI activist Shehla Masood was leading the protest. Shehla was killed four months later by an assassin's bullets on 16 August 2011. This was the day when Anna was stopped from going to JP Park for his second fast unto death. She was shot just as she was stepping out of her house. It was about then that Anna had been detained and was being taken to the officers' mess. In Mumbai, Saroj Kumar Sarangi, a fast-food business owner, said that he had initiated a campaign for wearing Gandhi caps with 'I Am Anna' inscribed on them. This was the beginning of a new fashion, the Anna cap, an instant hit from Kashmir to Kanyakumari. On my way to the Ramlila Maidan I saw young girls and boys selling these caps for ten rupees. On the way to Jantar Mantar and Ramlila Maidan I realized that all those people who used to beg at the traffic signals had suddenly found employment. I was told that a few young enterprising individuals had set up a small business for a short time. Young kids were seen running from one car to another and enthusiastically selling Anna caps. I also saw tricolours in their tiny hands and their parents directing them to potential customers. During the agitation, the Anna cap and the tricolour did brisk business for beggars and gave a new sense of patriotism to the common man, making him feel as if he had a big stake in this movement and in nation-building, as if he were doing something tremendous. One could describe this as a form of neo-activism, especially the youth who had never seen or participated in a people's movement before. India's young citizens have heard glorified stories of the freedom struggle or the JP movement but have never had the chance to be part of something similar themselves.

One such person, a young software engineer, Muhammad Imtiyaz, proudly said that he was Anna's soldier and with the Anna cap on his head he would mobilize people for the movement. He was not a political worker. Navjot, a student in Jammu, was beaming with confidence. He said that he would put an end to corruption along with Anna. In Jaipur, people burnt the effigy of corruption, and in IIT Kanpur and Kharagpur, students started a signature campaign in support of Anna's cause. One student, Shashi Shekhar, got very emotional and said that if a seventy-year-old could stand up for us, why couldn't we stand by him. In Ayodhya, Hindu religious leaders openly extended their support to Anna. In his home town, Ralegan Siddhi, villagers observed a bandh for him and burnt an effigy of the Shiv Sena leader Suresh Dada Jain, who had dared to criticize Anna. Suresh Dada Jain, once a senior minister in the Shiv Sena–BJP government in Maharashtra, had had to resign due to Anna's *anshan* against his corruption.

But this open display of patriotism and nationalism irked a section of the society – the high-profile intellectuals, film-makers, historians, senior journalists, editors, social activists. A few of them were genuinely convinced at the ideological and philosophical level of the wrongness of Anna's campaign, but a few knowingly or unknowingly became a part of the government-sponsored propaganda to discredit this movement. Leading this mass of people were celebrated writers and social activists, including Arundhati Roy, Mahesh Bhatt, K.N. Panikkar, Ramachandra Guha, Shabnam Hashmi, Shekhar Gupta, Aruna Roy, etc. Picking up on images from the day Anna sat on protest at Jantar Mantar, an attempt was made to give the movement a saffron colour. The picture of Mother India in the backdrop and the presence of a few Rashtriya Swayamsevak Sangh (RSS) leaders were cited as proof. For a few of these so-called intellectuals, who have a visceral hatred of anything that is even remotely linked to the RSS brand of nationalism, it became the subject of a hate campaign. In their opinion, a picture of Mother India and shouting slogans of

'*Bharat Mata ki Jai*' and '*Vande Mataram*' are not good signs for secularism. Shabnam Hashmi, who heads an organization called Act Now for Harmony and Democracy (ANHAD), said the movement had been stage-managed by the RSS and BJP since the very beginning. 'It has been clear in symbolism through the kind of leaflets that have been distributed across the country.' She added that the involvement of new-age gurus like Sri Sri Ravishankar and Ramdev proved that it was a truly right-wing agenda (*Communalism Watch*, 31 August 2011). Arundhati Roy also wrote later, 'We now have the back-story about Anna's old relationship with the RSS' (*The Hindu*, 21 August 2011). They were not alone. In those early days of the movement, I too wondered whether there was any link between the statements made by these intellectuals and the statements made by a few Congress leaders like Digvijay Singh. I have no direct proof, but as somebody who had been a journalist for twenty years, I could sense something beyond ideological compulsions.

From the second day onwards, when the government started getting feedback about the people's anger on the streets and the overwhelming support that Anna and his movement were receiving, I could hear bits and snatches of the whisper campaign in the corridors of power. I still remember the meeting of TV editors called by Information and Broadcasting Minister Ambika Soni, a pro-media minister, in her office. None of us had any clue about the agenda for the meeting, but the minute we entered her room, we were surprised by the presence of four very senior cabinet ministers. Ghulam Nabi Azad, Pawan Kumar Bansal, Salman Khurshid and Ambika Soni welcomed us. We knew immediately that the only agenda was Anna. Before this meeting, we had been subtly informed by the government that TV channels were going overboard in their coverage of Anna. They said we ought to be more balanced and that the government was being targeted unnecessarily. However, I must also confess that the government never sent us any communication to restrain us. Ghulam Nabi started the conversation. During the conversation, one of the ministers told us that Anna's ability to draw such a big crowd was no big deal and that, at any given point of time, any leader or party could organize a crowd of 20,000. We were also told how unfair Team Anna's demand to include members of the civil society in the drafting committee was – not only was this unprecedented, they said, it was also not possible to hand over the law-making process to people outside the Parliament. It was also hinted that the RSS had infiltrated the movement and that the BJP would benefit from this. After listening to the ministers' monologues, the editors decided to speak up. I told them that it was an unprecedented situation and it required unprecedented solutions from the government. I told them that, speaking for myself, I had never seen such an outpouring of people on the roads for any politician in my entire career. I warned them that it was easy to condemn this agitation, but the fact to remember was that this crowd had not been brought in by any political party; the people had come on their own. Other editors also agreed with me. Navika Kumar of Times Now and Vinay Tewari of CNN-IBN said that the government should not get mired in legality and technicality, but should find a political solution to a political problem. Some of us even suggested that Rahul or Sonia Gandhi should seize the initiative and go to Jantar Mantar to pledge their support in the fight against corruption, and request Anna to break his fast. The meeting lasted an hour. All of us had the impression that the government had a certain amount of derision for Team Anna and Anna's movement. But since it was now trapped in the web, this meeting had been an attempt to gauge the mood of the media and the people on the street. They probably got the message. That very evening, the process of communication was hastened on behalf of the government and, by the evening of 8 April gave me an insight into how a solution had been worked out.

This meeting gave me an insight about the government's mindset and I gleaned a few things. One, the government was looking for a bureaucratic solution to a political problem. They were able to solve the crisis at Jantar Mantar in record time because of Sonia Gandhi's initiative, as she had tried to find a political solution. But in her absence, the government did not have any solution to the agitation at the Ramlila Maidan for ten days. Two, the government had no respect for the movement and its leaders. After the agitation at Jantar Mantar, a government-sponsored malicious campaign was unleashed with the help of a section of the media. Three, the government was convinced that the RSS was the architect of the movement. Digvijay Singh's repeated statements that Anna and Ramdev were the *mukhauta* (masks) of the RSS was not just one man's diatribe. Anna's statement at the Press Club was misquoted to say that he had praised Gujarat chief minister Narendra Modi. Anna had then said that Modi and Nitish Kumar, the chief minister of Bihar, had done some good work at the panchayat level. I was there at that press conference. But prompted by Arvind, he also added that the Gujarat government did not do enough to control the 2002 riots. The damage, however, had been done.

Yes, it is true that Baba Ramdev and Sri Sri Ravishankar's association did not go down well with the left intellectuals. Even I thought that it gave the movement a religious tone and could have been avoided. But one has to understand that Arvind was trying to organize people for the movement and he did not have enough high-profile individuals who would volunteer for the anti-corruption movement. Sri Sri Ravishankar was one of the founder-members of the 'India against Corruption' campaign. He and his organization, Art of Living, were an integral part of the movement. According to a core member of Team Anna, even before the Jantar Mantar agitation, Sri Sri Ravishankar had been talking about corruption in his Art of Living sessions. Sri Sri had also instructed his followers to actively participate in the movement. His music teachers were specially loaned to the movement and were instrumental in keeping the crowd entertained throughout Anna's *anshan*, be it at Jantar Mantar or Tihar Jail or the Ramlila Maidan. Sri Sri's volunteers are quite adept at crowd management. Such volunteers were a great help in controlling the crowd.

History might judge Baba Ramdev differently, but the truth is that originally Baba was thought to be the face of the anti-corruption campaign. In October 2010 when Arvind and his team of RTI activists were planning to lodge a first information report (FIR) against Suresh Kalmadi, the chairman of the Organizing Committee of the Commonwealth Games, Anna was nowhere in the picture. In one such meeting, Kiran Bedi, the high-profile ex-cop, suggested that Baba Ramdev also be involved. Baba was already actively talking about the issues of black money and corruption. He had also hinted at launching a movement and had been touring India, trying to raise these issues in a big way at the all-India level. Baba was always suspected of having an understanding with the RSS on this issue. At Kiran Bedi's prompting, contact was established with Baba Ramdev. He agreed to take part in the march to Parliament Street on 14 November to file an FIR. Till then Arvind and his team had had good relations with Aruna Roy and her organization, the National Campaign for Peoples' Right to Information (NCPRI). A meeting was called and it was decided that the civil society would draft a Lokpal Bill because they believed that the government's Lokpal Bill draft was very weak. Arvind was the chairman of that civil society drafting committee. Arvind and his team were in a hurry, but the NCPRI wanted to move slowly. Differences cropped up. Arvind and his team decided to chart an independent path. Arvind and his team were very disappointed with Aruna Roy and NCPRI, and in Baba Ramdev they found a face and some help. The rally on 30 January at Ramlila Maidan was Ramdev's show. He was the face. 'But somehow he got the impression that Arvind and his team did not give him the credit he deserved,' a very senior member of Team Anna told me. According to him, 'Ramdev was very hurt.' So when the next move for the protest was discussed, Baba Ramdev refused to lead the movement.

The team was once again looking for a high-profile face and, as luck would have it, Anna emerged on the horizon. So there was truth in the rumours that there were differences between

Team Anna and Baba Ramdev and that was the reason that Baba didn't turn up at Jantar Mantar for the protest. Baba was really angry. He felt slighted. But when Anna's fast unto death gained unprecedented support, it became difficult for Baba Ramdev to keep a distance from the agitation. Now it was imperative for him to be seen with the movement; otherwise his public stand against corruption could be adversely affected. So on the fourth day, Baba Ramdev was seen at Jantar Mantar and denied any rift with Team Anna. He swore that he was very much a part of Team Anna. But he was not convincing and people did not believe him at all. At Jantar Mantar, in his own style, he tried to steal the limelight but, by then, it was too late. Baba Ramdev was perceived as overambitious. History had given its verdict and destiny had ditched him royally. Baba Ramdev lost an opportunity and, in hindsight, that was good for the movement.

Seeing the movement's might, the government too realized its mistake and opened up channels of communication. An important member of Team Anna, Swami Agnivesh, was already in touch with a senior member of the government. Contact had been established. Negotiations had started. On the third day of the *anshan*, Sonia herself appealed to Anna to break his fast. Kapil Sibal, minister for telecommunications, had two rounds of discussions with Swami Agnivesh and Arvind. The government was ready to make a joint drafting committee for the Lokpal Bill. Team Anna wanted five members from the civil society and five from the government. The government was adamant about nominating Finance Minister Pranab Mukherjee as the committee's chairman, whereas the civil society was pitching for Anna. The government did not want to issue a notification constituting such a committee for fear of constitutional impropriety. Anna later made it clear that he did not wish to head the committee and would prefer a Supreme Court judge. Anna also wanted the bill to be ready before 30 June which, in the government's opinion, was not feasible. The government also insisted on a minister being the chairperson and if that was not acceptable to the civil society, no minister would be a member, and their place would be filled by bureaucrats. Team Anna realized the futility of this exercise as bureaucrats would not be in a position to take decisions and finally the matter would have to go to the political bosses. So the team relented. On 8 April, decks were cleared for a breakthrough. Swami Agnivesh rightly declared that there might be good news. And after forty-four years the possibility of a proper Lokpal Bill would be a reality. So by the evening of the same day, a ten-member joint drafting committee had been agreed upon. Five members would be from Team Anna and, the other five, senior ministers from the government. Pranab Mukherjee would be the chairman and Shanti Bhushan would be the co-chairman. But things were still not clear. Anna wanted a written assurance and a government notification to be issued before he broke his fast. The government was hell-bent on issuing just an order; it did not want to be seen surrendering too much to the civil society as that would lower its esteem in the public's eye and would send wrong signals for the future. There was a deadlock yet again. People were anxious once again. Faces again fell at Jantar Mantar. Those who had been waiting for a victory celebration were now bracing for a long struggle. On the fourth day, by night-time, support for the movement had increased by leaps and bounds. Be it Jantar Mantar or the Azad Maidan in Mumbai or the Charminar in Hyderabad, Anna became an icon for the new Indian. In their eyes, he was a new mahatma who would cleanse the rotten Indian system. The pressure on the government was immense. The inputs they were getting showed increasing support for Anna. Finally, they relented – apparently on Sonia Gandhi's intervention. And then the government went out of its way to get a notification issued in the government gazette; I am sure that the official press must have burnt the midnight oil to achieve this.

The ninety-eight-hour-long fast was over and the next morning there were celebrations all over. Almost every city celebrated Diwali and Holi together. The film fraternity was a very important element of this movement. I had never seen this kind of euphoria in Bollywood. Anupam Kher and Shekhar Kapoor were leading the crowd. After Anna broke his fast, Anupam Kher said, 'To dream and to fulfil that dream is life.' This victory might not end corruption completely, but it was a glorious beginning. Team Anna knew that the fast had ended, but the battle was only half won, the war was still on: a war against the government's attitude, war against the mindset of the common man who accepted corruption as a normal part of life. The bigger question was whether things would change. It is no wonder then that, while breaking his fast, Anna warned the government that if by 15 August the bill did not become law, he would be forced to launch another agitation. Surely, the war was still on!

THE EMPIRE FIGHTS BACK

During the *anshan* at Jantar Mantar, Manish Tiwari had said, 'Everyone is free to go on hunger strike.' The official spokesperson Jayanti Natarajan had a slightly more nuanced opinion. She said, 'We respect Anna and we are committed to supporting Anna in his crusade against corruption.' Two statements from two different spokespersons of the Congress underline the contradiction within the party and the government. From the beginning, there were two approaches to the movement. One section of the Congress, the 'soft-liners', so to say, were more attuned politically and had their ears close to the ground. They were of the opinion that the issue needed subtle handling because corruption is an emotive issue and Team Anna had a far wider support than what the other section of the party envisaged. The other section of the party, which was primarily led by Home Minister P. Chidambaram and his friend and ally Kapil Sibal, could be categorized as 'hardliners'. From the first day, the hardliners had a very low opinion of Anna and his team. In fact, they were contemptuous of them from the beginning. In a private conversation with me, a senior cabinet minister said, 'You TV guys have given undue importance to these mohalla (local) type leaders and made them national figures.' In fact, he tried to convince me how we were trapped in a bigger conspiracy and were playing into the hands of those who had a dangerous agenda to destabilize the government and create anarchy in the country. In his opinion, the Anna movement was being used for this sinister design.

So it was no coincidence that, during the second dharna at Ramlila Maidan, Rashid Alvi, Congress's newly appointed spokesman, hinted, Indira Gandhi-style, at an American hand behind the Anna movement. I didn't need to be a political analyst to see the propaganda element in this statement, but, please believe me, a few conspiracy theorists within the Congress and the government were convinced that this movement was not as clean as a section of the media and society would have you believe, and that its real motive needed to be exposed to the world. There were two theories. One was propounded by the so-called secularists in the party and their cronies outside the party. They are of the firm opinion that since the government had exposed the RSS and the strong Hindutva hand behind a few terrorist attacks, Hindu fundamentalist forces were hell-bent on destabilizing the Manmohan Singh government to stop the bigger RSS names from surfacing and to save the RSS as an organization.

This theory is not unfounded. It has some solid basis. In fact, when the Hindu organization's name cropped up in connection with a terror blast and Sadhvi Prajna Singh and Colonel Purohit were arrested, the RSS had been very worried. Its leaders and the BJP tried to defend them. I still remember how Rajnath Singh, the then BJP president, not only supported Prajna Singh, but also went to meet her in jail; but as the investigation deepened, and Indresh Kumar's name appeared in connection with the Ajmer blast, the RSS's worry turned into a real scare. Indresh Kumar is a very senior functionary of the RSS and also a member of the highest decision-making body of the organization, the Pratinidhi Sabha. Hardliners in the Congress believe that allegations of Hindu terror have shaken the RSS and the organization now thinks that if this process is not stopped, the RSS will suffer the same fate as it did just after Independence. At that time, the RSS was blamed for Mahatma Gandhi's assassination and banned. It suffered a huge loss of credibility because of that stain and it took them nearly two decades to recover. That state of isolation and humiliation was also one of the main reasons why the RSS floated a political party to fight their battle.

I realized that the RSS was really shaken because of these disclosures, so even though there was initial support for Prajna Singh and Indresh Kumar, diktats were issued from Nagpur, the RSS headquarters, to distance the organization from such elements. It is also a fact that they panicked when Indresh Kumar was linked to them by government agencies. They were preparing their defence and were ready for any kind of government assault, but to assume that Anna and his movement was created by the RSS to checkmate the government's move was an ill-conceived notion with no basis in reality. As far as I know, the RSS has no direct links with this anti-corruption campaign, but yes the RSS's swayamsewaks are part of the campaign and there is no doubt about this. They are not at the forefront of the movement and none of the leading lights of the movement are active members of the RSS. Still, it has become difficult for Team Anna to counter this allegation and a section of the intelligentsia decided to maintain its distance from the Anna movement for this very reason.

In typical Mrs Gandhi-style, the hardliners' second theory is that this was a crisis created by an invisible foreign hand. The conspiracy theorist told reporters that since India was progressing so rapidly, powerful international players like America and China were jealous and wanted to halt India's forward economic march because India's unbridled growth would dwarf many economically powerful countries and would make India a serious power in world politics. So it was in their interest that India gets busy with its own internal crises.

Again, I should admit that this concern too has a basis in fact. 'As we all know, the world ignored India's economic liberalization in the early 1990s,' says Raghav Bahal, in his book *Super Power: The Amazing Race between China's Hare and India's Tortoise*. He goes on to say, 'India was a mysterious, mystical subcontinent buried under the weight of its anonymity; global risk capital simply chose to ignore this half-asleep, half-

stirring tortoise–elephant. Then one day in 2001 a missive
from Goldman Sachs in New York (which is popularly known
as BRICs report) changed the game.' According to this report,
India could become the third largest economy in the world in
2050 after the USA and China. It is true that international
politics is full of intrigue and our neighbours have long displayed
naked ambition, so yes, we ought to be vigilant. To assume,
however, that the movement is funded and guided by global
players is an insult to the average Indian's intelligence. This
assumption has serious fallacies – that Indians as a community
are comfortable with corruption, that the Indian democracy is
still immature and does not understand the true character of a
people's movement, that India is like the banana republics that
have no history of democracy to boast of. People like Arundhati
Roy have such a low opinion about the Indian people that they
thrust their ignorance on the bigger audience. For example,
when she writes, 'The campaign is being handled by people
who run a clutch of generously funded NGOs whose donors
include Coca-Cola and Lehman Brothers. Kabir, run by Arvind
Kejriwal and Manish Sisodia, key figures in Team Anna,
have received $400,000 from the Ford Foundation in the last
three years.'

So, convinced by the conspiracy theories, the hardliners were
adamant on crushing this movement, if possible in one go, and
if that was not possible, then step by step. The hardliners had
to keep a low profile during the Jantar Mantar agitation due to
Sonia Gandhi's presence, but their dirty tricks department was
active round the clock. A big controversy was drummed up just
as Anna broke his fast and announced the names of the five
members for the joint drafting committee. Questions were
raised about the presence in the committee of the father-and-
son duo, Shanti Bhushan and Prashant Bhushan. It was dubbed
favouritism. In no time at all, a non-issue became a national
issue. In the end, Anna had to make a statement. He said that it
was he who had nominated them and that they were the most
deserving candidates. Those who are familiar with the movement

know that the father and son were an integral part of the anti-corruption campaign from its incipient days. In fact, much before anybody thought of launching a movement, the Bhushans had been active in courts and had been raising serious issues of corruption in judiciary and in the government. Shanti Bhushan, one of the active members of the JP movement, was also the law minister in the Morarji government after the defeat of Indira Gandhi. In the legal fraternity, he is well known as a crusader and once he created quite a sensation by submitting a list of Chief Justices of India to the Supreme Court and informing the court that half of them were corrupt. The same was also true of his son Prashant Bhushan. He has been embarrassing the government on corruption issues with his PILs, particularly in the 2G and CVC Thomas cases. Prashant Bhushan was the member of the subcommittee that was to draft the Jan Lokpal Bill at the behest of NCPRI. Arvind was the chairman of the committee. So this controversy was the beginning of the canards that were spread to kill the movement by discrediting its leaders. Unfortunately, a leading English daily became a willing partner in this dirty game.

Today I am reminded of the conversation that I had with a very tired-looking Arvind at India Gate. It was the day that Anna had broken his fast and a massive victory rally had just concluded at India Gate. Arvind was sitting in one corner. I was to interview him for my weekly show. The time was fixed for 10 p.m. I was a bit early. Arvind was supposed to appear in Barkha Dutt's show, live, before recording for my programme. As the show began, a crowd gathered to watch and started hooting Barkha; it became difficult to continue the show live. It was a big embarrassment for her. The show had to be aborted after just five minutes. People were angry with Barkha because her name had figured in the Radia tapes; they were questioning her moral right to ask moral questions when she, in their opinion, was not clean. Arvind was waiting for me with his supporters. When I reached, he was already half asleep. While my camera team was setting up the equipment, I tried to keep him occupied (and awake) with conversation. I said that the agitation was over, but it would be difficult to sustain the momentum. Arvind agreed with me, adding, 'Difficult days are ahead.' In hindsight, his words proved to be prophetic. The controversy about the Bhushans being in the committee was only a trailer.

I was sitting with Aniruddha Bahal, one of the pioneers of sting operations in India, at Prashant Bhushan's residence. Shanti Bhushan also happened to be there. Suddenly, he referred to a phone call made by an *Indian Express* reporter enquiring about a CD and its contents, in which one could hear a conversation between Shanti Bhushan, Mulayam Singh Yadav (president of the Samajwadi Party) and Amar Singh (general secretary of the Samajwadi Party before he left it). In this CD one could allegedly hear Shanti Bhushan trying to strike a deal with Mulayam Singh Yadav for Prashant Bhushan to fix cases in courts for a few crores of rupees. The conversation went something like this:

> Shanti Bhushan: *Dekhiye*, Prashant PIL *karte hain* (Look, Prashant does PILs).
>
> MSY: *Hmm.*
>
> Shanti Bhushan: *Usse kuchh kamate nahi* (He doesn't earn anything from them).
>
> MSY: *Haan* (Yes).
>
> Shanti Bhushan: *Dekhiye hamne sab story sunli* (Look, we heard the entire story).
>
> MSY: *Hmm.*
>
> Shanti Bhushan: *Ek hi tareeka hai*, Prashant *bahut achha manage karte hain* (There's only one way, Prashant manages things very well).
>
> MSY: *Theek hai* (OK).
>
> Shanti Bhuhan: *Iske liye bahut zyada paise ki zaroorat nahi hai . . . chaar crore rupaye bahut hain* (For this we

don't need a lot of money . . . Rupees four crore will be enough).

The reporter wanted the Bhushans' reaction. The Bhushans immediately realized the seriousness of the matter. They complained to the police about the CD. They alleged that this CD was fabricated and needed to be investigated to find out who was behind it. The Bhushans did not have enough confidence in the government agencies and they were also aware that if it took time, their hard-earned reputation would be forever ruined. So they did not wait. They sent a copy of the CD to an American expert, George Papcun, who according to the Bhushans' press release, was one of the leading experts in the world in acoustic phonetics, and who had been employed by Los Alamos National Laboratory and the University of California. The press release claimed that, according to Papcun, the recording was not an authentic and valid representation of an original conversation and it had been tampered with.

Prashant Bhushan's two sons are very enterprising. One of them discovered that portions of the conversation in the CD were lifted from the tapes that Prashant himself had filed in the Supreme Court in 2006, asking the court to lift the injunction that restrained publicizing Amar Singh's intercepted phone conversations. Prashant claimed that all instances of the fabrication were lifted from a single three-minute conversation that Amar Singh had had with Mulayam Singh. I personally listened to both the conversations. And then I decided to break the story on IBN7 saying that the so-called CD might be fabricated and could be an attempt to malign their reputation. Amar Singh valiantly made several attempts to question the integrity of the Bhushans. Government agencies also sent the CD to three different forensic labs. The Delhi police claimed that the labs in Delhi and Hyderabad had concluded that the CD had not been tampered with, but the Chandigarh lab differed and wrote that the CD had been tampered with. The police filed a closure report in the Tees Hazari court. The reports were not made public. There was no investigation on who got the CD made, who circulated it and how it reached newspaper offices.

But there were many other mysteries that were to unfold. Within an interval of a few days, two newspapers, one English and one Hindi, both known for their proximity to the establishment, reported two stories of wrongdoings by the Bhushans. One report suggested how the Bhushans underpaid stamp duty for the purchase of a property in Allahabad and how the UP government had issued a notice to them regarding this. Another report tried to show how the Bhushans had availed themselves of two farm plots in Noida from Mayawati (chief minister of Uttar Pradesh) from her discretionary quota. The question raised in the report was that, since the Bhushans were fighting two PILs against the Mayawati government, attainment of this property from the discretionary quota raised a moral question. The Bhushans tried to defend themselves, issued press releases and claimed that this was a part of the malicious campaign by those corrupt influential people who were afraid that the presence of the Bhushans in the drafting committee might result in a tough law against corruption.

The Congress was ever more ecstatic with every new disclosure and exposé. Their spokesperson raised these controversies in every studio discussion on TV. Leaders like Digvijay Singh openly questioned the Bhushans' integrity and their moral right to be part of a committee which was to draft an anti-corruption bill. One senior members of the Congress party told me after one such studio discussion that we were wrong to defend civil society members. He also challenged me to air cases of corruption against civil society members and, when I had shown readiness, he narrated a few stories about them and promised me that he would hand over papers – those papers never landed on my table. Another senior Congress leader told me how journalists had become lazy and how he himself had to send them papers against civil society members.

So I was not surprised when reputed columnist Swapan Dasgupta wrote in his column in *Sunday Pioneer* on 26 April,

'What the country witnessed throughout this past week was the Congress, backed quietly by a section of the government, going on an overdrive to discredit the father-son duo of Shanti Bhushan and Prashant Bhushan, important civil society representatives nominated to the drafting committee of the Lokpal Bill by Anna Hazare.' He also wrote, 'There is no doubt that the sustained campaign has had the effect of showing the Bhushans as damaged goods and there have been calls for the duo to step down.'

It was an attempt to puncture the halo around Team Anna and also plant the seed of suspicion in the minds of other members of the team and their supporters. Team Anna were steadfast in this hour of crisis as was in evidence later when Anna sat at the Ramlila Maidan. Prashant played a very important role then. Very few people are aware that Anna had tremendous respect for Shanti Bhushan, who is probably the only one in the team who speaks like an equal to him. But the months of April and May were trying times for the movement. A senior member of Team Anna told me that the attempt was to provoke them to leave the joint drafting committee so that the government could get rid of them and draft a bill of their own liking. But the government did not succeed. On 16 April 2011, the first meeting of the joint drafting committee took place. Civil society members demanded a live telecast of the entire proceeding. Government members flatly refused, but agreed to an audio recording and to holding a public consultation before finalizing the draft.

THE FARCE THAT WAS RAMDEV

The attack on Team Anna proved that the success of the Jantar Mantar agitation contained the seeds of future turbulence. The collective ego of the government had taken a beating. They were having trouble digesting their self-inflicted defeat, a fact that would show up when Anna sat on another dharna in August. But trouble was brewing in the Anna camp too, in the form of Baba Ramdev, a development I had hinted at earlier. Baba Ramdev was a very ambitious man who for the past two years had been trying to launch himself into the big league. This was why, when he was contacted by Arvind and his team in the latter part of 2010, Ramdev was more than willing to lend his support to the anti-corruption campaign. He and his followers joined Team Anna in large numbers on 14 November for the rally at Parliament Street when an FIR was to be filed against Suresh Kalmadi in the CWG scam, and later at Ramlila ground on 30 January 2011. But for some reason, Ramdev had the impression that he did not get due recognition in the January rally. He thought of himself as the obvious choice for the leadership of the movement, but Arvind and his team had serious problems with the kind of language used at the January rally. They also thought that Ramdev had a dubious political agenda. The relationship between the two camps became so bad that Ramdev stopped responding to their phone calls. Several messages were sent to Ramdev to iron out the differences. Arvind and his team pleaded through others that Ramdev should talk to them, but he refused. Arvind did not yet want to dissociate Ramdev from the movement. One of Arvind's associates told me that the movement was not big enough then and any news about serious differences would have prematurely killed it. It was for this reason that Arvind had to be literally pushed into his car at one time to have a word with him but Ramdev was adamant. Ramdev was also unhappy about Sri Sri Ravishankar's presence, even though he was one of the founder-members of the India against Corruption campaign. Despite public posturing to the contrary, there was some rivalry between the two. Baba Ramdev once told them, 'Don't get involved with Sant politics.'

When Ramdev refused to be part of the movement, a serious attempt was made to bring Anna into the movement. Ramdev, meanwhile, was busy starting a parallel movement. I have met him many a time. One time, I was with him at Pragati Maidan. He had chalked out a political manifesto by then and was to announce that he would float a political party. While talking to me he declared that he would never contest elections or hold a public post. What he wanted to do was to mentor a political party and have his candidates to contest elections in all the 543 parliamentary constituencies. When I confronted him about the fact that in the Indian tradition sadhus and mahatmas and rishi-munis don't occupy seats of political power, he said that saints could not keep quiet when there was so much deterioration in politics and society. He cited examples from Indian traditions to prove that saints did advise kings and queens when required, and that kings and queens had always respected their opinions. Each time I met him I was more than convinced that he had political ambitions. He was very confident of the support that he had built through his yoga *shivirs*. In the last few years he had also cultivated very good contacts in all the political parties and in many social organizations. Neither did he have any dearth of money power. Ramdev was also close to the RSS and, whenever he was confronted with this question, he would always say that he had no problems with patriots. My sources

told me that he did seek support from the RSS to launch a
political party but the RSS refused to lend any support for this.
After he felt betrayed by Arvind and his team, he was even
more determined to begin his indefinite fast at Ramlila Maidan
on 4 June 2011. Anna's success was another motivating factor
for him. He was now more convinced than ever before that the
time was ripe for a movement and, if people could respond in
such a big way to Anna, he would create waves with his
organizational muscle power. Unlike Anna, Ramdev had been
touring India. He was better known than Anna. He was the
darling of the television media. He knew his presence always
ensured high TRP ratings. No TV channel could ignore his
presence and he had an opinion on all subjects, including
homosexuality, and was never shy about articulating his views
on news channels. In fact, as a TV professional, I loved his
combative style of articulation. Once I told him in jest that he
should reduce his appearances on TV or he would lose his
appeal. He just smiled. I knew that he did not take my advice
seriously. In fact, a few months before the 4 June programme,
he had started travelling with a customized OB (outdoor
broadcast) van. I have recorded his interviews live from Kohima
in Nagaland and Vidisha in Madhya Pradesh. He took his
success for granted. The government was also looking for an
opportunity to settle scores with Team Anna. The policy of
divide and rule brings succour to rulers everywhere.

The government was aware of the differences between the
two. A few senior ministers found this opportunity to divide
civil society and appropriate Baba Ramdev into the larger
scheme of things. They thought this would destabilize Team
Anna and prove that Anna and his team were not the sole
representatives of civil society. But they also did not want Baba
Ramdev to sit on a dharna beginning another 'circus' in the
capital. Representatives of the government decided to massage
Baba Ramdev's ego and convince him that, if the government
was willing to concede his demands, there was no point in
sitting on a fast. It was one of the most bizarre moments of my

entire career when I heard that Finance Minister Pranab Mukherjee, considered the de facto prime minister, would be going to airport to meet Baba Ramdev. At that time, I was in an Editors Guild meeting at the India International Centre. Pranab Mukherjee was the main speaker there. During the meeting I got a call from office: 'Can you confirm if Pranab Mukherjee is going to receive Baba at the airport?' I screamed at the caller, 'Are you out of your mind? How can you even think that Mr Mukherjee will go to receive Baba Ramdev? He is too senior a minister and Baba is not the head of the state of any nation, and even for a head of state, a junior minister is sent as per protocol, not such a senior person.' The caller responded, 'One of the news channels is flashing this news.' 'I am here. Mr Mukherjee is still with us and giving a talk on the Indian economy. So forget it.' I had barely taken a few breaths when my phone rang again. My executive editor was on the line. He asked me the same question, 'Is Mr Mukherjee still there?' 'Yes,' I said. 'But what is the matter?' 'Right now many channels are flashing the news that Mr Mukherjee has gone to the airport to see Baba Ramdev,' he replied. I was stunned to hear that. I said, 'Let them run.' Mr Mukherjee was right in front of me. He stayed there for another ten minutes. As he left, my phone rang again. I was very irritated and puzzled. What was happening? 'Don't run this unless I clear it,' I said. I was there with a few senior newspaper editors. All of them had the same opinion. 'Mr Mukherjee can't go to receive Baba Ramdev.' Within five minutes another senior reporter called me. 'Mr Mukherjee has reached the airport, I just saw his car. We should run this news.' Mr Mukherjee had indeed gone to the airport to meet Baba Ramdev. I had no other option. I reluctantly gave the go-ahead. I had no words to express what I was feeling. It was bizarre . . . just bizarre. Unprecedented. Mukherjee was not alone at the airport; the telecom minister, Kapil Sibal, parliamentary affairs minister, Pawan Kumar Bansal, and tourism minister, Subodh Kant Sahai, were also there. No leader, no head of government, no head of state had ever been given such a welcome at an airport in India. Even the American president and the president of the erstwhile USSR weren't accorded this privilege; Baba Ramdev had suddenly become very big and the government very small. A sure sign of panic. I imagine that they might have had a plan on paper and did not know how to execute it. Ideally, a junior functionary should have opened the door of negotiations. And finally, when things were settled, Baba Ramdev should have gone to meet Pranab Mukherjee for photo ops. But here, the government had already used its *brahmashtra* right at the start. Even then they could not stop Baba Ramdev from sitting on dharna. If the purpose was to send him back from the airport, it failed miserably and the government exposed itself badly.

I later inquired of a source in the Congress why Pranab Mukherjee had gone to the airport that day. I was sure it could not have been his brainchild. I was told by a senior leader of the party that Mukherjee was dead against it, but he could not say no when the prime minister personally requested him to go. I was told that Mukherjee was fuming after the meeting. Had it been left to Mukherjee, the government would not have faced what it did in the days to follow.

Baba Ramdev did sit on *anshan* on 4 June 2011 at Ramlila Maidan with more than 50,000 of his supporters. This *anshan* was immediately compared with Anna's fast. If Anna's *anshan* was on a footpath in front of 7 Jantar Mantar, under the sun, Baba Ramdev had five-star arrangements. Crores of rupees were spent on all the latest facilities. It was anything but Gandhian. The crowd was also different. If at Jantar Mantar, there were people from all walks of life who were genuinely concerned about the state of affairs in the country, Ramlila Maidan was filled with Baba Ramdev's committed followers who had been regulars at his yoga *shivirs*. My reporters later told me that there was hardly any crowd from Delhi. All of them seemed to have come from nearby places around Delhi. They were like well-trained members of a political party, whereas at Jantar Mantar one could easily see local Delhi residents, families, the young and the old. They were innocent faces, citizens of the Indian nation and not a committed cadre or the religious and devout. Baba Ramdev had obviously been planning to show his strength for a long time. During the day, he managed to partially pull it off, like all overly ambitious people, but he committed a mistake. He overestimated his strength and underestimated the government's wiliness.

A day before the *anshan*, the government had literally been on its knees before him, pleading with him not to sit on a fast. It had conceded almost all his demands at a supposedly secret meeting at Delhi's Claridges Hotel. The deal was almost done. TV channels had also conveyed to their viewers that some understanding had been reached between the two. Next day, Baba Ramdev sat on an indefinite fast. By afternoon, news started trickling in that this would not be a long affair. Ramdev was to hold a press conference in the evening. He was beaming with confidence. At the same time, telecom minister and the prime minister's blue-eyed boy, Kapil Sibal, was also to speak to the press. The government, which had insulted Pranab Mukherjee by sending him to the airport to talk Baba out of unleashing his yogic *anshan*, had a different script now. There was a twist in the tale. Baba was halfway through his presser. Just as he was announcing very proudly that the government had accepted ninety per cent of his demands, Kapil Sibal dropped the bombshell. He released a handwritten letter by Ramdev's second-in-command, Swami Bal Krishna, promising that he would end his fast. Kapil Sibal alleged that Ramdev had entered a written understanding with the government before starting his *anshan* – the understanding being that he would announce that very evening his decision to break his fast because the government had met all his demands. According to Kapil Sibal, the government waited for Baba Ramdev to announce the same. In fact, he made several calls to Baba Ramdev and when he did not get any semblance of a positive response, he decided to make Baba's letter public. There was mayhem in the newsroom. It was surreal. One minute Baba was smiling with victory, another minute he was crestfallen, and Kapil Sibal had a wicked smile. We did not know what to put on air. Baba was too cosy with the government, which had been determined to prove him bigger than Anna and was now out to cut him to size. It was not politics; it was bad politics. The government did not stop to think for a minute that if it ever had to enter into any negotiations in the future, they would be hard-pressed to engender trust in the other party. This was also probably why Anna ignored the Parliament's appeal to end his second fast. This event certainly eroded Baba's credibility in the eyes of the public. His fast now looked like a farce, a drama; he was playing a game with the government. Ramdev cried foul. He hardened his position to salvage his reputation. He said that now he would not accept the government's offer to form a committee to look into the issue of black money. In his opinion, the government would now have to promulgate an ordinance in place of forming a committee.

The government had clearly been too clever by half. They did not want Baba Ramdev to sit on a dharna. He did. And now the situation had become more complex – a so-called yogi, who is revered in the Hindu tradition, with more than 50,000 committed religious followers, was even more determined not to break his fast unto death unless the government conceded his demands. This was not the Anna crowd. A crowd with a religious mindset was more dangerous – a ticking bomb. Such a crowd always has a low threshold and a minor mistake could turn it into a volcano. So the government changed its strategy.

It was 12.45 a.m. The crowds at Ramlila Maidan were half asleep. Dozens of TV reporters were lazing around. Suddenly, policemen were spotted on the ground. I had just received a call from my assignment desk that Delhi Police had raided Ramlila Maidan to pick up Baba Ramdev. As I switched on the TV, I saw Baba Ramdev squatting on the shoulders of his followers. His followers were all around him. Baba was trying to calm his supporters and requesting them not to resort to violence. This drama continued for some time. I had no option but to rush to the office and marshal my resources. I immediately rang up my metro editor, Sandeep Kumar, and asked him to reach the ground with all the senior reporters. I was really scared. I told them this could lead to a stampede and hundreds of lives could be lost. The police had been stupid. Meanwhile, I received information that Baba Ramdev had disappeared. Nobody knew his whereabouts. There was no trace of him for a good two hours. The police were in a state of panic. By 4.00 a.m., news came in that Baba Ramdev had been caught fleeing dressed in a woman's attire. He was disguised in a traditional salwar-kameez. He was surrounded by three women who covered him as if shielding an injured companion who was being taken to the hospital. They had successfully come out of the ground and covered quite a distance. As they were about to disappear into the concrete jungle, a policeman got suspicious, stopped them, removed the dupatta and Baba Ramdev was caught. He was immediately taken to a safe guest house and from there sent to Dehra Dun in a Border Security Force (BSF) aircraft. From Dehra Dun, he was taken to his Patanjali Yogapeeth ashram in Haridwar.

Baba had made another blunder. For some reason, he had decided to run away from the police. If he had stayed back and let the police arrest him peacefully, he would have been a hero. He tried to justify his running away by saying that the police were out to kill him. Nobody believed him. This only showed how naive he was and how wrongly he was advised. He had not learnt the very important lesson that satyagrahis never fear for their lives. True Gandhians were never scared of going to jail or bearing the brunt of lathis. During the Salt Satyagraha, the police would hit protesters with lathis and, as they fell, their place was taken by others. This went on till all the protesters were on the ground, bleeding profusely. Baba was now exposed, twice in twenty-four hours. Though he continued with his fast for a few more days, his body was too weak to carry on an *anshan* in spite of his yoga practice. He had lost his moral fibre. And maybe he had no fight left in him. TV had made him, TV had killed him.

Prime Minister Manmohan Singh justified the police action. But all the political parties, including the BJP, and the civil society termed this action undemocratic. The National Human Rights Commission issued a notice to the Central government and the Delhi Police and the Supreme Court also pitched in. Everybody knew that this action was engineered by Union Home Minister P. Chidambaram and his friend and colleague, Kapil Sibal – the duo that later tried the same trick with Anna in August. Anna was outraged. Despite their open differences with Ramdev, Anna and his team announced that they would sit on a day-long dharna at Rajghat to protest the police action. The government was not in the least apologetic. Senior Congress leader Digvijay Singh openly called Baba Ramdev a cheat and a thug. The government was, it would appear, drunk on its success.

SONIA'S ABSENCE AND THE
CONGRESS ARROGANCE

Between 9 April and 16 August 2011, the situation had changed dramatically. Firstly, Sonia Gandhi was no longer physically fit to supervise and intervene if required. She was suffering from a mystery illness, which the Congress, for some reason, was trying to hide from the public under the guise of privacy. So secret was the affair that even senior cabinet ministers were not aware of her illness until she had taken off to New York for a major surgery. She had appointed a four-member committee comprising A.K. Antony (defence minister), Rahul Gandhi, Ahmed Patel (political advisor to the party president, i.e., Sonia Gandhi), and Janardan Dwivedi (general secretary, media) to handle party affairs in her absence. This led to a lot of speculation and also created the space for a power struggle within the Congress.

Secondly, the government had successfully vanquished Baba Ramdev. Ministers like P. Chidambaram and Kapil Sibal were now confident that they could handle any mass movement, including Anna's. Though they were criticized for the way Baba Ramdev was taken away from Ramlila Maidan in the middle of the night – a section in the Congress was also opposed to the method employed – the party was of the opinion that this was the minimum price one had to pay in order to avoid 'chaos, anarchy and blackmail in the capital'.

Thirdly, the crowd at Jantar Mantar in April had shaken the

government and they saw the possibility of an Egypt-like situation. The Congress knew there would be no violent mass upsurge because India was a democracy, but there would be electoral consequences. In the intervening period, five states had held assembly elections and, in three (Assam, West Bengal and Kerala), the Congress had come to power along with its allies. In Tamil Nadu, its ruling ally Dravida Munnetra Kazhagam (DMK) had lost badly, but that was attributed to the 2G scam and the A. Raja factor. In Puducherry, the Congress lost but that was inconsequential. So the spectre of electoral defeat was no longer looming over the government.

Fourthly, the Manmohan Singh government was confident about the two-pronged strategy it had devised to deal with Team Anna. The government had decided in principle that Anna would not be allowed to sit on an indefinite fast. They would also work to unsettle Team Anna; especially to scratch Anna's own moral aura.

So a new confrontation was brewing. One could sense that in the way government members in the joint drafting committee were dealing with Team Anna in the last few meetings. Finally, it led to both sides levelling allegations against each other. After the last joint drafting committee meeting in the third week of June, when Arvind announced that two drafts of the Lokpal Bill would be put before the cabinet, one drafted by the government and the other by civil society members, we all knew that the government would not succumb to Team Anna's demand for a strong Lokpal Bill. The government had promised to have the Lokpal Bill ready by 30 June and then it was to be introduced in Parliament. Anna had already threatened that if the Parliament did not pass a strong Lokpal Bill by 15 August he would start another *anshan*. These fruitless joint drafting committee meetings had virtually ensured that. It was just a matter of time. In an indication of how the government planned to deal with Anna's *anshan*, on 22 June, Digvijay Singh issued a veiled warning that Anna would be meted out the same treatment as Baba Ramdev was given.

I was therefore not surprised at the Delhi Police's attitude when Team Anna applied for permission to sit on a fast at JP Park in central Delhi. The Delhi Police asked them to give an undertaking agreeing to twenty-two conditions. Two were most contentious: one, the protest could be held only for three days, and two, the number of participants could not exceed 5,000. Team Anna refused to sign on the dotted line. On 13 August, Kiran Bedi called the undertaking a political document. I was told by my sources that Kiran Bedi was not wide of the mark. The idea was to frustrate and provoke Team Anna. The police commissioner of Delhi was taking instructions directly from the home ministry and P. Chidambaram was keeping a tab on each and every movement. Senior police officers candidly admitted that it was a political decision and permission would be granted only when the political masters so ordered. Anna held a press conference and warned that the protest would continue beyond three days and that, if the government were to use force, people would react strongly.

A showdown between the government and Team Anna was imminent. On 13 August, Anna wrote a letter to Prime Minister Manmohan Singh requesting him to intervene with the police. He exhorted the prime minister to 'show courage'. He wrote, 'You are seventy-nine years old and occupy the highest position in the country. What else do you want from life? Show some gumption and take concrete steps. We are willing to sacrifice our lives for the country and look to the leader of the country to give us an appropriate place.' By late night, the prime minister's office responded without any assurance. He wrote, 'My office does not in any way get involved with the decision-making process. I would request you to address your grievances to the statutory authorities concerned.'

The attack by the Congress got more and more aggressive as the day of the protest approached. Manish Tiwari will always remember – and always regret – what he said. He had been designated to speak to the media and had already discussed with his senior colleagues in the party. According to what a senior party member told me, there is an institutional mechanism in the Congress party to decide what is to be said to the press. The content is always pre-decided. Manish Tiwari had a clear brief to attack Anna and raise a moral question. As the official spokesperson of the ruling party, he said, '*Kisan Babu Rao Hazare urf Anna hum tumse poochhna chahte hain tum kis muh se bhrashtachar ke khilaf upwas par baithe ho. Tum khud ooper se neeche tak bhrashtachar me lipte ho, aur ye main nahi kah raha, ye supreme court ke poorva judge ki aguwai me bani ek janch kameti ne kaha hai.*' (We want to ask Kisan Babu Rao Hazare aka Anna what moral authority he has to fast in protest against corruption. You are corrupt from head to toe; I am not saying this, this has been said by a probe panel which was headed by a former Supreme Court judge.) This came as a boon in disguise for Team Anna. After the Jantar Mantar fast, Anna had acquired a stature that was unparalleled in contemporary India. He was seen as a mahatma, a saint who, at the age of seventy-four, was fighting against the central government. He was an icon for the common man on the street. But here was a Congressman who was being 'deliberately' disrespectful to a man his father's age.

Factually, Manish Tiwari was not wrong. The problem was with his tone and sarcasm and the use of the 'tum' form of address in Hindi. It offended the sensibilities of the Hindi heartland. People were outraged. I met dozens of people at Ramlila Maidan who hated him for what he said that day.

In Hindi, an elder is never addressed as 'tum' – the correct word would be the more respectful 'aap'. In English there is no such hierarchy. If he had spoken in English, there may not have been as much of a reaction. Manish Tiwari later told me that he never intend to insult Anna. His problem was language. He had been born and brought up in Punjab – where 'tum' is perfectly acceptable – and had been educated in English. He knew Hindi but it was not his native language. He candidly admitted that he just wanted to raise a moral question about how a man who had been accused of corrupt practices by a commission headed by a retired Supreme Court judge could claim to fight corruption. Manish Tiwari later apologized to Anna in writing but the damage was done.

It is true that the Justice P.B. Savant Commission has indicted Anna, along with four other National Congress Party (NCP) ministers, Padmasingh Patil, Suresh Dada Jain, Nawab Malik and Vijay Kumar Gavit. The Commission was appointed in September 2003 to probe allegations against the above-mentioned ministers and their counter-allegations against Anna. The Commission found Anna's Hind Swaraj Trust involved in illegally spending Rs 2.20 lakh of its funds on his birthday celebrations. The Hind Swaraj Trust was formed in 1995 and was to work in the areas of rural development and moral education.

In April 2005, a three-member task force headed by former chief secretary D.M. Sukthankar was appointed to recommend action if any loss was caused to the state government by the acts of all five persons, including Anna. In September 2005, the task force submitted its report. It had given an almost clean chit to Anna. The Sukthankar Task Force observed in its report, 'Although, as correctly pointed out by the Commission, the expenditure . . . amounted to misapplication of the funds of the Trust, was not authorized by the Trust Deed and was, therefore, beyond the authority of the Trust, we are not inclined to recommend any action, much less prosecution, against Sri Hazare for the reason that Sri Hazare's role is that of a whistle blower and he has been working in the spirit of a missionary to curb corruption by public servants, including ministers. This incident appears to us to be inadvertent. We feel that the observations made by the Commission against Sri Hazare are by themselves sufficient to chasten a person like him and to induce him to learn for the future to discipline and control his workers and followers.' The task force further added that, 'while the functioning of Hazare's Trusts had indeed shown breaches of various provisions of the Bombay Public Trusts Act, the offences are punishable with a fine of up to Rs 1,000.

With no intention whatever of belittling these provisions it cannot be gainsaid that these offences are relatively minor and are of a technical nature.' The report also said that such breaches were common in the rural areas of Maharashtra due to ignorance and lack of administrative support. Manish Tiwari is a true soldier of his party, so he quoted what suited his party's interest. He told a half-truth to the world, but the plan backfired.

This was not the only mistake that the Congress in all its arrogance made. Under the influence of the home ministry, Delhi Police withheld permission for the *anshan*. On the morning of 15 August, Prime Minister Manmohan Singh, through his speech from the ramparts of the Red Fort, tried to convince Anna of the fact that the power to make laws rests only with the Parliament. Manmohan Singh also reviewed the situation for two hours with his party colleagues at the Congress headquarters. The meeting was attended by Pranab Mukherjee, Information and Broadcasting Minister Ambika Soni, Janardan Dwivedi and Rahul Gandhi. It was decided that no personal attacks would be made on Anna.

Anna also reacted. He said that the prime minister was speaking Kapil Sibal's language. Anna warned the government to be prepared for any eventuality. If the Delhi Police had secret plans, so did Team Anna. Anna wanted to address a press conference in the evening before his fast. The news that Anna wanted to visit Rajghat to pay his respects to Bapu was cleverly leaked. It was Manish and Arvind's brainwave to take Anna to Rajghat. They did not know if Anna would be ready, but Anna promptly agreed. The news spread like wildfire. The media rushed to capture a glimpse of Anna. His supporters also reached in large numbers. In no time, Rajghat was filled with thousands of supporters and onlookers. The Delhi Police was caught unawares. Anna was sitting in front of Bapu Samadhi on the lush green grass. His eyes were closed. Tears were seen rolling down his cheeks. He seemed to be meditating. Nobody knew how long he would be there. It was already past six. Everybody was wondering what would happen if he decided to sit on a fast at Rajghat instead of JP Park. This was the one place where they would not dare use force to remove Anna. The home secretary had also reached the police headquarters. Anna's blood pressure was shooting up. Many senior police officers were convinced that they would lose their jobs if Anna continued to sit at Rajghat. Arvind realized the plight of the policemen and quietly informed them that Anna would leave the place by 6.45 p.m. Rajghat closes at 7.00 p.m. Anna got up at a quarter to seven and the Delhi Police breathed again. Anna left for the press conference at the Constitution Club.

Manish later explained that it had a lot of symbolism. Anna was an ardent supporter of Gandhiji. The idea was to convey to the larger audience that Anna was following the path of Mahatma Gandhi. He was also experimenting with truth, non-violence and peace in his fight against corruption. And the party which was burdened by history to carry the legacy of Gandhiji was seen to be forgetting the teachings of the Mahatma and conniving with the corrupt. The message was loud and clear. The stage was set for a battle that history would bear witness to. The next day was a very big day for both Team Anna and the government. A democratically elected government was up against its own citizens.

ANNA DETAINED

DAY 1 – 16 AUGUST

I was very tired the next morning. I had slept late, having had to organize and plan for the day. Anna was adamant about going to JP Park despite being denied permission by the Delhi Police. The police were also ready with its contingency plan. By late night we had information that the police would not allow Anna and his team to sit on a dharna. Now the question was what action the police would take to thwart Team Anna's plan. As a TV news channel, we had to be ready for every contingency. No reporter was to get any day off. Everybody was asked to be in office as early as 6.00 a.m., except those who had to manage the afternoon and night shifts. Anna and his senior team members had stayed put at Supreme Apartments, Mayur Vihar. Four of our teams were deployed to cover every single development. We were having our early morning cup of tea and anxiously waiting for the day to unfold. There was suspense and excitement in the newsroom. There was an argument in one corner. The crime reporter was of the view that '*police Anna ko uttha legi aur* arresting *me dal degi*' (the police would pick up Anna and would put him in jail). He was dead sure. He has solid contacts in the Delhi Police. Apparently, he had just spoken to some senior officer. A political reporter scoffed at him, 'You guys have no understanding of politics. This is not a simple crime story. It will have a political fallout. If Anna is arrested, there will be mayhem and unrest. The

Parliament is already in session. The government will have to face tough questions and might find it difficult to answer them.' He believed that with Sonia Gandhi away they would not chance such a major risk.

As the suspense deepened, a phone rang on the assignment desk. A reporter called from Anna's place. He was very excited. 'Anna has been detained.'

'What?'

'Yes. Anna has been detained by the Delhi Police. Please break this news.'

There was mayhem in the newsroom. I volunteered to go live for the analysis with other reporters. I also shouted that we had to get the visuals before any other channel did. The great game had just begun. What we did not realize then is that the roller-coaster ride that was to come would be the thirteen days that changed India.

At that time we had had very little information. We had no clue about when and how he had been arrested. But it had been confirmed that Anna, Arvind and Manish had been detained and would most probably be taken to the Gazetted Officers Mess in Civil Lines.

I was live on air, answering a question from the anchor in the studio. My cellphone was on the floor. As I finished my reply, I picked up the phone. There was an SMS. It was from Arvind Kejariwal. It was what we call breaking news.

'Anna was coming down from the lift to go to Rajghat when he was detained.' It was short and crisp; straight from the horse's mouth.

I jumped. I immediately told the assignment desk to note that down. The very next minute the information was on air. Another SMS popped up in my message box.

'Anna requested the police to take him to Rajghat but they refused.' Arvind had sent another one.

Reporters at ground zero were groping in the dark. Here I was, sitting in the newsroom, and I had first-hand knowledge of what had happened. There was frenzy at the output and assignment desks. No other channel had any such information. We were ahead of our competitors. I could easily imagine what was happening in the rival channels' newsrooms. There is no bigger kick than breaking bigger stories ahead of your competitors. We newsmen live for these few minutes of adrenalin. No drug can provide such a kick or professional high as this. By now I had realized that Arvind was also in police detention and he was discretely sending these messages.

'Anna asked them what his crime was; they said they were under orders.' Arvind could not have been more helpful; plus he clearly had news sense. This was also his way of communicating with his supporters through a news channel. He was telling them that Anna and his team were being detained illegally and against their will. And Anna was even denied the basic right to pay his respects to Mahatma Gandhi. Arvind was raising a question through his SMS: how insensitive this government was and how scared it was of Anna and his non-violent means of protest. I also did not lose the opportunity and I wrote back, 'What did Anna say when he was denied permission to go to Rajghat?'

Arvind replied, 'Anna said this was against the Constitution and this had never happened in last twenty years of his struggle.'

Anna was in the mood for a confrontation. This situation was indicative of his future resolve, his toughness. He was a warrior of innumerable agitations. But for the Delhi Police and its political masters it was a first of its kind experience.

I asked, 'What happened next?'

The reply was prompt. 'Anna and Arvind asked where they were being taken, they refused to tell.'

The police strategy was clear. They wanted to keep it a secret so that a crowd did not reach there and create a law-and-order problem.

Now I was curious to know where he had been shifted.

The Delhi Police Officers Mess at Civil Lines.

'*Anna not here.*'

Now his sentences were getting shorter. I could only presume that he was surrounded by a lot of policemen and could be caught messaging and leaking information. The two stalwarts were separated from each other.

I still persisted. 'Where is Anna? If you and Anna are under arrest, what will happen to the movement and who will lead it?'

Arvind was more than quick. He replied, '*Anna not with me. But anshan will take place in jail.*'

This was his last SMS. Later Arvind told me that his cellphone had been taken away by the police. The last SMS had thrown some light on Team Anna's strategy. They had an inkling that they might be arrested and had decided in advance to make the most of this arrest.

By now, details from other sources were also available. Anna and his team were denied permission to sit on a fast and Section 144 was imposed on areas adjoining JP Park. They had a hunch that they would not be allowed to go near the park. Team Anna was apprehensive about being picked up by the police on the night before the fast was scheduled to begin. In such a scenario, Anna and Arvind would not protest beyond a point. Manish Sisodia would have to ensure that he did not get caught and remained outside to coordinate and lead the movement. When this did not happen, they decided to go to Rajghat. Anna would sit there for four to five hours. A crowd would assemble and the movement would gain momentum and, from there, they would try to move to JP Park. The Team was sure that the police would not stop them from going to Rajghat. But they were mistaken.

By 7.12 a.m. they were out of the flat and walking towards the lift. The lift was downstairs. It stayed there for some time. There was a man on the stairs. As he saw them walking, he called someone. By 7.16 a.m. the lift came up; around five police officers emerged from it. Team Anna still did not expect to be arrested. The policemen requested them to go inside and went in with them to talk. Anna had no problem. Deputy Commissioner of Police (DCP) Ashok Chand was leading the police team.

He said, 'I have instructions to ensure that you don't go anywhere.'

Manish asked, 'Are you detaining us?'

Ashok Chand replied, 'Yes. Something like that.'

According to Manish, Anna protested and asked, 'What's my crime?'

Ashok Chand said, 'I have no idea but I have orders from above. If you are allowed to go to JP Park, there will be a law and order problem.'

When Anna requested them to take him to Rajghat, they promised to talk to their seniors. Manish could sense what was happening. As per the original plan, he tried to avoid being detained. He moved towards the stairs. An assistant commissioner of police (ACP)-rank officer asked him to come along. Manish tried to avoid him but the officer detained him with a firm hand on his shoulder. Everybody went down. They were gently shoved into police jeeps. Manish heard an officer talking to somebody on the phone, 'Sir, all of them are with us. Target 3 is with me.' Manish was giving some instruction on the phone and he was told to stop as he was under police detention. It was now apparent that the police was serious. Arvind was the first to reach the GO Mess at Civil Lines. It was 8.25 a.m. then. Not too long ago, at 8.00 a.m., Kiran Bedi, and soon after, Shanti Bhushan had also been detained at Rajghat. Home Minister P. Chidambaram admitted that he was aware of the developments but denied that he had put any extra pressure on the police to detain Team Anna.

Anna's detention infuriated people. They were ready to go to jail for him. People started coming out on to the roads. All the roads led to the GO Mess. The police was also prepared. A day before, they had worked out their plan. According to a senior police officer, 110 teams had been formed to arrest people were they to march on the roads. Each team was led by an inspector-rank officer with one sub-inspector and ten police personnel. Out of ten, four were lady constables, four male constables and two head constables. Each police personnel would have a helmet, body protector, a cane shield and a bullet-proof jacket. But they were not supposed to carry any kind of weapon; not even a lathi. They were under strict instructions not to use any kind of force and not to be discourteous to protestors. All the teams were to reach JP Park at 6.00 a.m. sharp. Every team would have an emergency response vehicle. According to ace IBN7 crime reporter, Alok Verma, 'Violence had to be avoided at any cost. Maintaining peace was the top priority.' It was apparent that the Central government did not want Team Anna to get any mileage. Probably, they had learnt a lesson or two from the Ramdev episode. The police had also identified fifteen stadia in the city where the arrested people were supposed to be put in an emergency situation. Additionally, two special executive magistrates were also requisitioned to be present in case anyone provoked violence and such people could be produced before the magistrate and sent to Tihar Jail.

In a situation like this, the newsroom is an ideal place to be in. I was getting information from all corners. Delhi was really volatile. Though the police had blocked two approach roads, one from the Ring Road and other from IP College, to the GO Mess where Anna was kept, and despite the heavy rain, supporters kept pouring in from all sides. By 10.00 a.m., the police were demanding more buses to carry protestors to the Chhatrasal Stadium, which had been converted into a temporary jail. It is another matter that the stadium looked more like a picnic spot the more it filled with protestors. All of them were singing patriotic songs and seemed to not mind being there at all. People from other parts of the country also spontaneously organized shows of their solidarity with Team Anna. Anna supporters resorted to blocking traffic, squatting on roads, organizing marches, sitting on dharnas and shouting anti-government slogans. People took casual leave to participate in the protest. In the absence of Anna, Arvind and Manish, Prashant Bhushan was asked to ensure that he did not get arrested and continued to lead the movement. A meeting was held at the Gandhi Peace Foundation. It was attended by the rest of the core committee members of Team Anna. The committee decided to hold a press conference and to challenge the government action in a court of law, which they did not pursue later. During the day, Kapil Sibal, who was attending a seminar in Delhi, was heckled and shown black flags.

The government was heavily criticized in the virtual world too. People used Facebook and Twitter to express themselves. Film personalities asked uncomfortable questions on Twitter. In this charged atmosphere how would the Parliament remain unaffected? The government knew it would be difficult to handle the Opposition. The Cabinet Committee on Political Affairs (CCPA) met just before the Parliament session was to begin. The National Democratic Alliance (NDA) was also busy fine-tuning its strategy. By all accounts the Parliament session was to be stormy.

By 11.00 a.m. the session started. The Opposition wanted to suspend the question hour and debate Anna's detention. The speaker disallowed notice for an adjournment motion on Anna. Sushma Swaraj insisted that those who had given notices should be permitted to briefly touch upon the subject. In a chorus, the entire Opposition demanded a statement from the prime minister. The Opposition said that the issue was not the Lokpal Bill, but the government's attitude. It was against the grain of a democratically elected government to not allow a peaceful, non-violent protest. They collectively opined that it was the fundamental right of a citizen to protest peacefully and that this right could not be snatched at any cost. After three disruptions, both the Houses of Parliament were adjourned for the day at noon. This event had much wider political ramifications for the government. It had united a divided Opposition. As far as I can remember, I had not seen this kind of an Opposition unity after the fall of the V.P. Singh government in 1990. It was a great political picture to see Sushma Swaraj in the company of Mulayam Singh Yadav, Lalu Yadav and leaders of TDP, CPI and CPM outside the parliament building. All the

Opposition leaders met in Sushma Swaraj's room at 2.00 p.m. and decided to attack the government together.

The government's ill-considered arrests had boomeranged. By the afternoon, it was nervous. The government's plan of action showed a clear lack of political understanding. Firstly, it made the mistake of equating Anna with Baba Ramdev. Anna had a much wider acceptability and a cleaner image. Secondly, the Parliament was in session and only a fool could have thought that the Opposition would keep quiet if something of this nature happened. In its arrogance, the government appeared to have forgotten that it had been heavily criticized for Ramdev's eviction from Ramlila Maidan. It was clear that a government led by a career bureaucrat and advised by two eminent but non-political lawyers was incapable of handling a political situation of this magnitude. Sonia Gandhi's absence had hurt the Congress badly.

As political momentum gained ground, the government readied its defence. Finance Minister Pranab Mukherjee said that the Opposition did not let the government reply. Around 1.00 p.m. the group of ministers in charge of the media had a meeting. After the meeting P. Chidambaram, Kapil Sibal and Ambika Soni decided to brief the press. In reply to a question, Chidambaram said that the government had nothing to do with the actions of the Delhi Police. Law was taking its own course. Obviously, by now the government was in damage control mode, and was trying to distance itself from the Delhi Police. But who would believe them?

Meanwhile, the crowd had been swelling at the GO Mess. According to the police, more than 1,500 people had been detained in Delhi alone. Anna and other members of the team who had been detained along with him were shifted to the DCP (West)'s office in Rajouri Garden. By 1.30 p.m. Anna and others had been formally arrested and produced before a magistrate. They were charged with disrupting peace and obstructing government servants in their duty under Sections 107 and 151 of the CrPC. All of them refused to sign bail bonds. By 3.20 p.m. they were sent to Tihar Jail. Team Anna sensed a big opportunity in the government's stupidity. Had they been detained and taken to some obscure area and released, their movement would have died. Arvind confessed to me that by arresting them the government was fulfilling their wishes. The government was so ill-advised that Team Anna was sent to Tihar Jail – notorious for keeping not only big terrorists and hardened criminals but also big-time alleged scamsters like A. Raja, Suresh Kalmadi, Kanimozhi and other senior officials from the telecom department as well as top executives of big corporate houses. It was difficult for the common man to comprehend what crime Anna had committed to have to share the jail with such people. In the public eye, the government was bracketing Anna, who was fighting corruption, with those against whom he had declared war; the message that went out was that the government was so blind that it did not see the difference between Anna and A. Raja.

There were eight people from Team Anna in jail. Anna and his secretary Suresh Pathare, Dada Pathare and Manish were together in jail number 4. Arvind was in jail number 3 with three other supporters. Their medical check-up was done and arrangements were made for Anna to rest. Manish took off his clothes and wore what was prescribed by the jail manual. Anna was still in his own clothes. Anna also expressed his desire to change his clothes, but the jail staff requested him with folded hands to not do so. As Manish told me later, the jail staff were extra polite with Anna and were heard saying that since they were duty-bound and were in uniform they were helpless; otherwise they were his supporters and would do anything for him. Anna would just smile. Manish was to have shared the cell with Anna. I could see the glint in his eyes when he narrated the story to me.

By evening, good sense prevailed upon the government. The top leadership of the government met. Prime Minister Manmohan Singh and Rahul Gandhi also consulted each other and it was decided to release Anna and his team. This message was conveyed to the jail authorities just before 9.00 p.m. An inspector went running to Anna and gave him the news. By 9.00 p.m., all the news channels were agog with the news of Anna's imminent release. The newsroom was once again filled with excitement. Speculation was rife of course. Somebody said that Rahul Gandhi was upset with the way the entire thing had been handled. Later, when I confronted senior members of the Congress, I did not get a clear answer. Was Rahul Gandhi consulted before Anna was arrested? In Sonia Gandhi's absence, Rahul was the most powerful leader. It was beyond my comprehension that he was not kept in the loop about such an important decision. But late at night Congressmen were busy telling the world that Rahul's intervention had got Anna released. But a few were also saying that it was at his insistence that Anna had been arrested. There was no independent confirmation of either statement.

Anyway, Anna was thinking along different lines. Even his team members had no idea. When he was informed about his release, he asked why he should leave. The jail staff were dumbstruck. They were used to dealing with individuals who would do anything to get out of jail. A smart inspector informed Anna with folded hands that the deputy inspector general (DIG) wanted to see him in his office and that they would come back after the meeting. This was a ploy to take Anna away from the jail premises. Anna went along with him. Once Anna reached there, the inspector refused to take him back. His job was done. Now he was in the DIG's office and was technically out of jail. When Anna realized that he had been tricked, he lost his cool. He asked, 'Where will I go? Will I be allowed to go to Ramlila Maidan?' Anna was adamant about demanding unconditional permission for his rally. The government was not willing to allow him to protest without agreeing to the conditions though they again offered him five places of his choice where he could sit on an *anshan*. When he was informed about the conditions that had been laid out he immediately announced that he was not going out of Tihar and would

continue his fast there itself. It was 11.00 p.m. Now it was time
for the seventy-four-year-old Anna to trick the government.
This angry old man foxed the government. He needed to be
handled with care, but with the natural arrogance of politicians,
care was in short supply. At the end of the day, the mighty
government was humbled by a humble man from Ralegan
Siddhi. Anna was resting in a corner of the DIG's office, which
had temporarily been converted into his rest house till he
decided to leave.

It was almost midnight. There were still a few protestors
sitting outside the jail. Arvind decided to stay back with Anna.
Manish was told to go out and explain to the supporters and
also to take charge of the movement. Manish came out. He sat
on a dharna. The crowd was not big. One could see less than a
hundred people. An appeal was immediately made on the
social media. Shivendra very proudly told me that a message
was floated on Facebook and Twitter that Tihar Jail was our
Tahrir Square and that people should assemble there in large
numbers, stay there, sleep there. Bulk SMSs were also used for
sending out an appeal. By 1.30 a.m. the roads outside Tihar
started filling up. A small loudspeaker and a mike were also
organized. Till then, the crowd had no leader. People had come
of their own accord; a few of them were holding fort till
Manish arrived. Now they had a seasoned leader. The
government did not know what was in store for it. And I was
exhausted in spite of the adrenalin that the news breaks had
pumped into my system.

ANNA DEFIANT. PEOPLE FURIOUS

DAY 2 – 17 AUGUST

'But there comes a time in the life of a nation when hard decisions have to be taken,' Indira Gandhi had said on 22 July 1975, when she appeared before the Rajya Sabha after having imposed Emergency on the country. Thirty-six years later, the man in her shoes had also taken a difficult decision – that of arresting Anna. But there was a difference. Mrs Gandhi did not change her decision despite national and international condemnation, but the Manmohan Singh government could not stand firm even for a day; within hours they had changed their mind and allowed Anna to leave jail. The tables had been turned; now the government was pleading with Anna and he was dictating the terms.

On 17 August, it was 8 o'clock in the morning. Anna was awake. He had had a good night's sleep. The director general of the Tihar Jail had come to see him. IBN7 reported in its 9.00 p.m. bulletin that the DG had requested Anna to leave the jail as there was a massive crowd outside and it was affecting the normal functioning of the jail. Anna refused point-blank. He said he would not move unless the government gave him a written unconditional assurance allowing him to protest. The DG tried his level best to convince Anna, but he just got up and left for his bath. Anna was in for the long haul. After the bath, Anna returned to the conference room, spread his mat on the floor and sat down to meditate.

It was 10.15 a.m., and by now the message had reached the government. It decided to give persuasion one more shot. The DCP of the Crime Branch, Delhi, also came with his team and tried to reason with Anna. He recounted the scene outside Tihar. There were people all around, especially in front of the main gate. Roads were choked and it was impossible for traffic to move. He also told Anna that it was disrupting the daily supplies to prisoners. Anna had the same answer. The DCP left without success. Medha Patkar had also joined the protesters by this time. Within an hour, Kiran Bedi was also seen addressing people.

It was now a battle of nerves. By 12 o'clock, the Delhi Police had another proposal. As reported by IBN7, the police was ready to allow him to protest at Ramlila Maidan for seven days and to extend on a daily basis after that. The police had also shown willingness to lift Section 144 of CrPC at Ramlila Maidan and adjoining areas. But Anna would not entertain any condition at all, be it of place or number of protestors or of the number of days. It was midday. The heat was scorching. People were sweating profusely. A few of the protestors could not bear the heat and fainted. They were provided temporary medical help by the young doctors who had gathered in support of Anna.

As the clock struck one, Anna requested the jail authorities to allow him to discuss a few things with his team members. By 1.30, his core team, comprising Kiran Bedi, Prashant Bhushan, Medha Patkar, Swami Agnivesh, Manish Sisodia, Akhil Gogoi and Art of Living coordinator Bharat went inside. By 2 o'clock, Sri Sri Ravishankar went in. It was at this time that Baba Ramdev was seen at the gate of the Tihar Jail. He was not in his element. The fiasco of the Ramlila rally was still writ large on his face. His trademark confidence was missing. For a while there were rumours that he wasn't allowed inside the gate. From a distance he seemed to be struggling at the gate. Conspiracy theorists immediately advocated that Anna did not want to see him. 'There was still enough bitterness between the two,' they were heard saying. But it was just a rumour. Within fifteen minutes he was with Anna and his team, discussing future strategies to take the movement forward. A few members were ready to accept the conditions laid down by the police. They were of the opinion that once permission was granted and Anna began the fast, it would be difficult for the police to take any action to evict them. But Anna was adamant. He wanted no conditions and was not willing to compromise on the issue of the written permission.

By 2.45 p.m., the core committee members came out. No solution had been reached. Prashant Bhushan announced that Anna wanted an unconditional exit from Tihar and if the police did not listen to him, he would continue his anshan inside the jail premises. He also appealed to the people to assemble at India Gate at 4.00 p.m. The social media was active once again. This was testing time for both the sides. There was a deadlock. Team Anna had spelt out its strategy; the government had to react.

Within seventy-five minutes, India Gate was full of people. India Gate, a national monument, was built in 1931 in the memory of 90,000 soldiers of the Indian Army, who laid down their lives during World War I, serving the British Raj. It was designed by Edwin Lutyens and inspired by the Arc de Triomphe in Paris. After Independence, this monument became the Indian Army's memorial to the unknown soldier, i.e., Amar Jawan Jyoti. On a normal day, this place is a favourite picnic spot for the Indian middle classes. Families come from faraway places in buses and the metro with their little children and their picnic baskets. This is also a place for families to meet prospective brides and grooms. Young girls and boys can be seen on the lush green lawns, stealing some cosy moments away from the hustle and bustle of Delhi life. But on that day the scene was different.

That day, India Gate was making a political statement; it was a place for a show of strength. People came there in large numbers to send a political message to the power establishment.

The protestors were restless and angry but not undisciplined. They were shouting anti-government slogans, but they were not abusive. This was a politically charged crowd, but it was against politicians. They were not carrying the flag of any political party – only the national flag. They had come to change India, not to create chaos. Anna was incidental.

Similar scenes were also seen at the Juhu Beach in Mumbai. In different forms, and in different shapes, thousands marched in a candlelight procession in Mumbai. In fact, similar displays of support were seen across India. Every city, in its own way, descended on the streets to support Anna. By 4.45 p.m., the anti-corruption campaigners marched from India Gate to Jantar Mantar via Parliament Street. Undoubtedly traffic was disrupted and people took hours to reach home. My reporters told me that nobody was complaining, if anything, they were cheering the marchers. Lutyens Delhi came to a halt. It was difficult to count the numbers as it was a moving crowd but, by any account, it was in thousands. I am sure the government agencies must have given their inputs to their masters. The clock was ticking. It was past 6.00 p.m. Kiran Bedi came out of Tihar – the same Tihar that she had at one time managed and administered. She had been DG, Tihar Jail, and was credited with major reforms in the jail. She had only this to say: Ramlila Maidan had been decided as the place for the *anshan* but Anna was not ready to leave yet. He did not want any conditions attached. Now it was certain that Anna would spend the night in Tihar.

Meanwhile, Parliament was witness to one of the harshest criticisms of the Anna movement by none other than Prime Minister Manmohan Singh during the day. Singh was of the opinion that the Anna movement was challenging a basic principle of the Indian democracy – that of the Parliament's authority to enact laws. He also insinuated that Anna and his team were playing into the hands of the forces that were opposed to the country's economic growth. In a way, it was the first structured critique of the Anna movement from the government and the PM was not mincing words. He very categorically said, 'As far as I am able to gather, Sri Anna Hazare questions these principles and claims a right to impose his Jan Lokpal Bill upon Parliament.' He further added, 'I acknowledge that Sri Anna Hazare may be inspired by high ideals in his campaign to set up a strong and effective Lokpal; however, the path he has chosen to impose his draft of a bill upon Parliament is totally misconceived and fraught with grave consequences for our parliamentary democracy.'

The prime minister also questioned another rhetoric of Team Anna and the movement. Team Anna had been saying time and again that the Parliament had stopped representing the will of the people and that people no longer related to MPs and MLAs. Those people had shown more trust in Anna and his team and that is why they were leading the movement on behalf of the people. The PM's attack was very sharp. He said, 'Those who believe that their voice, and their voice alone, represents the will of 1.2 billion people should reflect on that position. They must allow the elected representatives of the people in Parliament to do the job that they are elected for.' The prime minister's words held utter contempt for Team Anna and members of the civil society who claimed to be waging the war against corruption. But the prime minister was not alone. Booker Prize winner Arundhati Roy wrote (*The Hindu*, 21 August 2011), '"The People" only means the audience that has gathered to watch the spectacle of a seventy-four-year-old man threatening to starve himself to death if his Jan Lokpal Bill is not tabled and passed by Parliament. "The People" are the tens of thousands who have been miraculously multiplied into millions by our TV channels, like Christ multiplied the fishes and loaves to feed the hungry. "A billion voices have spoken", we are told. "India is Anna."'

Historian and social commentator Ramchandra Guha (*The Telegraph*, 27 August 2011) did not want to be left behind. He had this to say about Anna: 'He challenges and taunts the government and its ministers, wagging his fingers at the cameras.

Once Hazare was the voice and conscience of the village of Ralegan Siddhi; now he demands that he be seen as the saviour of the nation itself.' Guha further wrote, 'The population of the Delhi metropolitan areas is in excess of 10 million; yet at their height, the crowd in the Ram Lila ground has never exceeded 50,000.' He not only mocked Anna's wisdom, but also questioned people's support to the movement. In a way, the movement was not seen as a fight against corruption. It was instead perceived to be a challenge to the parliamentary democracy. RTI activist and member of the Sonia Gandhi-led National Advisory Council, Aruna Roy was more forthcoming. She said to *Indian Express* editor-in-chief, Shekhar Gupta, 'It is a very interesting period in the history of India, because it is a challenge to our ideas, it is a challenge to what we thought, it is a challenge to the future of democracy, it is a challenge to people's voice, it is a challenge to legislative processes.'

The prime minister and important members of the intellectual class were missing the point that there was rampant, all-pervasive corruption in the system, which was depriving the common man of his dignity. These people did not realize the fact that there was a genuine mass movement and that a movement could not be created out of nothing. Arvind was right that, in this case, anger against corruption was at the point of eruption (*The Hindu*, 31 August 2011). Baijayant 'Jay' Panda, MP from Orissa, admitted that the vast majority of the agitators were unfamiliar with the details of the Jan Lokpal Bill, neither were they keen on nuance. All they cared for was that they had had it with corruption, and were not going to tolerate it any more, and fully supported Anna and the Jan Lokpal version (*Indian Express*, 5 September 2011). B.G. Verghese, the doyen of Indian journalism, was most apt when he wrote, 'At last, it's good that people are mobilized around Anna Hazare who has raised the central issue of corruption, that people are excited to fight for their rights as citizens, that it's a warning to the government and members of Parliament who lied to the people on important issues.' (*Nai Duniya*, 31 August 2011)

The prime minister's response in Parliament looked at the problem from a purely legalistic point of view, whereas it was a political problem. Anna and his team were trying to find a political solution to a social crisis. Arun Jaitley was not wrong when he reacted to the PM's statement sarcastically: that the problem with the government was that it had too many lawyers advising it. The same sentiment was echoed by Ashutosh Varshney, professor at Brown University (*Indian Express*, 7 September 2011). Varshney was right in his observations about the government: 'When it makes arguments, it has relied on legalities . . . The moment was political not legal.'

But the PM did not stop there. He went on to say, 'India is an emerging economy. We are now emerging as one of the important players on the world stage. There are many forces that would not like to see India realize its true place in the committee of nations. We must not play into their hands. We must not create an environment in which our economic progress is hijacked by internal dissension.' The PM very cleverly indicated at the invisible foreign hand behind the agitation. His colleague Rashid Alvi had earlier hinted at an American conspiracy behind the Anna movement. He said that the sophisticated nature of the orchestrated campaign called for urgent attention to the hidden hand. Hinting at the US hand, Rashid Alvi said, 'The US had never spoken about any movement in India. This is the first time that it did. We show the path of democracy to others, what was the need for the US to say so.' A day before, the US had commented that the Government of India should be more responsive to democratic protests. After many, many years, the invisible foreign hand was back to haunt the establishment.

Manmohan Singh's speech reminded me of Indira Gandhi's broadcast to the nation on All India Radio on the morning of 26 June 1975. In the early hours of that morning, Mrs Gandhi had stunned her cabinet colleagues by informing them that Emergency had been imposed and they were required to endorse the proclamation. In her address to the nation, she went on to speak of the deep and widespread conspiracy that had been brewing ever since she began to introduce certain progressive measures of benefit to the common man and woman of India. (Katherine Frank, *Indira – The Life of Indira Nehru Gandhi*, p. 381) She claimed that she had been besieged on all sides. The right, the left, Hindu extremists, Naxalites, terrorists and a myriad other elements were all hell-bent on destroying the law of the land. The enemy was diverse, but it was led by the fascist JP movement, backed by a 'foreign hand'. Kathrine Frank writes in her book that Indira Gandhi was convinced that she would be overrun and destroyed in the same way as Chile's Salvador Allende was when the CIA-backed General Augusto Pinochet had staged a coup against him in 1973. Mrs Gandhi's insecurity was understandable. She knew she was high up on Richard Nixon's hate list, but what about Manmohan Singh? He was the darling of American politicians. Manmohan Singh has also never hidden his fascination with America. He had staked his chair to push the Indo-US nuclear deal through. And at a time when world leaders were avoiding George W. Bush, the whole world had heard Manmohan Singh saying how much Indians loved President Bush. I know Congress as a party has a great appetite for such things. Even a month after Anna broke his fast, one senior and respected Congress leader tried telling me about this foreign hand. But I did not believe it then, nor do I believe it today. In my opinion, it was a ploy to divert public attention from the movement and initiate a worthless debate.

The Opposition also did not believe the PM either. The BJP blamed the government of being intolerant to citizens' rights and creating an Emergency-like situation. NDA convenor Sharad Yadav was equally harsh, especially on Kapil Sibal. Yadav sarcastically advised Sibal to stop quoting provisions of law when dealing with political problems. He remarked, 'Heavens would not have fallen if the veteran Gandhian and supporters had been given a venue.' And clearly the country's citizens were unconvinced too. They were parking themselves outside Tihar with much gusto. By evening, the crowd was overflowing. All the approach roads were closed off. People were squatting all over the road. There was palpable excitement. Support for Anna was growing with every passing moment, as was the crowd. At times the crowd seemed unmanageable. Leaders of the agitation were worried. A volunteer informed Nitin Dabar that there was chaos at Tihar and something needed to be done. Nitin was working with Art of Living as a motivation teacher. He had done an MBA in finance. Before joining Sri Sri, Nitin had worked with reputed companies like *Hindustan Times*, American Express and Genpact as an executive. But he was more interested in music and social work. According to his father, the whole family was shocked when Nitin left his lucrative job and joined Art of Living, working for peanuts. But Nitin was happy. He had found peace. He was not a trained singer and had never sung before an audience from a public platform. But Sri Sri had recognized his talent and asked him to be a regular singer at his satsangs. Nitin was inclined toward spiritual singing. Since Sri Sri was one of the founder members of the India against Corruption campaign, Nitin also tagged along. Before this campaign he was also involved with the Clean Delhi drive. On 30 January, at the Ramlila Maidan, for the first time ever, he formally sang for India against Corruption from the dais. And he became an integral part of the anti-corruption campaign.

When he got a call from Tihar, he immediately consulted Sri Sri, who instructed him to rush and do what he could possibly do. Nitin and the poet Kumar Vishwas tried to control and entertain the crowd through music and poetry. It was quite a task. There was no music system. No mike. No platform to stand on and address people. No list of songs. He had trained himself to sing before a disciplined, peaceful, religious crowd in an air-conditioned ambience, where the atmosphere was spiritual and the mood sombre. It was a different scene in the stadium. It was hot and humid. People were sweating, sitting on the roads, on footpaths; a few had climbed trees. The atmosphere was charged. People were angry. Everybody was ready to make a statement. Slogan shouting was at its peak. There was no order; it could explode any minute. Nitin was there not to sing but to manage and motivate the crowd. He later confided in me that he had had no idea about what he would do or how he would do it. He knew how to sing; his voice was his only instrument. When he reached, there were more than ten thousand people. He looked around for an elevation. There was none. Then he discovered a tempo. He jumped on it. He asked the driver to remove the cover and took his bhopoo (horn). He hesitated for a second. Somebody from the crowd exhorted him to sing. *Hey man, you just start*. There was no leader, but the situation had thrown up a few. He could see a system emerging out of nothing. He collected himself, closed his eyes, lifted the bhopoo and let himself flow with that sea of humanity. He sang and sang and sang. Later he told me there was hardly any *sur tal*, but he was not bothered, he just continued. It was an open area. He was barely audible beyond a few metres. But within minutes one could feel order emerging out of the chaos. He had found his rhythm. This was the same Nitin who was seen at the Ramlila Maidan, singing, and only singing, every day, along with Anna. Music, spirituality and simplicity, wrote a new chapter in Indian history. Sadly, politicians were too complicated to see this.

DAY 3 – 18 AUGUST

By the time Nitin finished, it was 11.30 at night. He was a satisfied man and like millions of others was curious to know when Anna would emerge from jail.

The night was filled with suspense, but the morning brought a new dawn. Early on 18 August, Arvind announced that an understanding had been reached between the Delhi Police and Team Anna and they had got permission for a fifteen-day *anshan* at Ramlila Maidan without any preconditions. Somebody commented that Anna's demand had been for thirty days. It was explained that in its original application for the Maidan, Team Anna had requested fifteen days' permission only and now the Delhi Police had agreed to honour that. It was not a mean achievement. The Delhi Police had been willing to grant only three days to begin with. Anna had no faith in the government doctors who were to be in charge of his check-up during the fast. So a new character entered this saga – internationally renowned doctor, Naresh Trehan. From now on, Dr Trehan and his team of doctors would examine Anna thrice a day and he would fast as long as Dr Trehan felt he should. Home Secretary R.K. Singh also announced that an agreement had been reached between Team Anna and the Delhi Police. One deadlock was broken. There were many other hurdles.

Meanwhile, Swami Agnivesh spoke to the news agency PTI and hinted that Anna could come out any minute. There was commotion all over. It was 11.00 a.m., but the big question was, where would he go? Ramlila Maidan was not yet ready for the protestors. Because of the rains, it was slushy. The Municipal Corporation of Delhi (MCD) was trying hard to get things in order. Officials promised to hand over half the ground by noon. But, within minutes, the MCD revised its deadline to 3.00 p.m. Swami Agnivesh was confronted by reporters. He clarified that he hoped Anna would be out soon. It was expected that Anna would leave Tihar around 7.00 p.m. But at 3.00 p.m., when Team Anna went to the Ramlila Maidan for inspection, they realized that it would be difficult to prepare the stage, install CCTV cameras for security, a sound system for communication and organize other facilities like toilets and restrooms in such a short time. It was decided that Anna would spend another night in Tihar and he would reach Ramlila Maidan the next day.

Unfortunately, this did not mean that reporters could pack up for the day. From nowhere, a TV screen suddenly showed Anna in Tihar. He seemed relaxed and was talking. There was a scramble in the newsroom. Phones started ringing. Beat reporters were scurrying for cover. Vikrant Yadav who had been entrusted with staying in touch with Team Anna 24x7 had no answers. He promised to get back. He called in a few minutes, angry and complaining. 'I had already informed our office about this video clip during the day and also to keep an eye on YouTube.' He was a conscientious reporter and he had information that Kiran Bedi had shot this video message of Anna last night and was planning to pass it on to a rival channel. Vikrant created a ruckus and also warned them that it was not fair to favour one channel over another. He claimed that this was why Kiran Bedi had to put this clip up on YouTube; that particular channel had probably picked it up from there. Anyway, by this time, young cyber soldiers at the assignment desk had already downloaded the Anna clip and, in no time, the video message was on our channel too. In order not to lag behind in this blind race, we decided to drop a scheduled programme and use the Anna clip to maximum. The logic was simple. '*Log abhi Anna ko sunna aur dekhna chahte hain*' (People want to hear and watch Anna at the moment). It was not exclusive but it was the first visual of him after he went to Tihar and sat on a fast. Another battle was also on, other than the one between Team Anna and the government. There was nothing but Anna on TV channels.

Anna did not say anything earth-shattering in the video. He was talking to Kiran Bedi and said, 'Fifteen days' fast will pass by easily and I will continue till the Jan Lokpal Bill is passed . . . I will meet you all on Friday at Ramlila Maidan. I am getting energized by your support and feeling much better.' Then Anna made a political statement, 'I am convinced now that the Lokpal Bill cannot be stopped and if it does not come in fifteen days, I will extend my fast by seven days.' His voice had a tinge of sadness when he spoke about the government. 'The government had promised us that they would forward the positive points from the bill to the cabinet, but they betrayed us and, till it is formed, I will not stop.' And in the end he declared, 'If I die in the process, I will be happy as it is for the good of the society.'

The government and a section of the intellectual class that is,

I imagine, not familiar with the Gandhian method of satyagraha cried foul. They saw Anna as putting a pistol to his own head and asking for his wish to be fulfilled. Some people had a problem with another statement of his as well: 'Don't forget Bhagat Singh, Sukhdev and Rajguru who shouted slogans till minutes before they were hanged.' *Anna claims to be Gandhian, talks about non-violence and praises those who practised violence.* The problem was not with Anna; the problem was with those who were still caught in a time warp. Varshney put it succinctly: 'Thus far, the government has basically used the stock principles of old politics . . . faced with a novel moment, not comprehensible in older frameworks, a political imagination is the best way forward for the government and the politicians' (*Indian Express*, 7 September 2011). But was there any new imagination?

ANNA AT RAMLILA GROUNDS

DAY 4 – 19 AUGUST

You can call me an Anna supporter, but above everything else, I want corruption to be rooted out from the body politic, from the social fabric and from the national consciousness of the country. It is killing this country and as long as this disease afflicts us, we can never be proud citizens. So I was among those anxiously waiting for Anna to come out of jail. Equally, I was curious about what turn this movement would take and how the government would respond. Would there be a solution or, like many other movements in the past, would this one peter out too? As everybody was waiting for Anna to emerge, I was thinking about the past. Specifically, a video clip made by the India against Corruption team on 30 March. The roughly four-minute video was an appeal to the people to join Anna on 5 April when he was to go on an indefinite fast. The clip starts with the national flag in the backdrop of the Parliament and then a line: '*There is a scam when roads are made.*' This is followed by the details of the CWG scam, the 2G and other scams, and then the frame is filled with bold letters: '*Har taraf bhrashtachar, hahakar.*' These are very powerful words in Hindi and difficult to translate into English: there is corruption everywhere; anguished cries all around. The motive of the campaign was established with the very first picture. Then Kumar Vishwas is seen outside Parliament. He quotes the famous Urdu poet Allama Iqbal's words: '*Watan ki fikr kar nadan, museebat aane wali hai. Teri barbadiyon ke mashware hain asmano mein, tumhari dastan bhi na hogi dastanon mein'* (Worry about the country, O naive one, trouble is afoot, the skies foretell your destruction, nobody will remember you even in stories). And he fades into new graphics. *'Bhrashtachar ke khilaf, ek sakht kanoon lana hai. Jan Lokpal Bill ke liye, 5 April ko Jantar Mantar par Anna Hazare ka amaran anshan'* (A strong law has to be promulgated against corruption. Anna Hazare will sit on an indefinite hunger strike at Jantar Mantar on 5 April for the Jan Lokpal Bill).

Kumar Vishwas, a well-known Hindi poet, was born and brought up in Pilakhuwa, a place not very far from Delhi, and belongs to a class of poets that is very popular in kavi sammelans. He is a professor of Hindi literature and teaches in a college in Ghaziabad. As a young poet, he became a sensation in kavi sammelans with poems like: *'Koi deewana kahta hai, koi pagal samajhta hai, magar dharti ki bechaini ko bas badal samajhta hai'* (Somebody calls him besotted, somebody thinks he is mad, but only the clouds understand the earth's anxiety.) Now he is trying his hand in the Mumbai film industry as a lyricist. He had been involved with the India against Corruption campaign. When his good friend Manish broached the subject of Anna's *anshan* with him, he was excited and, at a meeting in his home in Vasundhara, Ghaziabad, on the day of Holi, they decided to make a video film to inform, attract and provoke people to think about corruption and to inspire them to come to Jantar Mantar and join the movement.

Kumar had just got over the professional isolation he had been facing due to the jealousy of his fellow poets and was in a good mood. Arvind thought that, given his popularity with the Hindi-speaking, small-town, middle-class youth, he could help introduce Anna to the Hindi belt. In the video, Kumar comes across as someone who introduces the subject, warns about the dangers of the problem – *'Tumhari dastan bhi na hogi dastano mein'* – and then provides the solution, probably inspired by the Buddhist saying 'there is misery, there is reason for the misery and finally a cure for the misery'. Kumar was acting as a *sutradhar*, a narrator; his job was to introduce the unknown hero, the debutant in Delhi, Anna. And then enters the real hero. Anna's introduction starts with the claim that his last fast resulted in the removal of six ministers and the suspension of 400 government officials. His profile in the video is less dramatic but powerful. '*Na banglay, na gadi, na bank balance. Niwas: gaon ke mandir ka ek kamra. Pariwar: poora desh. Kamai: sadgi, samarpan and sewa.* (No bunglow, no car, no bank balance. Residence: a room in a village temple. Family: the whole country. Income: simplicity, dedication and service.) And then Anna is seen sitting under a big tree, in black-and-white ambience, lost in a trance. He was projected as an antithesis of the modern-day politician. Standing in front of the Parliament he says: '*Jab tak ye bhrasht mantri aur varishth afsar jail nahin jayenge tab tak corruption par break nahi lagega*' (As long as these corrupt ministers and senior officers are not sent to jail, there will be no respite from corruption). He goes on to say, 'Jan Lokpal Bill should be made with people's participation.'

Then Anna gives a new twist to the entire debate, taking the campaign to an altogether different level. He says, 'This is the second freedom struggle.' He appeals to a new generation, people who have never seen the freedom struggle, people who have known the freedom struggle only through books, and invites them to be participants in a very big project, the project of a new freedom struggle; he pitches this as an opportunity to be part of a new history. Yes, it does strike a chord. There were emotional appeals of a different kind as well. A small child says, 'At this age, Anna is taking a giant stride – for whom?' This child of about five years simply says, 'I am keeping a fast, will you?' There is another appeal: 'An old man of seventy-eight years is sitting on a fast, what will we do?' The Hindi is more direct, '*Athahttar saal ka booddha upwas par baitha hai, hum kya karenge?*' It hits you. You end up asking yourself a question: 'What will I do? What should I do?' That video ends with a resolve that, together, we will change the world.

The world may not have changed, but millions now hope that nothing is impossible.

Anna had still not come out of jail. Meanwhile, a lot needed to be done at the Ramlila Maidan. The previous day, in a meeting at Prashant Bhushan's basement room in Jangpura, Arvind had declared that the ground had to be ready by ten the next morning. Kumar was given the responsibility of preparing the dais where Anna would sit and address the public. Kumar later told me that earlier, at Jantar Mantar, volunteers had merely been told to make a backdrop. Nothing was discussed. Left intellectuals tore into that backdrop and called it the visual evidence of Team Anna's link with the RSS. The backdrop was a large map of India with the symbolic representation of Mother India on it, along with stamp-size pictures of Mahatma Gandhi, Babasaheb Ambedkar, Bhagat Singh, Sukhdev, Rajguru, Chandra Shekhar Azad, Laxmibai, etc. Anna was seen with the picture of Mother India looming large over him. It could easily be confused with Goddess Durga holding the national flag in her hand, instead of some *shashtra* (weapon). Left intellectuals had a problem with this picture of Mother India. The picture was purported to have been borrowed from the RSS. The RSS uses such a picture to inspire its brand of nationalism in the cadre.

Anna had always talked about non-violence and proclaimed himself to be a follower of Gandhi. Therefore, questions were raised as to why pictures of Bhagat Singh, Sukhdev and Rajguru, who practised violence, were there. The answer was simple: they belonged to a different stream of the freedom struggle, but they were part of the same great project and they too inspired people with their supreme sacrifices. Despite the differences in ideology, Gandhiji and Bhagat Singh were fellow-travellers in the same journey, not enemies. But there was no denying the fact that it did create a confusion at the ideological level which was avoidable in terms of pure symbolism.

At Jantar Mantar, Anna was an unknown commodity, but in four months since the situation had changed. Now Anna was very big and his team much smarter. Anna now had to be treated differently as also his visual image. In this context, the look of the dais was very important. During the fast, that is the vantage point Anna would be seen from; so his look had to be smartly crafted, especially for TV, because TV speaks through images. An effort was also made to avoid controversy. It was a big challenge for Kumar and his friends. They decided on a look that would reflect Anna's simplicity and the gravity of the cause. It was decided to put up only Gandhi's portrait and do away with other icons of the freedom struggle. Now the question was, which portrait of Gandhi would suit the occasion? Initially, they decided to keep Gandhi's picture in one corner and keep a lot of space blank with a sentence in Hindi – *Jan Lokpal kanoon lao* – on top and below it in small letters, 'India against Corruption'. This backdrop was put up, but somehow it did not look aesthetically or politically appealing. So it was removed and another one was designed. Anna had reached the Ramlila Maidan by then, but he had not been consulted on this. The new backdrop was a lot better. A very imposing, larger-than-life image of Gandhi in the middle with '*Jan Lokpal Bill lao*' on top and 'India against Corruption' was deleted from the frame. Earlier, a coloured picture of Gandhi was used, but this backdrop used a black-and-white image. According to Kumar Vishwas, a coloured picture seemed to have a streak of violence, whereas a black-and-white picture looked serene and pure. He had derived the idea of Gandhi from the time that Anna had sat in front of the Gandhi Samadhi at Rajghat on the evening of 15 August. Anna had seemed to have been in silent communication with Gandhi. The new stage immediately struck me. It had more clarity, was uncluttered, simple, there was no ideological confusion and seemed very peaceful. It looked as if Gandhi had taken Anna under his wing was constantly blessing him.

The team also decided on a raised dais to discretely convey the idea that Anna was no longer an ordinary person. Nobody was allowed to walk on with their footwear on to maintain the purity of the place. There was only one entry and one exit point so as to maintain discipline. And entry to the dais was only from the back, not from the front. This was again a way to pay respect to Anna because one could not walk with one's back to Anna. At Jantar Mantar, Anna's platform was very close to the audience; anyone could have just walked up to him as if he were one of them. But at Ramlila Maidan, the team ensured that not everybody could reach him. To reach Anna, one had to get through the trusted members of his team. A proper scanning was done and permission from Anna's secretariat was required. A distance was deliberately maintained between him and the crowd. There were three layers. One was just next to the platform, for his team and special guests. Next to this was a place for the media. After the media, an empty space was left to avoid commotion. This arrangement was also important from the security point of view.

Ramlila Maidan was waiting for Anna, but that was in the future. In the present, honestly speaking, when Arvind visited my office just before the *anshan*, I was not sure if history would repeat itself, and Anna would be received with as much fanfare as he had received in April. I asked Arvind what the movement's next exit point was. He said, 'Withdrawal of the bill.' I was not convinced. I was keeping my fingers crossed, but I was extremely sceptical. But the last three days had been phenomenal. History had repeated itself neither as farce, nor as tragedy. I did not want to miss a beat and so was glued to the TV. Anna was about to emerge from jail. It had rained in the morning, the roads were wet and the reporters drenched. The sun had disappeared. It was perfect light for the cameras. But there was no respite for the reporters. It had started to drizzle. Suddenly, the cameras started shaking and the decibel level went up. I figured that Anna was somewhere in the vicinity. He was there, outside the gate. The clock has just struck 11.42 a.m. He held himself tight, raised his fist and his voice and shouted *Bharat Mata Ki Jai, Vande Mataram*. He repeated it.

He had not eaten for the past three-and-a-half days, but did not look tired. It was electrifying. The crowd went berserk.

There was madness in the newsroom as well. I had not seen something like this for a very long time. The closest parallels would be Lal Krishna Advani at the peak of the Ayodhya movement or V.P. Singh during Bofors. Anna had climbed atop a truck which had been specially brought to take him to Ramlila Maidan. He briefly addressed the crowd. Without much ado, he appealed to people to observe non-violence and not to block traffic. He even said that if anyone disrupted traffic, he or she would not be a part of the movement. At some level, he was hurt by the government's conduct. It showed in his address when he ridiculed the government saying, 'What kind of law is this? Whenever you want, you put in jail, and whenever you want, you release.'

The cavalcade started moving. Manish was next to Anna. Anna asked for a tricolour. The very next minute, he was vigorously waving the national flag. It was raining heavily, but still there was no place to stand on either side of the road. People had assembled since morning to get a glimpse of Anna. From Tihar, the cavalcade was to go to Mayapuri, which is hardly a two-kilometre drive. At 12.20 p.m. the truck reached Mayapuri. Word had already spread that Anna had left Tihar Jail and was on his way to Rajghat. The whole city came to a standstill. At 1.32 p.m. he was at Rajghat. As he was getting off the truck, it started pouring again. That was an unbelievable scene, which is permanently etched in my memory. Anna had started sprinting. Initially, the policemen escorting him could not understand what was happening. As they realized, they also ran after him. He stayed there for half an hour. And then he proceeded to the final destination. Ramlila Maidan was waiting for him.

And here he committed a mistake. He had probably not imagined such an overwhelming response. He got carried away and in his speech he said something which he should not have. He dropped a bombshell. His team members were also taken aback. Anna declared that he would not break his fast unless the Jan Lokpal Bill was passed by the Parliament by

30 August. According to a very senior member of the team, Anna should not have said this. This was never discussed and was not part of the strategy. Rather, it weakened their position. Opponents of the movement got an opportunity to call them immature, a bunch of megalomaniacs, who had no respect for Parliament; to say that they were so drunk on success that they were putting a gun to the government's head and were dictating terms to the Parliament. Ramchandra Guha wrote, 'His understanding remains that of a village patriarch' (*The Telegraph*, 27 August 2011). Veteran journalist, editor and now member of Parliament, H.K. Dua, wrote in *Hindustan Times*, 31 August 2011, 'The demand that Parliament must pass the Jan Lokpal bill by August 30 made the members of Parliament believe that the authorities of the Parliament and the constitution were under threat.' The team was also disappointed with Anna. This underlined the fact that Anna was also human and had weaknesses. But there were people like Narayana Murthy, mentor of Infosys, who had faith in him and his movement. Murthy said, 'We can't say they are undemocratic because Nehru, in August 1962, almost fifty years ago, said democracy is not just about Parliament at the top; democracy is all about empowering people at the lowest level ... it is not proper to say it is undemocratic' (*Indian Express*, 2 September 2011). Nevertheless, the damage was done.

By 2.40 p.m., the doctors had checked on him. He was perfectly alright. No danger to his life; his vital organs were normal. It did not look like he had not eaten for three-and-a-half days. I also decided to get out of the luxury of my air-conditioned office and be with the people and to gauge the mood. It had rained during the day but the sun had reappeared in the afternoon. The humidity was beyond description. My skin was itching and I was cursing myself and the weather gods. I mingled with the crowd. I was very impressed with the quality of the people. I could sense both innocence and hope. These were not people who had been bought over by any inducement. They were not paid to be there, like the crowd of a modern-day political rally. People had come on their own; they were troubled by rampant corruption. Many had never heard about the Jan Lokpal Bill, but they had faith in Anna and felt that this was their one opportunity to be rid of corruption.

Arundhati Roy was rather naive when she wrote that this was a bloodless Gandhian coup, led by a freshly minted saint and an army of largely urban, and certainly better-off people. I wish Roy had troubled herself to go to Ramlila Maidan the way she took the trouble to visit the den of Maoists to understand the Naxalite problem. Even then I did not agree with her understanding, nor did I this time. I don't blame her. It's a problem of the class that she belongs to. For them poverty and radicalism are romantic ideas that cleanse their upper-caste, upper-class guilt. Noted academic Sunil Khilnani wrote in the *Times of India* (27 August 2011), 'Those taking to the streets are not typically the masses of certain historical precedents, but members of the middle class.' Political scientist Yogendra Yadav had made several efforts to mingle with the crowd at Ramlila Maidan. He was very categorical that the assembled were not only urban, better-off people. In his opinion, the proportion of self-organized and self-mobilized people was very large. He agreed that a large number were indeed middle class, but then which movement was not led by a conscious middle class? He did not agree with the thesis that it was only the middle class that drove the movement. He was of the opinion that there was a good mix of people; if there were the urban middle classes, there were also hundreds of faces that were clearly from nearby villages.

I was there for more than a week, from early morning to late at night. I interacted with quite a lot of people from the crowd. It is true that all of them were carrying cellphones but that was no certificate of affluence. Cellphones have broken all caste and class boundaries. If there are more than seventy-five crore cellphone subscribers in India, they have to be from all the sections of the society. I could say they were a hungry people and an angry people. Those present at the Ramlila Maidan had a hunger for honesty and were angry with the corruption all around. I met young girls and boys, and all of them had the same question, *'Kya kuchh hoga'* (Will something change)? *'Saheb bahut corruption hai. Kuchh kariye'* (There is too much corruption, please do something). I had no answers to their questions; I too was looking for an answer. But those innocent faces held hope. The Anna movement had given them the hope that the traditional power structures and political parties had denied them.

I was amazed at the patience of the people present there. It was not a normal situation out there. It was very hot, extremely humid and every now and then, it would rain. In that hot and humid condition, to sit there for more than five hours was not a joke and it was not a normal sitting; everybody was touching everybody, and rubbing into each other's skin. The body odour must have been nauseating. And please remember it was not a professional crowd. For a majority of them, this was the first time they had ever been to a political rally. I met three generations of families there together. If there were engineers, doctors, management professionals, young entrepreneurs, one could also see the God-fearing, not too well-educated rural folks in typical rural attire speaking in local dialects. So, to brave that kind of weather and to continuously respond to the slogans and speeches made from the rostrum, were proofs of their commitment. Unlike a typical political rally, they were not there for a particular time period after which they could go back home. It was an indefinite fast. There was no time limit and there was no guarantee on when it would get over. For a political party to organize a crowd is not a big thing. Many bigwigs of the Congress party had been boasting that they could plan bigger rallies any time, bigger than Anna's, but to sustain this crowd for days together, 24x7, was stupendous. It needed commitment, honesty of purpose, and a moral and ethical glue to connect the leadership to the movement.

I noticed another remarkable thing. I noticed 'discipline'. The conduct of the crowd was exemplary. Delhi roads are anything but a disciplined. Rudeness, hot-headedness, anger, short temper, impatience and abuse are the order of the day, part of the living culture. I have been living in Delhi for more than twenty years, I love this city and I owe everything to this metropolis, but I have never been able to understand why its threshold of tolerance is so low. And it is decreasing each day. Maybe because it's a city of immigrants, maybe because it's a city of upstarts. Every time one ventures out, the city scares one with its brazenness and its beauty. But in all those days, Delhi looked different. No one lost their temper. There were a fair number of girls and women in that crowd, and they mingled freely in the crowd; but I didn't hear of a single instance of eve-teasing. Was it possible that Delhi was changing? Or were they scared of Gandhi, who loomed large over Anna?

It was no different on 19 August. By then, a section in the government and the Congress was in an introspective mood. Sandeep Dikshit, Delhi MP and son of Delhi Chief Minister Sheila Dikshit, was the first one to rebel. He openly said that arresting Anna had been a mistake. There were many in the party who shared his opinion, but were more circumspect. Salman Khurshid (law minister) was still articulating the government's more hawkish viewpoint. He said, 'If one has to become an alternative to the government, one has to contest elections.' No matter how strongly they denied it, a very strong signal had gone out to the government and they had to take note.

Something unusual was also happening in Mumbai. The dabbawalas did not distribute food that day. This apparently had happened for the first time in their 120-year history. The dabbawala is a service that provides food to more than two lakh Mumbaiwalas. Every day they deliver dabbas to their respective clients without fail, come hell or fire. But that day, they observed a bandh in support of Anna. There was hunger and anger of a different nature in the air that day; that day, food was not the priority.

OVERWHELMING SUPPORT

DAY 5 – 20 AUGUST

With Anna reaching Ramlila Maidan, the first phase of the movement was over. Round one, Anna. The government had given Team Anna a walkover. Anna had come to Ramlila Maidan on the afternoon of 19 August. The next three days were very important. Three consecutive holidays followed, 20 and 21 August constituting the weekend and 22 being Krishna Janmashthami. In these days Team Anna had to prove that the mass mobilization at Tihar was not a fluke; that people did not go there out of sympathy for Anna's arrest. A movement needs a show of strength. There was no denying the fact that people felt strongly about Anna and his team and also for the cause. But they did have their daily lives to get along with. Sure, they could show up in large numbers on a weekend, but what about working days? Would people show the same level of commitment? The success of the movement depended on the number of people that showed up consistently. Government agencies were monitoring the situation closely. The intelligence wing was fully geared up. Chidambaram and Kapil Sibal were holding the fort on behalf of the government and were briefed about minor details. The government kept quiet till Tuesday, the first working day after three consecutive holidays. In an off-camera media briefing, Chidambaram said that he was confident that the crowd would thin now and that Anna would not be able to sustain his fast for very long due to old age – and that would be the ideal time for the government to strike. So he wanted to tire Team Anna and force them to make a desperate move. As it happened, the Manmohan Singh government was betting on the wrong horses.

I decided to spend an entire day at the Ramlila Maidan to understand the dynamics of the movement better. Although I had gone there for a few hours the previous day. I had visited Jantar Mantar while Anna was on *anshan* there. I had also gone to Rajghat when he sat on a day-long fast to protest the lathi charge on Baba Ramdev and his supporters. But now I wanted to set my editor's hat aside for a while and wear my reporter's cap. I spent the entire day of 20 August at the Ramlila Maidan. It was a sunny morning. As I turned my car in towards the Ramlila Maidan, I could smell the change in the air. I was still almost a kilometre away, but the road was packed. There were a few cars and four-wheelers there but, mostly, people were walking with the national flag in their hands and an Anna cap on their heads as if they were going to attend a mela. The car was going dead slow. It took me ten minutes to cover a distance that would have been a five-minute walk. There was no chaos, but traffic was moving slowly. Police had barricaded the entire area. As I moved to the main crossing, on the right I could see OB vans of all shapes and sizes. Their generators were continuously spewing smoke. Normally, local residents would object to these loud OB vans and make sure they leave as early as possible. I was told that they had been there for more than twenty hours – and would remain stationed there for another hundred hours or so – but nobody objected. I asked my driver to drop me at the nearest entrance and asked him to find parking space. I was walking towards the metal detector with a cap on, when I was stopped by an elderly couple. They had recognized me. '*Kab tak ye chalega? Kya sarkar Anna ki baat manegi?*' they asked. (How long will it continue? Will the government listen to Anna?) I politely told them that I had no idea. I was as clueless as they were. A few moments later, I got a call from Mumbai. A not-so-young MP was on the line. He wanted my assessment of the movement. I told him the government should hurry up and try to find a solution as early as possible or the Congress would be in deep trouble. He agreed with me. He seemed disgusted with the leadership and was very unhappy with the way the situation had been handled. Anyway, I passed through the security drill and entered into the main ground. It was not yet full. There was plenty of empty space. I made my way through the dozens of raised platforms made by TV channels for their live broadcasts and found my team. My team was the closest to Anna's platform. I couldn't see more than 10,000 people. Though people were still pouring in, I was not sure the ground would fill up. I left the media enclosure and moved towards the common area. I walked further through the barricade. Now I was among Anna supporters, I was one of them. As I looked back I saw the raised platform and also what looked like a few flying metal animals; from a distance they could look like flying snakes, with their tongues out, spitting venom. They are called Zimi-Zibs. Zimi-Zibs are iron ladders, on top of which a camera is fitted and remote-controlled from a makeshift station on the ground. This camera would get us the top-angle shot, helpful in capturing the mood of the crowd from above. As a kid, I was fascinated by kites. That day I felt like the entire area had turned into a kite competition and every Zimi-Zib was a kite, flying to get the best out of every shot. Like a well-choreographed dance, the movement of the Zimi-Zib was synchronized to the movement of the crowd on the ground. Everybody wanted to be captured by the TV cameras at least once. A few camera-crazy people were looking into the cameras, shouting slogans. Others were making noises just for the cameras and a few had painted their faces with the tricolour. Then there were the truly enterprising ones who had dressed up in fancy dress. A few dressed as Hanuman, another was Ravan of corruption, play-acting his own killing by the forces of righteousness. There was one gentleman who was dressed as Gandhi in loincloth and wearing the Gandhi glasses. He also had a walking stick in his hand. He was trying to walk like Gandhi, with long strides. My generation has not seen Gandhi in the flesh-and-blood. We have been introduced to him only through films and photographs, so feel free to take my opinion with a pinch of salt when I say he was not a bad copy.

I moved further into the crowd. On the left there was an enclosure for women where one could see women from all walks of life, and from urban and semi-urban areas. I met a woman who was seventy-three years old. She was very excited and had come to see Anna. She had faith that, in him, she would find answers to her questions. This woman could barely speak proper Hindi. I presumed she had come from Haryana. Next to her was a young lady. She introduced herself as a doctor. Not far from her, a mother and a daughter were busy shouting slogans. When I asked them, the older one told me that she was not well and had gone to fetch medicine for herself when, unable to resist, she came over to the Ramlila Maidan. Now she was feeling better. She had hope, '*Gooskhori khatam hogi*' (Bribing will be wiped out). The daughter's eyes were shining bright. I was just randomly walking around, observing faces. They had names but nobody knew them. All of them wanted to say something, all of them wanted to register their protest. They aspired to be heard, but in the cacophony of economic reforms and high-sounding corporate lingo, they were left alone with their own voices. In Anna, they had found their words. Those words had found a touch, a touch of optimism, of hope, a hope that finally this system would change and their sons and daughters would not have to pay for their birth and death certificates.

The other side of the crowd, the men's section, was also as hopeful. They were fathers, sons and grandfathers. They were more aggressive than the mothers, daughters and grandmothers. I found a few men talking bitterly about Manmohan Singh. *Saheb, ye sarkar bahut corrupt hai. Poora kha legi aur dakaregi bhi nahi* (Sir, this government is very corrupt; it will eat up everything and not even burp). That was the general refrain. All of them were invariably carrying cellphones. All of them had a viewpoint. Not all of them were from posh south Delhi. There were many from Seelampur, Nandnagri, Nangloi, etc. I was trying to get to the end of the ground. So far, there had been cotton mats on the ground and a good water-resistant tent over the head. But I walked further, suddenly I felt the surface go slushy and wet. That part was not ready. By now I was feeling hungry. In the distance I saw a few food stalls.

People were standing around eating puri and sabzi. I entered one such stall. It was run by the organizers. I asked someone there who was running all these stalls. I was born and brought up in small towns and have also lived in my village. I have seen time and time and again that, if there is an occasion, people and organizations would come in from nowhere. These were people who might not get involved directly but are ready to render any service free of cost because they found the cause *pavitra* (sacred). For them it is *punya ka kaam* (sacred work), *dharm ka kaam* (religious work), *daan dakshina dene se janam sudhar jaata hai* (giving alms will make their lives better), *paap kam hota hai* (lessen the burden of sin), *kyonki jo kiya hai wahi agle janam mein bhogna hai* (because whatever is sown in this life is the harvest in the next life). They are interesting people. They might spend lakhs of rupees in charity, but may not necessarily be willing to help a poor person on another occasion. Such public service is a kind of investment for this life and, for the next, a bribe to the gods to make up for their sins. All part of the odd mix that is India.

Hunger dealt with, I was walking back, a little tired and sleepy, when suddenly I felt something hit my ears. I strained and heard a sound. It was coming from the raised platform. I must confess I am not a music buff. I prefer the music of silence to the music of sound. Not that the former was to be had. But the sound was not bad either. For the first time I noticed that the crowd there was in some kind of a legitimate relationship with the sound. Anna was too far and he was fasting. He couldn't talk to them all the time. Neither could his team. But there were speakers as there are at all rallies and public gatherings. This was a political agitation, speeches made at the Ramlila Maidan were also political in nature; some of those speeches had great content but was stated softly, others lacked the imagery of words and made up with higher decibels. But the question was, how long could people listen to the same speeches? So Nitin Dabar had the onerous job of keeping them engaged and entertained and of keeping the energy levels high.

Young Nitin had good company in Kumar Vishwas, a not so young poet, whose responsibility as a moderator was to keep the show going without a dull moment; a thankless job, but he turned it into a fine art. His experience at kavi sammelans came in handy. This occasion helped me understand the power of music and poetry, and its impact on people.

After my many days at the Maidan, I can say with conviction that honesty of purpose and purity of music were two key elements for the success of the movement. Music kept the momentum going and kept people engaged with what was happening on the dais. When I asked Nitin whose idea it was to have music, he simply said that while India against Corruption had a special interest in music, there was no elaborate plan for a musical programme. A day before the 30 January rally, Arvind had asked him to sing from the dais. Before that, he had created a theme song for the Clean Delhi campaign a few months ago. So when he was asked to sing again, he let his imagination soar. On 29 January 2011, on his way home, Nitin wrote the Lokpal song. He wrote it on his mobile: *Lokpal, Lokpal pass karo Jan Lokpal.*

This song became the anthem for the movement and was an instant hit. When he told the team about the song, Kiran Bedi asked him where it was. He said that it was on his mobile. Arvind told him to get it recorded.

Phir se nayi subah aaye
Duur ho kaala andhera
Janlokpal ki awaaz lagaye
Bharat desh hai mera
Mera desh meri jaan
Meri shaan meri aan
Lokpal Lokpal

Nitin later told me that the idea was very simple. Lokpal is a legal thing and very complicated for the common man, so one needed something simple that would convey the purpose of the movement and inform people about the need for the Jan Lokpal. It was a success. Even I used to hum it when I was there!

I asked him how he chose other songs.He told me that it was done very carefully. He used devotional songs for the fervour of the movement and purity of the ambience. The songs of the Sarva Dharma Prarthana Sabha were specially added to establish the link of the movement with Gandhi.

Ishwar Allah tero naam
Sabko sanmati de bhagwan

And

Raghupati Raghav Raja Ram
Patit pavan Sita Ram

The two are historically very important and were sung every day in Gandhi's Sarva Dharma Prarthana Sabha. With Gandhi's picture in the backdrop looming large over Anna, these songs evoked Gandhi and added a certain purity and spirituality to the ambience; maybe this is why the crowd behaved so decorously, as if Gandhiji was nearby and watching them. Devotional songs like these were good for setting the mood, but to keep people enthused, energized and focused on the movement, they would need some variety. But raw energy was not what the organizers wanted from people – the idea was not to make people violent but to make them more committed. So patriotic songs from movies were chosen, but violent and aggressive ones were avoided. Songs that had a certain social message were preferred over others.

1. *Bharat humko jaan se pyaara hai*
2. *Des meray des meray, meri jaan hai tu*
3. *Mitwa, tujhko kya darr hai*
4. *Suno gaur se duniyawalon, buri nazar na humpe dalon*
5. *Mera rang de basanti chola*
6. *Dil diya hai jaan bhi denge, aye watan teray liye*
7. *Mera mulk mera desh, mera yeh watan*
8. *Ye hausla kaise thamey*
9. *Aye meray watan ke logon*
10. *Aye meray pyare watan*

The mood of the crowd was gauged and then songs were selected. During the day, when the crowd looked a little sluggish, patriotic songs were played, and the next minute one could feel the charge in the atmosphere. And when the crowd seemed so charged that it could lead to chaos and disruption, devotional songs did wonders to bring people back to sanity.

Nitin wrote a special song for Anna. Nitin says he is not a professional writer. He writes what comes to him naturally. He wrote this for Anna:

Dekho mera desh chala
Anna terey saath mein
Main bhi Anna, tub hi Anna
Ab toh sara desh hai Anna

He had written this in the car on his way back from the *anshan* on the fourth day. Later, he added a few more lines:

Woh hai ek lakh hazaron mein
Jaise ki chanda sitaron mein
Woh hai sabke dulare
Woh hai Anna Hazare

No great imagery, simple lines and simple music:

Bhrashtachar, bhrashtachar, band karo yeh bhrashtachar
Desh hai mera imaan yaaron
Desh hai meri shaan
Desh ho raha hai katal
Ki itna badh gaya bhrashtachar
Aao milkar desh bachaye
Milkar karey agaaz

When the movement felt less than secure about its success, at such moments, sounds of optimism would sweeten the air:

Har sant kahe, sadho kahe
Sach aur sahas ho jiske mann mein
Anth mein jeet usi ki rahey

Or

Yeh hausla kaise jhuke
Yeh aansoon kaise ruke
Manzil mushkil toh kya
Dhundla sahin toh kya
Tanha yeh dil toh kya

Raah mein kaaten bikhre agar
Uspar toh phir bhi chalna hi hai
Shaam chhupa le suraj magar
Raat ko ek din dhalna hi hai
Rut yeh tal jaayegi
Himmat rang layegi
Subah phir aayegi

And remember there was no elaborate music system. They were singing with only a guitar, a dholak and an octopad. Only three instruments, with no ultra-modern sound arrangement. It was rhythm, pure rhythm and nothing else.

But none of this was music to the government's ears. This was the hub that the whole world was watching live. By

20 August, Ramlila Maidan was another Tahrir Square. Only, this was not a rebellion to establish democracy but to strengthen it. Unfortunately, the government thought otherwise. V. Narayanasami, minister of state in the prime minister's office, and Rajiv Shukla, minister of state for parliamentary affairs, were singing a different tune. Shukla said, 'The way people are talking about the government and Parliament from the stage, only God knows what will happen to the movement.'

Team Anna was slightly irritated with the parliamentary standing committee. Newspapers that morning had carried full-page advertisements on behalf of the committee asking people to send in their suggestions on the Lokpal Bill within fifteen days. Team Anna found the advertisement offensive. It was a hint that, as far as the government was concerned, they were not the only ones whose opinion was important, other members of the civil society were also to be consulted and it would not happen in a day or two. By 9.40 a.m., Arvind had reacted. He said, 'It is pointless to invite comments when the government bill is of no use.'

The first positive signal came from the prime minister around 2 p.m. when he said that the government was ready to talk but the deadline of 30 August was unacceptable. Arvind reacted on behalf of Team Anna saying, 'We are ready for talks, but it's only the government which can tell us when, where and with whom to talk.' Even if the talks themselves were far away, at least both sides were talking about talks. Meanwhile, support was increasing on the fifth day of Anna's *anshan*. By evening, Ramlila Maidan was overflowing with people and the Zimi-Zibs were relaying their messages to the government. If Ramlila Maidan was full, there was resonance in other cities too. In Anna's village, Ralegan Siddhi, students made a human chain. In Pune, effigies of political leaders were burnt. Jaipur was organizing a yajna; if in Bhopal people were sitting on a fast, in Bangalore, software engineers and doctors were joining the stir in large numbers. Everybody was worried about Anna's health. According to the doctors, Anna was keeping well, all his vital signs were fine. He had lost three kilograms of weight. His pulse rate and blood pressure were both normal. And the presence of more than 80,000 people on the grounds that evening was a great motivation for Anna to remain fit.

DAY 6 – 21 AUGUST

There were some murmurs at Ramlila Maidan that a back-channel communication had been established between the government and Team Anna, but nobody was confirming it. The next day, we came to know that a bureaucrat from Maharashtra, Umesh Sarangi, and a local dharma guru, Bhayuji Maharaj, part of Narendra Modi's Sadbhavna mission, had met Anna and discussed a few things with him. Parliamentary affairs minister Harish Rawat confirmed in Dehra Dun that talks were on. Sarangi had on previous occasions also been instrumental in breaking Anna's *anshan*. Arvind too confirmed the meeting, but said that there had been no concrete proposal from the government. Bhayuji is considered close to cabinet ministers from Maharashtra, Sushil Kumar Shinde and Vilas Rao Deshmukh. That very day, Bhayuji and Sarangi met with Kapil Sibal and it looked like the deadlock might just break, but nobody had a clue what the solution would be. This was despite Anna's renewed threat that, if the Jan Lokpal Bill was not passed by 30 August, the country would witness a movement the likes of which it had never seen.

On the sixth day of his fast, Anna decided to intensify the agitation. He instructed his followers to go in large numbers to their MPs and convince them about the Jan Lokpal Bill. He did not use the word 'gherao', but the message was clear. Although Anna had stressed that they should use only Gandhian methods, the government panicked and immediately rushed extra forces to the ground. Anna supporters wasted no time in reaching the PM's residence; police stopped them at a distance and dozens of them were detained. UPA chairperson Sonia Gandhi's local office in Rae Bareilly was gheraoed. Central ministers like

Salman Khurshid in Firozabad, Sriprakash Jaiswal in Kanpur and Pawan Bansal in Chandigarh bore the brunt of the Anna followers. Chief Minister Sheila Dikshit and her cabinet colleague Raj Kumar in Delhi were not spared either. By sunset, Ramlila Maidan was overflowing with people and, according to the police estimate, there were more than a lakh people there – a strong signal to the government that if it did not dance to the tune of We the People, there was grave danger ahead. But there were signs that the government was also besieged from within. Pranab Mukherjee had said that he did not wish to comment on the movement; questions should be directed to the home minister, he said. A power struggle was on and the prime minister was a mute spectator. Sonia Gandhi's absence had complicated things.

ANNA, RSS AND MUSLIMS

Rajiv Gandhi was still alive. The RSS mobilization on the Ayodhya issue was peaking. I was in JNU, studying international politics. The campus was untouched by religious polarization because student politics was dominated by the students' wings of left parties. The Students' Federation of India (SFI) was the leading force. JNU was a very open and liberal campus. Gender equality was a big thing and violence was anathema. The National Students' Union of India (NSUI) and Akhil Bharatiya Vidyarthi Parishad (ABVP) and their vices had no presence at all. These organizations existed only on paper; to be affiliated with them was to be labelled lumpen and retrograde. I had come from Allahabad University, where student politics was all about caste and community mobilization. To be a student leader, one had to be either a Brahmin or a Thakur, the two dominant castes in eastern Uttar Pradesh. Other middle and lower castes had very little hope for success. There were a few other radical organizations, but their presence was marginal. So when I entered JNU, I found myself in a wonderland. I will freely admit that we were living in an ideal world, a utopia. Our interactions with the outside world were always a little uncomfortable. So even at the peak of the communal mobilization in India, we were not affected and the campus was not divided along Hindu–Muslim lines. Though the Ayodhya issue was at the forefront of campus discussions and debates, our opinions were not divided – we believed that the

Ayodhya mobilization was an attack on the secular fabric of the country.

I had started freelancing for *Saptahik Hindustan*, the weekly Hindi magazine of the Hindustan Times Group. The Communist Party of India (CPI) had called for a rally at Ayodhya to protest communal mobilization. Rajeshwar Rao was the general secretary of the party. I had many friends who were members of AISF (All India Students' Federation, the student wing of the CPI). They were going to Ayodhya by train. I tagged along. Naushad was also with me. He belonged to Faizabad, a few kilometres from Ayodhya. It was at this time that the shila poojan ceremony was to take place at Ramjanmabhumi at the behest of the Vishwa Hindu Parishad (VHP). The train was full of kar sewaks; the ambience outside the campus was charged with an alien energy. Those young kar sewaks were very aggressive and my friend S.N. Prasad and I, in the best JNU tradition, were trying to engage them in a discussion. But a contrary viewpoint was not welcome; for them, the only truth was that Lord Ram had been born there and Babar, the Mughal emperor, had demolished the temple to build a mosque and it was their religious duty to see a temple rebuilt at Ram's birthplace. I could sense that a discussion could be dangerous but, I would invariably get drawn in and many a time almost got beaten up. Naushad kept quiet through the whole thing. We heard some of the worst anti-Muslim slogans and they were so bad that I dare not repeat them now. I later learnt that in those days such slogans were quite common; I certainly never saw any VHP or BJP leader asking the crowd not to raise them.

Naushad, a member of the AISF, was full of enthusiasm and energy when he had got onto the train but, as the train inched closer to Ayodhya, I could see his body shrinking and face dropping. But we were also quite a few in number, so he felt safe enough to go. We got off the train at Ayodhya. From there, we had to walk. I said I would join the rally later as I wanted to visit the place where the shila poojan had been done.

I was surprised and happy when Naushad volunteered to join me. Once we started walking, I could feel that Naushad had realized his mistake and wanted to wriggle out. He told me that he was not feeling well and would like to go back. I did not insist. I was not very comfortable either; with every step the situation was getting more and more tense. When I finally reached the spot, the ceremony had already been wrapped up and there was no one there, except for an old man from Indore. He had come all the way for Ram Lalla's darshan. I asked 'Baba, *Kaisa lag raha?*' He looked at me and tears started rolling down his cheeks. I could not understand. He just said, '*Aaj agar Rajiv Gandhi aa jate to amar ho jate*' (If Rajiv Gandhi had come today, he would have become immortal). He was a simple soul, an innocent man with no malice. He had been told that Bhagwan had no roof over his head as his place had been demolished long ago and the time had come to construct a temple for him. I had no words. I walked back quietly.

I was very young but had a fire in my belly. This visit had changed my perception of politics and of the communalism vs secularism debate. The old man was not communal, he had no political agenda like the VHP and the BJP leaders, or like the kar sevaks in the train who were motivated and trained supporters of the Sangh Parivar. A state can tackle political leadership and their army of followers, but no army can handle innocent souls like that old man who was genuinely concerned about Ram, and he was not alone. There were millions of them. Neither did I forget Naushad's face when he said he was not feeling well and wanted to go back. It was brave of him to even have come all the way to Ayodhya in that surcharged atmosphere. But even such a braveheart had lost courage and could not walk to the shila poojan sthal.

Both were innocent and both were suffering. They were victims of circumstances. The old man was crying and Naushad was scared. Since then, I have often wondered what kind of society we had made where a Hindu feels his God is homeless and a Muslim feels unsafe. As a student then and as a hard-core professional now, this has not been a communalism vs secularism question. Both are politics, both are vote banks. It is an existential question. No society can live without its gods, without its religion. The history of the Soviet Union is witness to the fact that even seventy years of living with no religion, under a strict communist regime, gods did not disappear from the hearts of the Russian people. It was, in fact, the most potent unifying factor. The left-liberal brigade of Indian intellectuals and historians should redefine their understanding of secularism to incorporate religion. Secularism has to accommodate that old man.

Hindutva militants should also realize that there are millions of Naushads who want to understand Hinduism, who want to communicate with their Hindu brethren, but are scared because of the atmosphere created by communal elements. He fears for his life. He fears for his existence. He fears for his identity. The Sangh Parivar needs to understand that its brand of politics will not survive because it does not accommodate the millions of Naushads who are as innocent as that old man.

Even after all these years, that incident keeps coming back to me. So, on 20 August, when the Shahi Imam of Jama Masjid, Syed Ahmed Bukhari, made a statement that Anna's stir was anti-Islam and Muslims should not participate in it, I was worried again. The Shahi Imam said, 'Islam does not condone the worship of the nation or land. It does not even condone worship of the mother who nurtures a child in her womb' (*Times of India*, 22 August 2011). Bukhari further said, 'How can Muslims then join his stir with a war cry that is against the basic tenets of Islam. I have advised them to stay away.' Syed Bukhari is not known for his secular credentials so his statement alarmed me. The process of communalizing had begun and this issue ultimately, people like Naushad and that old man would be the worst sufferers.

From the very first day, Anna's agitation was accused of harbouring Hindu communal elements and of being sponsored by the RSS. If you remember the first day of Anna's agitation at

Jantar Mantar, three objections secularists had raised; first, the presence of two senior RSS leaders on stage; second, the Mother India as goddess in the backdrop, which was said to be the classic picture used by the RSS in its functions and ceremonies to train and motivate its cadres; and third, the raising of slogans like Bharat Mata Ki Jai and Vande Mataram. Arundhati Roy, the writer and civil rights activist, indirectly raised the question of the use of Vande Mataram and the picture of Bharat Mata in the movement and then reached the conclusion that Anna's movement was dangerous. When she was asked by Sagarika Ghose in an interview on CNN-IBN if the Anna movement was an RSS-sponsored Hindu rightist movement, Arundhati did not give a straight answer. She said, 'I am not saying that, but the symbols used in the agitation are interesting.' She elaborated, 'Vande Matram was first used in Bankim Chandra Chatterjee's novel in 1882 and went on to become a slogan during Bengal's partition; and in 1937, Rabindranath Tagore said that its use as a national song was not correct as it was divisive and had a long communal history.' Arundhati did not stop here. She said, 'You first used a picture of Bharat Mata and then a picture of Gandhi. You had people who were openly members of a Manuvadi agitation. So you had a cocktail of dangerous things and it would have been more dangerous if it had not ended the way it did' (*Nai Duniya*, 2 September 2011).

Ramchandra Guha takes a circuitous route to hint that the RSS is the mastermind of the Anna movement. Drawing a parallel with JP, he wrote, 'The materials of history thus suggest that the parallel between JP and Anna is less comforting than we suppose. The front organizations of Jan Sangh's successor, BJP, are now playing a much active role in India against Corruption' (*Hindustan Times*, 23 August 2011). In another article, he very smartly quoted Mukul Sharma, an environmental journalist, who he said found Anna's approach deeply brahmanical (*The Telegraph*, 10 September 2011). But other secularists were more forthright in their allegations. Film personality Mahesh Bhatt, social activist Shabnam Hashmi, academic Ram Puniyani and others held a press conference in Mumbai on 23 August 2011 and openly accused Team Anna of being fascist and the RSS of being the mobilizing force for Anna. 'The RSS and BJP are mobilizing people on the ground,' Hashmi alleged, adding that since the Gujarat chief minister was close to being prosecuted, 'the Sangh is trying to build a cult figure like Anna.' She also said, 'Anna is surrounded by people who are fascist to the core.' These allegations weren't new. Even before the Ramlila *anshan*, Congress general secretary Digvijay Singh had said quite openly that Baba Ramdev and Anna were masks of the RSS. He never proffered any proof and every time Anna was asked this question he had always denied it. So when RSS chief Mohan Bhagwat openly extended support to the Anna agitation on the eve of his indefinite fast on 15 August, the Congress and the secularists got another opportunity to rubbish the movement. It is in this context that, when Anna was asked about the RSS connection yet again, and it was suggested that it was for this reason that a section of the minority community was not part of the agitation, he lost his cool and said that those who ask such questions should be sent to a lunatic asylum. I was there when Anna and his team were facing questions from the press. It was the fifth day of his fast and he was sitting on the stage while Arvind and Prashant Bhushan were holding the presser. This question had been directed at them. Arvind was about to reply when Anna snatched the mike from Arvind and responded angrily.

I could understand his anger. Anna and his team believed that this was an attempt to malign the movement and was done at the behest of the Congress and the government. In the beginning they accepted the allegations as a part of politics, but Shahi Imam Bukhari's statement had come as a bolt from the blue. It was seen by the leaders of the agitation as an attempt to communalize the anti-corruption stir and to brand the whole movement as an upper-class, upper-caste agitation. It was also perceived as an attempt to confuse the right-minded liberal

Hindus. Urgent remedial steps were taken to minimize the damage. So, by the afternoon of 20 August, there were Muslims on the dais and, from that day onwards, a few Muslims were lined up to break their Roza in full public glare. In my opinion, this symbolism looked like a cheap political gimmick. People can see through such a farce.

I have also been told that Arvind and Kiran Bedi visited Bukhari and tried to explain the nature of the movement but Bukhari was unmoved. This again, in my opinion, was uncalled for. Neither does Bukhari represent the entire Muslim community nor does he carry any credibility. There was a time when the word of the Shahi Imam of Jama Masjid carried a lot of weight but, over a period of time, India's Muslims have come to see that the Imam had used them for his narrow interests. That Bukhari's statement did not carry weight was evident from the fact that he did not get enough support from other leaders of his community. In fact, Mufti Mukarram, Shahi Imam of Fatehpuri Masjid in Delhi, who subscribes to the Barelvi school of Sunni Islam, which is what the vast majority of Muslims in the Indian subcontinent adhere to, categorically rejected Bukhari's statement. He said that Islam had nothing to do with the Anna movement, which was for a noble cause, and he appealed to his brethren to join the movement (*Eurasia Review*, 23 September 2011).

The Muslim Personal Law Board also distanced itself from Bukhari's statement. The spokesperson of the Board, A.Q.R. Illyas said, 'I do not agree with Imam Bukhari. Chanting Vande Mataram is not an issue.' He said, 'In principle we agree with what Anna Hazare is campaigning for, but we are not for dictating terms to Parliament.' His colleague on the Board, Jafaryab Jilani, explained that the Board had decided to stay away from Anna's campaign due to its political overtones and that their organization believed that this issue did not come under its purview. The Deoband was also of the same opinion. Mohatamim of Darul Uloom Deoband, Mufti Abdul Qasim Nomani, clarified, 'Corruption is a serious issue and is a matter of concern for everyone but Deoband is a religious institution and does not get involved with political matters' (as reported by www.milligazette.com, dated 27 August 2011). For the two biggest institutions of the Muslim community, Anna's movement was not a communal issue.

Even in the virtual world, Bukhari's words did not go down well with Muslim readers. One Javed Saikia from Bangalore reacted on India TV's website below a report on Bukhari's statement, 'Another Jinnah is on the rise; they don't represent the Muslims of this country. Imam Sahib, please do not mix this noble cause with religion.' Sayeed Khan from Pune wrote, 'Bharata mata ki jai, Vande Mataram and supporting Anna Hazare.' Rehan from Delhi was furious, 'If you can't say anything positive about Annaji's Movement, keep your mouth shut, please don't do dirty politics.' Mohammad Firoze Qureshi from Mumbai just hated what was said, '*Bukhari sahib, apko kitne paise mile hain Anna sahib ke khilaf bolne ke?*' (Mr Bukhari, how much have you been paid to speak against Anna)?

True, some Muslim leaders did express their apprehension that the RSS might be trying to hijack the agitation, but none of them said it was led by Hindu fundamentalists. Jafaryab Jilani said, 'There is an allegation that the movement is actually backed by the RSS from behind the curtain. The leaders of the anti-graft movement are yet to give evidence to prove that they are not motivated politically.' Now this is a fair point. And Team Anna should try to explain their position and say where they stand on the RSS. One of the senior leaders of the Jamaat-e-Ulema-e-Hind, who refused to be identified, said that in his personal capacity he supported the movement and felt that it was a golden opportunity for Muslims to fight along with their Hindu brothers and prove that on a question of national importance they think alike. But he did admit that allegations of an RSS link had created confusion in the minority community.

The editor of the Urdu weekly *Nai Duniya*, ex-member of Parliament, Shahid Siddiqi, also said that the alleged RSS link did force Muslims to think about the movement. He also added that Anna's alleged praise for Narendra Modi (which Team Anna later denied) also preyed on the minds of Muslims. Despite these apprehensions, a section of the Muslim community openly supported Anna. The India Ulema Council, the Pasmanda Muslim Mahaj, All India Muslim Women Personal Law Board and the All India Muslim Majlish-a-Mushawarat had no hesitation in supporting the anti-corruption campaign (*Eurasia Review*, 23 September 2011).

So it is not true that Muslims as a community boycotted the movement. One can only conclude that a section of Muslims did not take part in the Anna agitation. It is also true that there have been serious apprehensions in the community in view of the propaganda unleashed by vested interests that the RSS might be controlling the movement behind the scenes. But I would argue that an overwhelming majority of the community did not buy Bukhari's argument. This goes to prove the point that some secular intellectuals are still seeing the world with their old mindset. They need to change because Indian society today is changing very fast.

During my research, a few so-called Muslim intellectuals tried telling me that Muslims, being a minority community, have always struggled with the basic issues of identity and security. There is a very strong belief in the community that they have been left behind and, if they don't take the issue of education seriously and become a partner in the economic development of the country, they have no future. Given this background, Team Anna should have tried to answer their questions. As far as I could see, Team Anna never did try to integrate the minority community into its movement. They thought that corruption being an issue that affected everyone, irrespective of religion, the movement would get support from everyone; but they did not account for the complexities of Indian society. I remember that the leader of Jamaat-e-Ulema-e-Hind, Mehmood Madni, was present on the stage on 30 January when the first rally took place at the Ramlila Maidan. But he was lost somewhere in the movement and was never seen again. If an effort had been made to integrate him into the movement and its leadership, it would have blunted the attack by people like Digvijay Singh after Mohan Bhagwat's speech on Dussehra, when he said that the RSS cadre had worked for the success of the Anna movement. Arvind realized that this statement would be misunderstood, so he too made a statement. He said, 'The RSS should not try to take credit for the success of the movement. If they want to take credit, they should take credit for the Gujarat riots . . .' Bhagwat reacted to this and said that the RSS did not want to steal credit, but they were always against corruption and would always support any such movement (www.timesofindia.com, 11 October 2011). The matter should end here, but knowing our leaders, I am sure attempts will be made to communalize the movement further. That is where the real danger lies and that is why I am worried whenever I hear statements by Shahi Imam Bukhari, Digvijay Singh and Mohan Bhagwat, because I know that ultimately the victims of such divisive politics will be Naushad and that old man from Indore.

SIBAL UNWANTED

DAY 7 – 22 AUGUST

The angry old man from Ralegan Siddhi had shaken everyone out of their deep slumber, but the government continued to pretend to be asleep. Krishna Janmashtami was the last day of the extended holidays. As expected, Ramlila Maidan was overflowing. Since morning, the mood at Ramlila Maidan had been upbeat and people kept coming in. I met a lady doctor who was in her early thirties. Good-looking, wearing specs, still in her lab coat. I asked her, 'What are you doing here? Are you a member of the medical team?' She answered, 'No.' 'Then what are you doing here?' I persisted. She smiled and said, 'I wanted to come here since the day Annaji sat on fast, but you know the nature of my profession and so I could not get time. Today I had decided, come what may, I will go to Ramlila Maidan. I finished my work and drove down here right after.' She was not mesmerized by the electronic media, she did not want to be interviewed for TV unlike many in the grounds who were desperate to be featured on television. She was not a regular TV news watcher either. But during this *anshan*, she could not keep away from TV. She had a busy schedule attending to patients, keep changing news channels whenever she had a moment just to know what was happening to Anna. She was not alone. I used to come across many such stories every day. There was a young man of twenty-five. He was working in Chicago, USA, as a software engineer. He had been tracking the Anna movement for a long time and, when he read about Anna's second indefinite fast, he planned in advance, applied for leave and came all the way to Delhi and became a volunteer. He did not go home throughout the *anshan*. His mother also joined him as a volunteer. This mother-and-son duo were in charge of managing the crowd. The mother was in the ladies' enclosure and the son, Kuldeep, was an interface between the media and the first row of the public. One day I asked if he didn't get tired; he said that the first three days had been very difficult but now he was okay. He worked from 6.00 a.m. to 11.00 p.m. and had no time to sit down and rest. There was no one to relieve him and he was not paid for his services.

So when I would hear senior members of the Congress or cabinet ministers running down the movement, I would smile at their foolishness. Cabinet Minister Veer Bhadra Singh said, '*Koi bhi madari tamasha kar le, bheed to jut hi jaati hai*' (If a showman does a trick, a crowd is bound to gather). Once Digvijay Singh asked me what was so great about a crowd assembling around Anna; he could easily organize more than a lakh of people as and when he wanted. I just smiled. If politicians had not forgotten being in the crowd, the public would not have gone to Ramlila Maidan to see Anna. I have not met someone as committed as the doctor I mentioned earlier in any political rally. So anybody who said that it was not a mass movement was living in a fool's paradise. Anna had proved his point. People were with him. And they were coming out of concern, not compulsion. Ramlila Maidan was equally packed on 22 August and it is my guess that the number of people there probably crossed a lakh by sunset and if I were to add the numbers that gathered through the day, it would no doubt be an even more impressive figure. This was the most successful day in terms of crowd size at Ramlila Maidan and I am not counting the people outside the ground and elsewhere in the country. The movement had entered its most crucial phase and a solution had to be found very soon; a slight mistake could have shattered the momentum. But the massive turnout all over India, and especially at Ramlila Maidan, had made it clear that it could not be dealt with in the way the government had handled Ramdev's agitation. At the Maidan, I could feel the crowd getting restive. But there were many questions: Was this government keen on a peaceful and dignified solution? Did they have a strategy to tackle Anna and his team? Were they aware of the ground reality? Were they competent enough to deal with this kind of a political problem? And did they have a plan B in case plan A failed?

A very senior member of the Congress told me that the government had no clue about the seriousness of the issue, and they had underestimated Team Anna's strength and resilience. Home Minister P. Chidambaram was of the view that, given his old age, Anna would break down in a few days and, once the three consecutive holidays were over, support for Anna would dwindle and that would be the ideal time to strike. Chidambaram kept waiting for the right time. As it happens, the government saw reason. He was removed from the team that was dealing with Anna. Despite his age, Anna was more tenacious than Ramdev who was almost half his age and a yogi. On the ninth day of his fast Anna was heard saying that he could continue for another nine days, and on the eleventh day, when the whole country was worried about his health, doctors who were monitoring him were puzzled and happy. Dr K.K. Kasliwal, a very seasoned doctor, told IBN7 reporter Maushami Singh that Anna's health was normal except for a weight loss of seven kilograms. His pulse rate was normal, his heart was functioning properly. Dangerous ketone levels in his body were also neutralized by a heavy intake of water. Moreover, the crowds did not stop coming to Ramlila Maidan even after the holidays. As per police estimate, after 22 August, at no time was the number of people in the ground was less than 20,000, and the number steadily increased throughout the day, reaching dramatic proportions around sunset.

This senior Congressman I quoted earlier also told me that the wrong people were given the responsibility of handling the situation. In his opinion, it was not such a difficult and complicated case as it turned out to be. He said, 'P. Chidambaram and Kapil Sibal are eminent lawyers and very competent as cabinet ministers, but unfortunately, it is not a legal issue and they from the beginning had treated it like another case in a court of law.' I was convinced that lawyers could win cases but not political battles. There is this old saying in my home town about lawyers: '*Case to jitwa dega lekin ghar bhi bikwa dega*' (They will win the case but the client will be bankrupt at the end).

The government was also severely handicapped by the absence of Sonia Gandhi. She was ill and was not in a position to exercise her duties as party president and as guardian of the government. A four-member committee which was supposed to take decisions on her behalf had shown no leadership. Either it was not competent to take decisions or was too involved with the internal power struggle that was playing out. Most importantly, the government was led by a prime minister who had no claim to politics. He is a career bureaucrat who was at the right time at the right place. There is no denying the fact that Manmohan Singh has contributed greatly in making India a future superpower. I fully agree with him when on 24 August he said in the Parliament, 'I as a finance minister inherited an economy with a bankrupt treasury, with foreign exchange reserves totally exhausted, with the creditworthiness of our country seriously in doubt. We turned around that economy. We have ensured that this economy, the bankrupt economy that we inherited, has become one of the fastest-growing economies of the world.' Manmohan Singh is not pompous by nature; he is shy, and normally he does not brag about his contributions, but that day he was very hurt by the personal attack made by PAC chief Murli Manohar Joshi. He proclaimed, 'India is respected all over the world . . . and I did make a small contribution in my own way to enhance the prestige of this country.' Manmohan Singh had been an excellent finance minister and he also had a great tenure as prime minister in his first innings; he is a great economist, but politics is not his cup of tea. He did not see that this issue needed political handling, not a bureaucratic solution. The party and the government will have to suffer because of his failing, and maybe he too will have to pay the price?

Even a week later, the government could not decide what to do with Anna. It did not have a strategy. No official channel of communication had been opened. Umesh Sarangi and Bhayuji did meet Team Anna but Anna was not willing to take them seriously. The government did not realize that, as long as it was trying to find a solution through Kapil Sibal, there was no hope for negotiation. On 22 August Anna made it very clear that he could not trust Kapil Sibal because of his conduct during the joint drafting committee meetings. We also got a hint that Sri Sri Ravishankar was trying to act as a go-between. Sri Sri did indicate that good news might be round the corner but it did not happen. Till then everything was in limbo. Team Anna wanted a solid proposal from the government and also the name of a credible negotiator, but the government was in no position to commit anything. The government was waiting for the prime minister to come back to the capital to take charge of the situation.

Meanwhile the country was concerned about Anna's health. In seven days he had lost five kilograms. He was looking tired, and dangerous levels of ketones were found in his blood and urine. In medical terms, when the body does not receive enough glucose from outside, it breaks down inner-body fats, and in this process an acid called ketone is secreted, which is dangerous for the body. Anna did not address the public even once through the day. This was unusual. His supporters were worried. Everybody was praying for his health. The atmosphere was tense, but there was no sign of reconciliation in the air. However, a section of Congressmen were very upset with the leadership. The Congress was being seen as a party that was not interested in tackling corruption. In Mumbai, Priya Dutt interacted with Anna supporters and Sanjay Nirupam wore an Anna cap. Anil Shashtri tweeted that the government should not underestimate the strength of the movement and should immediately start negotiations. But on that day, the most important question that everyone was asking was what would happen to Anna if the government did not move fast?

DAY 8 – 23 AUGUST

On 23 August, when the sun reappeared on the horizon, it brought hope. For the first time in the last eight days, a breakthrough seemed imminent. The prime minister was back from West Bengal. He took control of the situation and the process of consultation began. This is how it went:

10.00 a.m.: Manmohan Singh reached Parliament. The first visitor was Abhishek Manu Singhvi, the chairman of the standing committee on law and justice which was studying the Lokpal Bill.

11.30 a.m.: Kapil Sibal and Salman Khurshid met the prime minister. They briefed him about the movement and also about the results of the meetings that Umesh Sarangi and Bhayuji Maharaj had with Team Anna. Khurshid told waiting reporters that the government was concerned about Anna Hazare's health.

12.15 p.m.: Delhi Chief Minister Sheila Dikshit spoke to the prime minister. Apparently, Dikshit cautioned the PM about the growing support for Anna and also told him that, if the situation was not properly dealt with, it could be dangerous. She also hinted that the operative team ought to be changed. She said that there were many competent leaders in the government who could find a way out. So far, Chidambaram and Sibal were handling the affair. It was not an easy choice for the prime minister. In Delhi, law and order comes under the purview of the central home ministry and the Anna movement was Chidambaram's direct responsibility. Kapil Sibal was the prime minister's blue-eyed boy. In the 2G case he was the prime minister's troubleshooter and in this battle he was Chidambaram's best buddy. They were a team. One senior bureaucrat told me that Chidamabaram was very strong-headed and once he made up his mind, there was no arguing with him. During the crisis Kapil Sibal was the only one who could help him change his opinion.

1.15 p.m.: The most awaited, high-profile meeting began. The prime minister was closeted with Pranab Mukherjee, A.K. Antony and P. Chidambaram. During the meeting it was leaked that Sonia Gandhi had been briefed in detail while she was still in the hospital; and it was at her initiative that the team was changed and Pranab Mukherjee was brought in as the chief negotiator to talk to Team Anna. As per my information, Sonia Gandhi's name was deliberately floated to crush rumours about her illness and to give credibility to the government's new initiative – that it was serious about a solution. Sources told me during my research for this book that Sonia Gandhi was too ill to be informed or to intervene. It was also decided in the meeting that the PM would write a letter to Anna.

3.15 p.m.: The first official dialogue between the government and Team Anna took place. Arvind met Congress MP Sandeep Dikshit alone at his residence after taking Anna's permission. Sandeep took him to meet Salman Khurshid.

5.00 p.m.: The PM wrote a letter to Anna. In his letter the prime minister told Anna, 'I have maintained that your and our objective is identical, viz., to reduce significantly, if not eliminate, the scourge of corruption from this country. At worst, our paths and methodology may differ, though I do believe that even those differences have been exaggerated.' Team Anna had been demanding the withdrawal of the government's Lokpal Bill from the Parliament and the introduction of the Jan Lokpal Bill. The PM in his letter did not commit to anything of this kind. He wrote, 'We are ready to talk to anybody. However, we will have to keep in mind parliamentary supremacy and constitutional obligations in matters of legislation.' He said categorically, 'Our government is prepared to request the speaker to formally refer the Jan Lokpal Bill also to the standing committee for their holistic consideration along with everything else.' Then he appealed to Anna to break his fast. Team Anna did not find the PM's letter exciting, but at least it had prepared a ground for talk. The deadlock was broken. Both the teams started talking; that was the success story of the day. There was a trust deficit between the two, but with the new initiatives, that gap was narrowing, and that was a good sign.

7.30 p.m.: Arvind, Prashant Bhushan and Kiran Bedi went to North Block for a discussion with Pranab Mukherjee. Everybody waited with bated breath. Anna supporters in Ramlila Maidan asked me, 'What will happen? Will the government agree to the Jan Lokpal Bill?' These were innocent souls with hopes and concerns, with bright eyes and fatigued legs; for them the future of India was at stake, the India of their dreams, a corruption-free India, an India they could feel proud of.

9.56 p.m.: The meeting was over and everything looked hunkydory.

10.02 p.m.: Outside the meeting venue, Salman Khurshid said that it had been a good session, and that they were not looking at specific issues.

10.09 p.m.: Outside the meeting venue, Prashant Bhushan said that the talks were constructive and held in a good environment. But it would be difficult to persuade Anna to break his fast without a written commitment. Arvind said that they had had a good meeting; the government had promised to get back to them after a discussion with the PM. They had also been told that there could be many more meetings.

10.11 p.m.: Prashant reiterated that the government should present, vote and pass the Jan Lokpal Bill in that very session of Parliament.

10.27 p.m.: Prashant, Arvind and Kiran reached Ramlila Maidan. They briefed Anna about the talks with Pranab Mukherjee.

10.30 p.m.: Pranab Mukherjee appealed to Anna to break his fast, saying that his life was precious; the matter would be discussed in an all-party meeting the next day. The dialogue would continue and he remained hopeful that a mutually acceptable solution would be found. The ball was rolling too fast. From no hope of a breakthrough we were now moving at breakneck speed. Was it the genius of one man named Pranab Mukherjee? But this did not bode well for some people in the Congress. At stake here were careers – careers of very powerful people. Time was running out for them. It was midnight and no one was in sleep mode. A meeting was scheduled after midnight at 7 Race Course Road (the prime minister's residence).

DAY 9 – 24 AUGUST

12.24 a.m.: Ministers were entering 7 Race Course Road for a meeting of the cabinet committee on political affairs, the highest body to make decisions on political matters in the cabinet.

12.29 a.m.: Meeting of the core committee of the India against Corruption, Team Anna, to discuss the content of the discussion with Pranab Mukherjee, the chief interlocutor for the government.

12.49 a.m.: Kiran Bedi briefed the media about their decision. She said that Anna would only accept a written assurance and, as soon as that was received in writing, a decision would be taken about Anna's fast. This was the clearest indication that the talks had gone very well for Team Anna. It looked like Anna would be breaking his fast sooner than his team had thought possible.

12.58 a.m.: The meeting at 7 Race Course Road ended, ministers started coming out, no news, no media briefing. They all looked tense.

1.02 a.m.: The Congress core committee meeting began. Ahmed Patel, political advisor to party president Sonia Gandhi and member of the four-member committee nominated by Sonia to take decisions on her behalf, also joined them.

We were all waiting for the meeting to wind up. Outside 7 Race Course Road there were only the security personnel on duty and the media. Anxiety, suspense and restlessness were palpable in the atmosphere. We journalists have a knack for reading ominous signs. The body language of some of the ministers who came out told a different story that we were unable to read correctly. All we could do was to make a few conjectures. The question was whether we should wait for the meeting to get over or go home and get back early in the morning. Most reporters called their respective channels for instructions and got a terse reply that they were not to budge from there till the cat was out of the bag. A few sleepy faces roundly abused their bosses, took out cigarettes, sent up their anger in smoke and settled to waiting for their breaking story. But the angry old man had gone to sleep.

He was also tired. He had had a long day as well. He was fighting with the government and also with his doctors. During the day, his medical team, led by Dr Trehan was insisting that there were complications in his body due to lack of food and he needed either to be taken to the hospital or an intravenous (IV) drip was to be administered at the Ramlila Maidan itself. He said as much at 8.30 p.m. in his medical bulletin to Anna supporters at the Maidan. Later, Manish told me an interesting story. According to him, Dr Trehan had spoken to Anna during the day and had explained to him why his body required the IV drip. He promised that he would not force anything on him and everything would be done with his permission. He convinced Anna to put on a cannula (the medical equipment through which drip was administered). Anna agreed. A cannula was put in. Suddenly, word spread that Anna was being administered a drip. A few news channels also flashed this news. There was panic among Team Anna. Anna was furious. He asked to speak to the doctors. A junior doctor came. Anna asked him to remove the cannula. The doctor refused. Dr Trehan was called immediately. Team Anna promised the doctor that if it was really urgent and the doctors so advised, the team would take a decision on the drip. Manish went to the dais and clarified that Anna had refused to take the drip and that the news being shown on TV channels stating otherwise was wrong. There were unconfirmed reports that the government was pressuring Dr Trehan to convince Anna to accept the drip. After the first official meeting too, Salman Khurshid had called Arvind to request that Anna be administered a drip. Arvind told him that in order to do that, they needed a written request and an assurance about the Jan Lokpal Bill, which Salman Khurshid was in no position to oblige with.

Disturbed by these developments, Anna decided to speak to the people from the stage. At 9.15 p.m. Anna addressed his supporters. '*Meri antaratma ne kaha hai ki is waqt koi bhi IV dawai lena galat hoga. Ek taraf mai kehta hun ki mai samaj ke liye jiyunga ya marunga, aur doosri taraf maut se daroon; ye galat hoga*' (My conscience says that it would be wrong to accept an IV drip or any medication. My refrain is that I will live or die for my community . . . so it isn't right that I should be afraid of death (*Indian Express*, 24 August 2011). Anna was angry and sensed something. He said, '*Agar mujhe koi yahan se uthane aye to gate ke saamne khade ho jana, kisi ko andar mat aane dena. Par is andolan mein jo bhi karen, ahimsa ke saath kariyega*' (If anyone tries to take me away from here forcibly, don't allow them to enter . . . but don't resort to violence.) Not that his supporters needed that warning – the agitation had been peaceful, not a single stone had been thrown except one incident in the early morning when a few hoodlums from nearby areas had come there drunk and unleashed violence on the policemen. If anything, his call could have incited the crowd if any policemen tried approaching the dais. In these situations, there is always the possibility of mischief from both sides, and the police could have used that to discredit the movement. Anna was later counselled and the next day he took

back that statement. But he was angry and the world was to see
the full force of his anger the very next day. Only, this was not
the anger of arrogance like that of some cabinet ministers who
were fuming about the turn that events had taken.

POWER STRUGGLE AND
HIDDEN AGENDAS

DAY 9 CONTINUES

It was 11.30 at night. The date was 24 August. Anna was seething with anger. His entire team was with him on stage and the tense crowd was listening to them. Normally, at this hour Anna would go to sleep and the mikes would be switched off. But today the atmosphere had changed. Anna was saying, 'After nine days, the real face of the government has been exposed. Which face? The face of a black Englishman, the face of dictatorship . . . I am not scared. Do whatever you want to do.' He continued in anger, 'This government is showing dictatorial tendencies and wants to forcibly pick me up. Don't stop them. The other day I had said, "Don't let them come near me, stand in their way if they come to pick me." But today I am saying "Don't do that. Let them come here, don't you lose your patience. The government wants violence here, let the government take me away; don't indulge in violence."'

I was also amazed to see this. I had just got back from the Ramlila Maidan. The minute I got home, I got a call from office saying that there was an emergency press conference at the Ramlila Maidan and that anything could happen. I immediately switched on the TV. What I saw on screen was unbelievable. The situation was very tense. I was very hungry and was about to eat my dinner, all laid out on the table. But I could barely eat as I was constantly receiving phone calls from the office and from reporters on the field. Or I was calling them to check with them.

During the day I had gathered that something was amiss, though nobody was willing to spill the beans. At 10.05 p.m. I left the Ramlila Maidan, along with Prabhanjan Verma and Vikrant Yadav, I got a call. It was Prabal. He had information that Anna might be forcibly picked up by the police later that night. The two senior reporters who had been assigned to constantly monitor the activity of the Delhi Police and other agencies concerned had passed on information that there was a definite plan in place. The police were waiting for a clearance from their political master, i.e., the home minister. We had moved just half a kilometre towards Ajmeri Gate. I asked the driver to stop the car by the kerb and requested Prabhanjan and Vikrant to confirm the news. Prabhanjan called up a senior doctor in Dr Trehan's team who was keeping a close watch on Anna. The doctor told him that all arrangements had been made at the Medanta Hospital and doctors there were ready for any eventuality. He was a good source and hinted that Anna might be brought in that very night. Meanwhile, Vikrant spoke to a junior police officer of that area. Junior officers are often more cooperative than their tight-lipped seniors, who are likely to talk only if they are really close friends or they deliberately want to leak a story. The officer on the other side of the phone, said candidly that it was worthwhile to stay back at the Maidan. '*Kuchh* action *ho sakta hai*' (Some action is possible).

Two different sources were hinting at some action. And the only action possible at midnight was a Ramdev-style pick up, that is to say, Anna would be forcibly taken to Medanta Hospital in Gurgaon. My reporters, Alok and Nitish, had already confirmed the probability of this happening. I decided to go to office and plan for a late-night emergency. Prabhanjan and Vikrant volunteered to go back to the Ramlila Maidan. I really felt bad for them. I knew they had been at Ramlila Maidan since 7 a.m. every day and were looking forward to a

good dinner and a good night's sleep. They were dead tired.
But for a journalist nothing is more exciting than participating
in a big news story. Back in office, my team and I analysed the
situation. I was sure nothing would happen before 2 a.m. So I
went home to have dinner and thought I would come back
later, but by the time I reached home, the film had changed
dramatically.

Anna had called upon his supporters to move to their
respective MPs' residences in the thousands and sit there, court
arrest and go to jail if the police were to pick him up. He
cautioned them, 'Don't indulge in violence. Don't damage
public property.' And exhorted them, 'I will go to jail; you all
don't sit idle, go to jail, court arrest from tomorrow.' He was in
full flow, 'If they come to take me away, our slogan will be
Dilli Chalo (Let's go to Delhi). The government has refused to
honour the Lokpal Bill, we have to gherao the Parliament.' It
was the ninth day of his hunger strike and he had been advised
to speak less, to conserve energy, but this was the fifth time
that he was addressing the public that day. He was still charged.
Kiran Bedi was also speaking in her own style about the day's
events, 'There was lot of difference between yesterday and
today.' Arvind interjected, 'Today Pranab Mukherjee was a
different person. Yesterday he was very respectful, today he
was behaving differently. *Kal woh sun rahe the, aaj woh hame
suna rahe the*' (Yesterday he was listening to us, and today he
was lecturing us). Arvind said, 'A day ago he had accepted the
Jan Lokpal Bill, but today he rejected the Jan Lokpal Bill. He
said that the government would draft a fresh bill and if we
wanted to add something we should just let them know.'
According to Arvind, he, Prashant and Kiran were taken aback.
It had come as a shock to them.

The talks had broken down. Politics was fighting back.
Something had happened in the last twenty-four hours that we
didn't know about, though we did have an ominous feeling
about the CCPA meeting the night before. But none of us had
imagined that things would go from breakthrough to

breakdown. In the meeting with Team Anna the day before, there was an agreement on all issues, except questions of lower bureaucracy, citizen's charter and appointment of Lokayukta. Even these issues, Pranab Mukherjee had promised he would discuss with the PM and get back to them in an hour. Team Anna was very hopeful. They were expecting some major announcement that night itself. The team waited for the phone call. They waited till three in the morning and when the call did not come, they went to sleep. The next morning, Pawan Kheda called Arvind. Pawan works with Sheila Dikshit as officer on special duty. He is also friends with her son Sandeep Dikshit, a member of Parliament. Arvind and Sandeep had known each other for years. Both had worked in the NGO sector and it was through Sandeep that contact had been established with Arvind. Once Pranab Mukherjee took charge of the matter, Pawan was the one who called Arvind for any discussion with Sandeep. Pawan did hint at what had happened the previous night, but it was Salman Khurshid who gave him all the details. He said that everything that had been discussed and decided with Team Anna was rejected in the CCPA meeting. Kapil Sibal and P. Chidambaram were furious. Sibal had apparently even shouted at Khurshid. They said that there could be no compromise with constitutional procedures. Chidambaram and Sibal had bragged that that they needed only an hour to throw Anna and his team out of Ramlila Maidan. This happened in front of Manmohan Singh who had been silent most of the time and had avoided taking sides. Finally, Chidambaram and Sibal won, much to Pranab Mukherjee's embarrassment. He was no ordinary minister. He had been informally labelled the de facto prime minister. Clearly, there was a serious power struggle in the cabinet. Such a snub to Pranab Mukherjee was no ordinary matter. It was an indication of something much more serious.

Let's look at it another way. Chidambaram and Sibal were handling the crisis from day one. The prime minister decided to take the charge away from them and gave the responsibility to

Pranab Mukherjee, the second most powerful cabinet minister after the PM. Mukherjee roped in Salman Khurshid and Sandeep Dikshit. In a matter of hours, they managed to achieve a breakthrough, which proved that Chidambaram and Sibal had messed up and could not tactfully handle the crisis that was proving to be detrimental to the party and the government.

So, shouting at Khurshid had meant an open snub to Mukherjee, the PM-appointed interlocutor. Now there could be only two things. Either these two ministers snubbed Pranab Mukherjee at the PM's behest or they are so powerful that they don't need to heed the PM. It was unlikely that the PM would have instigated something like this because ultimately he would be the loser. And if he was not backing them, who was? Because they wouldn't dare do something like this on their own. They were not mass leaders. Sonia Gandhi was not around. So what was going on? And was it not for this reason that later an open war broke out between Pranab Mukherjee and Chidambaram on the issue of 2G?

After the meeting, Pranab Mukherjee had been upset and humiliated but, like a seasoned politician, he knew that this was a very sensitive time and needed careful handling. He also knew that it was the ninth day of Anna's fast and that this phase was critical for Anna's health. So he did not break ties with Team Anna. At 8 a.m. the next day, he instructed Salman Khurshid to be in touch with Team Anna. Despite the internal tension and uncertainty, meetings took place one after the other. The all-party meeting was also scheduled on this very day. At 9.50 a.m., the parliamentary affairs minister, Pawan Bansal, announced that it was not possible to stick to the deadline of 30 August for the passage of the bill. At 10 a.m., Salman Khurshid reached Sandeep Dikshit's residence. They prepared a few points for Pranab Mukherjee. At 10.55, Salman Khurshid and Sandeep Dikshit reached Parliament, where they were joined by Pawan Bansal and the minister of state for parliamentary affairs, Rajiv Shukla, and Pranab Mukherjee. In between, Kiran Bedi, Arvind and Prashant Bhushan stepped out to meet Khurshid at his residence. The meeting began around 11.30 a.m. and continued till 1.30 p.m. They made a draft resolution, which was to be passed in Parliament. Khurshid took that draft with him and showed it to Mukherjee. By now we had information that Anna's deadline of 30 August had no meaning. The all-party meeting began at 3.30 p.m. and continued for three hours. In the meantime, minister of state in the PMO, Narayanaswami, informed reporters that the Jan Lokpal Bill had been sent to the standing committee along with Aruna Roy's and Loksatta Party chief, Jayaprakash Narayan's Lokpal Bills. This was immediately rejected by Team Anna. They reiterated that the government's Lokpal Bill should be withdrawn from the Parliament, the Jan Lokpal Bill be introduced and then discussed.

The all-party meeting had no solution to the problem; rather it complicated matters for Team Anna. Its recommendation was not that the Jan Lokpal Bill be introduced in Parliament, but that the government bill be amended in light of Team Anna's bill. And, on behalf of all the parties, an appeal was made to Anna to break his fast, which of course Anna ignored. By now there were enough hints that the government had hardened its stand and once again Pranab Mukherjee's soft line had been put on the back-burner. The government was, in fact, emboldened because it now had the backing of all the political parties. It was ready for an open confrontation.

Every day, my fellow reporters and I stepped out of the Ramlila Maidan to have a cup of tea and unwind. On 24 August as I stepped out of the premises, I could see extra police. I thought that it must be due to complaints of hooliganism around the ground. I didn't give it much thought. But later in the evening one of the core committee members of Team Anna confided in me that there was some suspicious movement around the stage and in the ground. I still remained unconvinced. I believe political workers and agitationists always carry a few conspiracy theories in their pocket. But after sunset the rumour intensified and everybody could sense some suspicious movements. Anna had also seemed restless throughout the day. Till the final assault at midnight, Anna had been constantly holding the mike and stressing to the people there that if something were to happen to him they should be patient.

After much research, I can confidently say that there had been a definite plan to forcibly pick up Anna and to take him to Medanta, and the rumour was not just a rumour. The home ministry was hell-bent on not letting Anna continue his fast. It was a day full of suspense and action on 24 August. I was told that once the CCPA meeting had rejected Pranab Mukherjee's plan and it was decided that no concession would be made to Team Anna, the only option left was to forcibly pick up Anna. The police arrangement had been stepped up that morning. By 11 a.m. the Rapid Action Force (RAF) had been summoned and was stationed near the stage in different groups. Two hundred policemen of the Special Operations Squad (SOS) were also deployed. A stretcher had been bought from a medical store in Kamla Market to carry Anna to an ambulance. A Maruti Versa had been specially converted into an ambulance to hoodwink Anna's supporters. A team of forty inspectors was constituted to carry out the operation. The route from Ramlila Maidan to Medanta had been properly assessed. The ministry was in regular touch with Dr Trehan. On 24 August, three dry runs were done for the route by three different teams between 6 p.m. and 7.30 p.m. It was also decided to avoid the usual route to Gurgaon and to take the Mehrauli route, which was shorter as well. This operation was to be carried out at four in the morning and all the members of the operation were required to report to the Kamla Market police station by 3 a.m. for a final rehearsal. Till then, Team Anna and Delhi Police had had an excellent relationship and they had been in touch with each other on a regular basis. On 24 August, when all the preparations had been made, the home ministry was informed about the police's readiness. Now the police was only waiting for a green signal from the home ministry. Home Minister P. Chidambaram had been briefed about every minute detail of the operation. It was he who had to say yes.

So when Arvind, Prashant Bhushan and Kiran Bedi went to see Pranab Mukherjee for the second round of discussions around 9 p.m., at the finance minister's North Block office, it was a very tricky situation. Before leaving for the meeting Arvind had checked with the Delhi Police who had assured them that nothing would be done without Anna's prior permission and Arvind had announced the police assurance from the stage. The future of the movement was dependent on the outcome of this meeting. The public at the Ramlila Maidan were very restless. I had not witnessed such collective anxiety earlier. People were asking each other, 'What will happen?' All eyes were on North Block. Fast, protest marches and rallies were being held as usual in other parts of the country too. Mumbai was equally volatile. The Suburban Railway Passengers Association had also joined the protest and, on this day, started a train morcha. In Bangalore, citizens had made a fifteen-kilometre-long human chain across the city. Youngsters had taken out bike rallies in Chennai. In Jammu, the hearing-and-speech-impaired had come out on the streets. Ralegan Siddhi was extremely worried about Anna's health. Young boys and girls working with Team Anna were very tense; I saw a few even crying out of concern for him. But Anna was adamant. At 7.30 p.m. he said to the people gathered, 'I am not seventy-four years old, I am young. I fought with Pakistani soldiers once and now I am fighting with the enemies within. This fight is on.'

At 9.51 p.m., Salman Khurshid came out. He said, 'We are trying to understand each other.' Kiran Bedi was overheard saying, 'Yesterday he was listening, today he was shouting at us. He rejected the Jan Lokpal Bill.' Talks had broken down. Arvind later told me that, during the meeting, Kiran Bedi had been getting innumerable SMSs from her friends and juniors in the police department. The messages had been crisp. 'At 4 a.m. the police will forcibly pick Anna from Ramlila Maidan.'

Arvind directly asked Pranab Mukherjee, 'Will you pick us up forcibly from the grounds?'

According to Arvind, Pranab Mukherjee lost his cool. He said, 'Don't talk to me like this.'

Arvind persisted. 'Anna will not get up. You are not saying anything. What should we do?'

'I am not authorized to; ask the home minister,' Pranab Mukherjee retorted.

'What should we say to Anna? What about his fast?'

Team Anna wanted a final answer from the finance minister of the country.

Pranab Mukherjee was very curt, 'That is your problem. Did he ask me before sitting on a fast?'

The most powerful minister was saying that Anna's fast was not his problem. He forgot that, a few hours ago, the prime minister of the country had appealed to Anna in Parliament to end his fast. He had said, 'I applaud him. I salute him. His life is much too precious and, therefore, I would urge Sri Anna Hazare to end his fast.' Now the minister said something quite different.

That was the end of the discussion. The movement was at crossroads. Kiran Bedi rightly said, 'The movement had come back to the point from where it started.' It went back in time. Now at stake was the future, the future of the movement, a movement which had given hope to millions, millions who were on the streets all over India, resolved after sixty-four years of independence to fight corruption.

Team Anna was back at the Ramlila Maidan. It was past ten. Anna had gone to sleep. He was woken up and briefed. He was also upset. An urgent meeting of the Team Anna core committee was called to discuss the future of the movement. Arvind wanted to intensify the movement. He was of the opinion that they should give a call for Dilli Chalo. 'Let's call for a civil disobedience movement right away,' he said. Prashant was not in favour of this. Arvind had lost his cool and was angry with Prashant. He said, 'What should we do? Let them loot the country?' There had been a heated argument between the two. Prashant did not like Arvind's statements. He had reacted very sharply and said, 'I am walking off.' Arvind regained his composure and, according to a senior member of the movement, apologized to Prashant. Both realized that unity was the need of the hour. Until then, they had worked as a team and had tremendous respect for each other. The difference was in their approach and their backgrounds. Arvind was a product of social movements. Since he left his job as joint commissioner of income tax, he had been involved in some social movement or the other and had been mobilizing people. Prashant, on the other hand, was a lawyer by profession. In the legal fraternity, he was well known as an activist lawyer, a radical who had taken the establishment head on. Unlike Arvind, he had not been fighting in the street, his battleground was the court of law. He was used to challenging the system from within. He used petitions to correct the system, not demolish it. One team member put it aptly, 'Prashant was a chamber activist and Arvind was a street fighter.' But Anna was there to bridge this gap; he was the neutralizer, the assimilationist, the radical sanyasi, the moral vanguard of the movement. Finally, they had decided to go to the public and tell them the truth. Arvind later told me that transparency had been their biggest strength. His approach was simple: whenever in doubt, face the people. They had all gathered on stage. Anna was also there. Arvind and Kiran Bedi placed in public all the details of the meeting with Pranab Mukherjee. The angry old man of seventy-four years declared war against the government. He gave the Dilli Chalo call. It was 11.30 at night.

*

The whole world saw Team Anna's angry outburst. The public was very charged. The government was perceived to be sheltering corruption. The damage was done. Another angry old man in the North Block was once again in action. He was also on TV channels and gave a long phone-in interview to CNN-IBN. Mr Pranab Mukherjee clarified, 'My statement has been misquoted. I never said Anna's fast is his problem. It is a national problem. I appeal to Anna to end his fast as soon as possible.' It was 12.30 at night. I had never seen Pranab Mukherjee giving phone-in interviews to channels so late at night. He is not fluent in Hindi; he was answering questions posed by the IBN7 anchor in Hindi. This got me thinking; was it the genius of this old man of the North Block to escalate the crisis to this level to counter his friends/opponents? Was he trying to make them realize that they were playing with fire which could have engulfed the entire nation and the loser would have been the party, or was it just one of those moments which happen in history for which there is no explanation? Only God knows or Mr Mukherjee does. Anyway, the police did not execute its plan to forcibly hospitalize Anna. Do I need to spell out why? Maybe Mr Chidambaram has the answer.

DEADLOCK ENDS

DAY 10 – 25 AUGUST

Now the 'real' politicians had entered the fray. From deadlock to breakthrough and then back to a deadlock, so the morning of 25 August dawned a little tense. I had reached Ramlila Maidan slightly early. I was shaken by the overreaction of the two angry old men. Frankly, I thought that both of them had lost it. Of course, Pranab Mukherjee should not have said those words about Anna and his fast unto death. But we all know what Mukherjee is like. He is burdened with so many responsibilities that even he cannot count them. He is entrusted with any political matter or administrative issue that others cannot handle. There are not enough senior persons in the party who have that kind of experience, expertise or goodwill, and those who are competent are conveniently sidelined. People like Ghulam Nabi Azad, Ambika Soni or even the likes of H.R. Bhardwaj, who could have been assets for the Manmohan Singh cabinet, are either given insignificant ministries or non-political posts.

The Manmohan Singh cabinet has nine former chief ministers and, of these, seven belong to the Congress, but their talent is not utilized. One very seasoned cabinet minister told me that if politics was handled by theories learnt in Harvard, Oxford or IIT, this government had no future. He was no doubt unhappy with the way things were run at the party and government level. He was not alone; an overwhelming majority of leaders were extremely unhappy with the way Anna's *anshan* was handled from the very first day. But they would not open their mouths and, don't forget, many of them are hard-core Sonia loyalists.

Another minister told me that, over a period of time, Sonia had become inaccessible, so much so that cabinet ministers and chief ministers had to wait for long to even meet her. All the senior leaders hate the party bureaucracy. They feel humiliated that they must seek permission from their juniors to meet Sonia Gandhi. Several leaders openly told me that people who have no grassroots experience are given prominence because of their Harvard, Oxford and IIT backgrounds, and the party bureaucracy does not feel threatened by them. According to one senior leader, Indira Gandhi and Rajiv Gandhi were also surrounded by a coterie of *chamchas*, but they did not stop meeting or interacting with party leaders or grassroots workers. With Sonia, that link is broken and, in their opinion, Rahul Gandhi is also taking the same route. Once, I asked a senior member of the Nationalist Congress Party (NCP), 'When the issue of Sonia Gandhi's foreign origin is no longer relevant, why don't you merge your party with the Congress?' He candidly replied, 'Do you expect Sharad Pawarji to stand in queue at Ahmed Patel's office to seek an appointment to see Sonia Gandhi?' It was this malaise that was chiefly responsible for the mishandling of the Anna issue. I was really surprised by Pranab Mukherjee's outburst in the meeting with Team Anna. But when I thought about it, it occurred to me that it might have been a deliberate ploy to send a message to the entire 'non-political establishment' that if the issue was not handled with finesse and speed, the party and the government would face serious consequences.

When I heard that Vilas Rao Deshmukh had entered the ring, I told myself that a solution was now round the corner. Vilas Rao is a very seasoned politician from Maharashtra; he had been chief minister twice, speaks Marathi and has dealt successfully with Anna's *anshan* many a time in the past. He has known Anna for the last thirty years and the two of them are on good terms. Vilas Rao should have been the one to take charge at the very outset. Instead, he was sitting in his bungalow at 14 Akbar Road, watching the game. Is that not a comment on the functioning of this government? During my research, I got to know that, when Anna had sat on an indefinite fast at Jantar Mantar, Sharad Pawar had personally told Manmohan Singh to involve Vilas Rao Deshmukh. Pawar had said frankly, 'I don't have a good equation with Anna and Vilas Rao is the only one who can deal with him.' Pawar was not much off the mark. Readers may recall that Pawar was the first one to resign from the group of ministers (GOM) on corruption as he was attacked by Team Anna in April 2011.

Vilas Rao is probably the only cabinet minister who has had held all the posts that a people's representative should. At the age of twenty-eight, he was elected sarpanch of his village and then he became a member of the Zila Panchayat, then an MLA, an MP, the chief minister and, finally, a cabinet minister. He does not feel comfortable in Delhi and his heart has always been in Maharashtra. Although Vilas Rao had not been contacted by the government or the party, he took the initiative himself. His close associates told me that, after a week, when there had been no solution in sight, Anna's relatives and his core supporters from Ralegan Siddhi had approached Vilas Rao and pleaded with him to do something. Two of Anna's doctors from his village were also amongst them. They said that they could not trust Anna's close associates in Delhi and were very worried about Anna's health. Initially, Vilas Rao ignored the request, but when the pressure from Maharashtra became too much, he contacted Pranab Mukherjee and offered to talk to Anna. Chidambaram and Sibal had been diehard opponents of Anna and his movement, and Team Anna disliked them. As long as they were there solution was difficult. Fortunately, Chidambaram and Sibal had been removed from the scene and Mukherjee had been given the charge. Mukherjee told him to go ahead. Vilas Rao had a two-pronged strategy:

1) To not meet Anna in the full glare of the public; 2) To talk directly to Anna, and not involve any go-between. In my opinion, after Pranab Mukherjee's taking charge of the situation, Vilas Rao's entry was the second most important development during the entire crisis as far as the government's role goes.

Vilas Rao got cracking immediately. He established contact with Anna on the phone and wished to meet him. Anna had no problem. The only condition that Vilas Rao had was that he wanted to meet Anna and talk to him alone, not in the presence of his close confidantes, like Arvind, Prashant Bhushan and Kiran Bedi. Anna had no problem. Vilas Rao went to meet Anna on 25 August at 2.45 p.m. The whole conversation took place in Marathi. This meeting took place just after Parliament had appealed to Anna to break his fast.

In the end Vilas Rao said, 'Anna, the national capital has given you so much respect, the whole country is with you, the PM has saluted you, the all-party meeting and the Parliament have appealed to you to break your fast. What more do you want?' Anna's face brightened despite not having eaten for the last ten days. Vilas Rao knew his words had had an impact. He continued, 'This is the most opportune time, Anna. You should end your fast. What more do you want?'

Anna, like a seasoned politician, raised three fingers and said, 'Ask the government to accept these three demands and I will get up.'

Vilas Rao said, 'What are these?'

Anna elaborated, 'The corruption of the lower bureaucracy should be put under the purview of the Lokpal, the citizens' charter should be made in each government department for a time-bound delivery of people's work and grievances, and the establishment of Lokayuktas in states should be under the aegis of the Lokpal.'

This was a major climbdown for Anna and a great face-saver for the government. Till then, Anna had been demanding that the government's Lokpal Bill should be withdrawn, the Jan Lokpal Bill should be introduced and then Parliament should discuss the bill.

This was Anna's reply to all those who had been defaming the movement saying that Anna was a dictator who wanted to blackmail Parliament and the people's representatives, and all he wanted was to pass the 'monstrous' Jan Lokpal Bill by pointing a gun at the government. This allegation was partly brought about by the propaganda unleashed by the government and partly due to a lack of understanding about the nature of the movement. I know for a fact that some serious intellectuals were really worried because they believed that Anna only wanted his Lokpal Bill to be passed as it was, without any alterations. The problem with these intellectuals was that, in the last two decades, this country had not seen any big non-violent social and political movement and, over a period of time, the trade union movement has also weakened due to the government's liberal economic policies. A successful agitation must have a much higher pitch and bigger demands and an even much larger objective. The objective of this movement was to remove corruption, which Anna elevated to a higher level, calling it the second freedom struggle, which in turn gave a sense of importance to the ordinary citizen. They believed that they were contributors to the nation-building process, like the freedom fighters were in an earlier era. If all they had was a vague idea that India must be corruption-free, no government would have given them the time of the day. From the beginning, Team Anna had projected the Jan Lokpal Bill as something that was non-negotiable. But as the bargaining gained momentum, they showed their true cards and compromised with the bill, narrowing it down to the three basic demands that I believe were the soul of the bill and that perfectly fit the grammar of the negotiations. One always starts bargaining from the higher position and then comes down to accommodate the rival's viewpoint to reach a middle ground. There is always a give and take in the process. BJD's young MP Jay Panda had said, quite aptly, 'He and his team has always been depicted as demagogues whose rigid approach defied rational discussion . . . The reality is that Team Anna was never as intransient as it was portrayed. There had all along been signals that they would engage in give and take; but as long as the government stuck to its unbending position, it made perfect negotiating sense for them to do the same' (*Indian Express*, 5 September 2011). So I think Shakeel Ahmed, spokesperson of the Congress, was wrong when he tried to project Anna's climbdown as a defeat (*Hindustan*, 7 September 2011). I was following Anna's speech very closely. Anna had always focused on the daily sufferings of the common man caused by corruption at the lower level of bureaucracy. He wanted an assurance from the government that these three demands had to be incorporated in the Lokpal Bill. While reporting for IBN7, I asked people on camera about their experiences with corruption. Here is what they had to say:

> 'I paid Rs 25,000 for the job in Delhi.'
> 'I paid Rs 500 to the traffic police in Delhi.'
> 'I paid Rs 5 lakh to get a job in the police department in Karnal.'
> 'I paid Rs 3,000 for a small work in Karnataka.'
> 'I had to pay money for a small work in a school in Samastipur.'
> 'I paid Rs 1,500 for a driving licence in Delhi.'
> 'I paid a bribe to get my arrears passed in Meerut.'

In this country, the *aam admi* is paying a bribe for every little thing that needs to be done in a government department. He has to pay a bribe even to move his file. Anna had also mentioned this in his letter to the prime minister, 'I can't tolerate it when a common man struggles because of corruption. To prevent the common man from being a victim of corruption, the Jan Lokpal Bill has three provisions.' Unfortunately, the intellectuals in this country don't have to face this on a daily basis, so they don't feel the pain of the common man. Shaqeel Ahmed is part of that elitist understanding, but one of his senior colleagues, who did not want to be identified, echoed what Jay Panda had written. He said, 'These demands were not so big, could have been agreed upon, and all three were very genuine and affect the common man.'

So the moment Anna showed his cards, Vilas Rao saw the light at the end of the tunnel. The crisis was suddenly solvable. Vilas Rao said, 'It's OK with me, I will inform the prime minister.' After a twenty-five-minute conversation with Anna, Vilas Rao went straight to Mukherjee. It was 3.20 p.m. Mukherjee advised him to meet the prime minister. Word spread like fire. Consultations reached a fever pitch. At 4.40 p.m., Salman Khurshid and Sandeep Dikshit met Mukherjee. At 5 p.m. Chidambaram reached 7 Race Course Road and was joined by Vilas Rao at 5.15 p.m. Vilas Rao gave the PM the details of his talks with Anna. The PM did not look convinced, perhaps because of the belligerence shown by Team Anna so far, or because, until then, he had been getting a different kind of feedback. The PM wanted to be sure, so he asked Vilas Rao to request Anna for a letter confirming this. Meanwhile, at 5.35 p.m., Anna announced that, if the government agreed to initiate a discussion on the draft of the Jan Lokpal Bill in Parliament and all the parties were in agreement, he would break his fast. Now there was scope for no scepticism. The PM called a high-powered meeting of senior ministers, where it was decided that the three demands made by Anna would be accepted and the issue would be discussed in Parliament. Now the government and Anna were seemingly on the same page and the end of the crisis looked very close. In less than twenty-four hours things changed dramatically again. It was like a roller-coaster ride.

But the day did not start so bright. Arvind was very bitter in the morning. He blamed Chidambaram and Sibal for trying to derail the negotiations. He said that these two ministers were hell-bent on sabotaging the entire process and did not want any solution to the crisis. Arvind was right. There were serious differences in the cabinet and also in the party. One not-so-senior leader told me that ninety per cent of the party members believed that

1) Anna's arrest had been wrong;
2) the no-negotiation attitude in the beginning had been wrong; and

3) the government should have introduced a much stronger Lokpal Bill than what it did in the monsoon session after the meetings of the joint drafting committee.

The junior leaders and ministers were furious and puzzled about why the government was so adamant and arrogant. They were sure that the prime minister could not be so impractical and that it had to be the fault of the Chidambaram–Sibal duo. By now Arvind had emerged as a hardliner in the Anna camp, but I was still surprised by his statement. This was a purely political statement, probably aimed at neutralizing the two ministers. The message was loud and clear: that Pranab Mukherjee and Salman Khurshid were searching for a truce and the other two were playing obstructionists. I have no doubt that Arvind made a politically loaded statement and I have strong reasons to believe that it was done at the behest of 'somebody'. Who? I leave that to your imagination.

Despite the late night political earthquake of 24 August and the early morning bitterness on 25 August, the day went smoothly and Parliament was gracious and dignified in making an appeal to Anna to break his fast. On the tenth day of Anna's *anshan*, Prime Minister Manmohan Singh, while speaking on corruption in the Lok Sabha had said, 'Corruption is a collective national responsibility and there is a need to find a credible solution to tackle it. I want the Jan Lokpal Bill to be given due consideration by the parliamentary standing committee.' The prime minister also said, 'We will find effective ways and means to discuss the Jan Lokpal Bill along with the government's version of the bill, along with Aruna Roy's and Jayaprakash Narayan's. All ideas should be discussed and debated to get the best possible bill to help us deal with corruption.' The prime minister set the agenda thus: that the government was ready to discuss the Jan Lokpal Bill, but with the rider that it would be discussed with Aruna Roy's and Jayaprakash Narayan's draft bills. And then the PM made a historic statement, 'I applaud Anna, I salute Anna, I would urge Anna to end this fast. I request all to request Anna that his point has been registered and we will take note of it.' Leader of the Opposition Sushma Swaraj immediately endorsed the PM's appeal. And on behalf of the entire house, Speaker Meira Kumar made an appeal to Anna to end his fast.

This was truly a historic moment. No other individual had been accorded this privilege in Indian parliamentary history. Anna, in his letter to the prime minister, said, 'I have the highest regard for our Parliament. Our Parliament is the sacred temple of our democracy.' As a goodwill gesture he also apologized. He wrote to the PM, 'If anything that I or my associates said during this movement has offended you or anyone else, I apologize for that. To hurt anyone is not our intention.' But to my utter disappointment, Anna and his team ignored the Speaker's appeal. I believe that, despite all his misgivings about elected representatives, Anna should have shown respect to the Parliament as an institution and as a symbol of Indian democracy, and ended his fast, thereby providing the Parliament an opportunity to reciprocate the same sentiments to the will of the people by establishing a strong Lokpal on the lines of the Jan Lokpal Bill. This was especially necessary because a lot of critics believed that the movement had questioned the sovereignty of the Parliament. One of the senior editors in the country, H.K. Dua, wrote in the *Hindustan Times* (31 August 2011): 'The demands that Parliament must pass the Jan Lokpal bill by August 30 made members of Parliament come to believe that the authorities of the Parliament and the constitution were under threat . . . It is not that people do not put pressure on the government to demand reforms, but dictating laws to Parliament amounts to acquiring extra-constitutional authority, which no reasonable citizen can accept – it is a sheer case of overreach.' But people like S.L. Rao had defended the Anna agitation. He wrote in *The Telegraph*, (4 September 2011): 'If many people who feel strongly about an issue led with determination and single-minded objectives and agitate non-violently it will be difficult in the future to refuse to consider their demands.' Like Dua, I am not questioning the motive of the movement, but Team Anna did commit some mistakes and this was one such moment. I have no hesitation in saying that, after the PM's appeal, it would have been impossible for the government to go back on their assurance. If it did, the government would have lost the moral right to further accuse Team Anna, and Anna always had the option of sitting on an indefinite *anshan* again.

Even in Team Anna, there was a minuscule minority that did not agree with the leadership on this question. Swami Agnivesh was one such person who had at one point been at the forefront of the movement, but was slowly being marginalized. He was caught on camera passing derogatory remarks about Team Anna. He had been provoked by Team Anna's rejection of the Parliament's appeal. He was heard talking to one Kapil, who everyone concluded was Kapil Sibal, despite Swami Agnivesh's vehement denial. Swami Agnivesh was saying:

Jay ho Kapilji, jay ho Maharaj.

(Listens to the other side.)

Bahut zaroori hai Kapilji, nahin to ye paagal ki tarah ho rahe hain jaise koi haathi ho . . .

(Listens to the other side.)

Haan bahut . . . lekin jitna concede *karti jaati hai* government *utna hi ye sir par chadh rahe hain.*

(Listens to the other side.)

Kuchh karna chahiye . . . Further ground *bilkul nahin* concede *karna chahiye,* firm *hokar . . . haan haan . . .*

Haan bilkul firm *hokar kahiye, koi sarkaar ko is tarah se kare yeh buri baat hai , mujhe sharm mehsoos ho rahi hai ki hamari sarkaar kitni kamzor ho rahi hai.*

Dekhiye na itni badi appeal *karne ke baad Anna* fast *nahin todte, itni badi cheez kah di, saari* Parliament *ne kah diya . . . haan . . . aur itne unche shabdon mein pradhanmantri ne kahaa . . .*

This was a sixty-nine-second clip. Swami Agnivesh was heard complaining to Kapil that despite the prime minister's and the Parliament's appeal, Team Anna was behaving like a mad elephant and he was ashamed that the government had become very weak and that it should be firm and not concede further ground.

Swami Agnivesh was one of the founder members of the movement. And during the first *anshan* he was one of the negotiators with the government. But he got upset that his name was not proposed by Anna as a member of the joint drafting committee. In the eyes of Team Anna, he was suspect. The team perceived him as a mole who was leaking important information to the government. But he was still not sidelined. The team thought that doing so would have sent a wrong signal. Therefore, he was active in the month of August as well. He was very visible on TV channels and was vehemently defending the movement. But he became furious when his name was missing from the list of negotiators who were to talk to the government. He had complained to Anna. Anna had flatly refused to nominate him. Agnivesh asked, 'What will my role be?' Anna told him to work for the movement. Agnivesh felt humiliated. He threatened to leave the movement. Anna said that he could do as he wished. He left the agitation. So when Team Anna got to know about this video clip, they were very angry. They felt betrayed. One of the team members asked me if I could provide them the clip. I said it was not possible for me to share it with them as it would be unethical because it had been recorded without Swami Agnivesh's knowledge.

They were also advised by their well-wishers to forget this incident, as the movement had become too big to take cognizance of such trivial things. Later, this clip found its way into newspapers and TV channels. Once it became a front-page story and turned into a big controversy, I had no other option but to run it on my channel too. Still, I say that Swami Agnivesh had raised a valid question in a vulgar fashion. The point at hand was of respect for the Parliament and its supremacy. By not accepting the appeal made by the Parliament, a perception had gained ground in a section of society that Team Anna was too high-handed and had no respect for the Parliament which had affected the fine balance between the sovereignty of the Parliament and the dignity of the movement. In my opinion this tenuous balance is important for the survival of democracy and Anna should have taken that extra caution. Despite this, the big-ticket story of the day was that peace, truce and reconciliation was in the air and both sides were willing to walk the extra mile like 'real' politicians.

RAHUL GANDHI — STAGE FRIGHT?

My first memory of Rahul Gandhi was that of a small child standing with his father along with his sister Priyanka. All three were glum. Mrs Indira Gandhi, Rahul Gandhi's grandmother and prime minister of India, had been shot dead by her own bodyguards outside her own residence. She was to be interviewed by a foreign TV network. Those were different days. There were no 24x7 TV channels, no internet, no virtual media, no Facebook, no Twitter, no cellphone, no iPad, no iPhone, no Blackberry, no Skype, no SMS, no MMS. All India Radio and Doordarshan, both public service broadcasters, were the only source of news. I was in Allahabad. At about 3.30 p.m. as I was going to the university for my evening classes, I found that the roads were empty and the normally busy University Road was deserted. I had reached one of the university hostels. My friends told me that Mrs Gandhi had been shot and that 'apparently she was dead'. There had been no confirmation. Some of us tried to tune in to BBC radio. A friend told me that the news was true. My home town, Mirzapur, was eighty kilometres from Allahabad. I became a little tense. I was expecting the worst now. I rushed back to my room. This time, the roads were different. Apparently, people had heard about Mrs Gandhi's death through Doordarshan. People on the streets were agitated. Angry mobs had started pelting stones and shops were forced to shut. I started pedalling my bicycle faster. I reached my room very nervous and frightened. My first priority was to somehow reach the railway station to catch a train to Mirzapur, but by the time I could plan things out, curfew had been imposed in the entire city. I was convinced that something most unfortunate was going to happen.

TV had just entered the Indian skies, thanks to the 1982 Asian Games. I was watching the most unforgettable moments of Indian history. Mrs Gandhi's pyre was burning, and through the smoke I could see hazy pictures of Rahul Gandhi and Rajiv Gandhi who had just been appointed prime minister. That young boy remained with me throughout my journey from boyhood to adulthood. He looked soft yet slightly stern; was royal in demeanour but slightly unapproachable.

Another picture of his which remains etched in my memory was of Rahul helping his mother Sonia as she managed her husband's funeral cavalcade after he was blown into pieces by a suicide squad of the Liberation Tigers of Tamil Eelam (LTTE). By now Rahul Gandhi was seven years older and was a good-looking young man, but he looked even more reserved than before. Rahul was not in politics and neither was his mother. Sonia Gandhi was a housewife. I still remember a very senior journalist from a national Hindi daily, saying that a division in the Congress was on the cards and the RSS and the BJP, as well as the whole nation, was waiting to find out if Sonia Gandhi would contest the elections from Amethi, a seat vacated by Rajiv Gandhi's death. The RSS was watching this because a 'no' from Sonia Gandhi would herald a new era in Indian politics without the Nehru-Gandhi family; it would mean the end of dynastic politics, and the weakening of the Congress would be a great opportunity for the Sangh Parivar to foist its ideological agenda on India. Sonia Gandhi did not succumb to pressure from Congressmen at that point, but she had to take the plunge later, when it was almost certain that if Sitaram Kesri continued as party president, there would be no hope for the Congress. By that time, I was a few years into journalism. We all knew that Sonia Gandhi was a stop-gap arrangement and finally one of her kids would take over. It was a guessing game for all of us as to who would jump into politics – Rahul or Priyanka. Our generation was more fascinated by Priyanka. We all thought that she had inherited her grandmother's charisma. As a result, we were all deeply disappointed when Priyanka decided to take a backseat and Rahul contested elections from Amethi in 2004.

Contrary to our expectations, Rahul made no forceful intervention in Parliament. He was like a fresher who was learning the art of politics – the politics of patience.

Unlike Sitaram Kesri, this young man was not in a hurry. Everyone wanted him to make his presence felt. He took his time. On 24 September 2007, the man whom everyone was waiting to see as prime minister was appointed the general secretary of the party. He was in charge of the student and youth wings. The world had to wait another year to see him speak forcefully in Parliament during the confidence vote in the Lok Sabha in 2008 – and that speech will always be remembered for Kalavati of Vidarbha. This was the first hint to the outside world of his non-traditional approach to politics.

While speaking on the Indo-US nuclear deal, he had said, 'Three days ago, I went to Vidarbha and met a young woman who had three sons. She is a landless labourer and earns Rs 60 a day; her husband works in the field and earns Rs 90. With their total income, they ensure that their three children go to a private school. I spent an hour with them. They live in a slum.' He went on to say, 'The eldest son dreams of being a district collector, while the middle one dreams of becoming an engineer. And the youngest wants to do a private job.' Ignoring Opposition interruptions, he continued, 'Poverty is directly connected to energy security. As I was walking out, I noticed no electricity in the house. I asked the children, how do you study? They pointed to a little brass lamp and said we study by that lamp.'

Rahul then began narrating the story of another woman called Kalavati, who had nine children and whose farmer husband was one of the many in Vidarbha to have committed suicide. He could not complete the story as his speech was cut short. But he had made a political point that he was different and wanted to do politics differently. Though a lot of people rubbished him, I was impressed. I felt vindicated when he went to Dalit *bastis*, spent nights there and did manual work. In the elections of 2009, he took a big gamble and did not align with Mulayam Singh Yadav in Uttar Pradesh. Everybody had thought he would be doomed, but the party won twenty-one seats. He had arrived. His role increased tremendously in the party and very often there would be conjecture about him becoming the prime minister. Even the PM said that he had offered Rahul Gandhi a cabinet berth, but he was not interested. Manmohan Singh was still at the helm of affairs when Anna took control of Delhi.

Therefore, when we got to know that Sonia Gandhi was suffering from a mysterious illness and had gone to New York for treatment, we all thought that Rahul Gandhi would take over the party. But I was greatly disappointed that he was not assertive during the crisis. It was true that Sonia Gandhi was very ill and Rahul was shuttling between the US and India, but one of the tragedies of being in public life is that national duties have to get precedence over private ones. On 16 August we were told that Anna was released from the jail on Rahul Gandhi's instructions. But after this, he was just not visible. The rumour in the political corridors was that throughout the crisis he had backed Chidambaram and Sibal. One senior member of the party told me that, since the Baba Ramdev operation at Ramlila Maidan, there was a collective understanding in the party that the government had to be tough with Anna and not allow him to sit on an indefinite fast. When I asked, 'What was Rahul's opinion?' I was told, 'It was the party's decision.' But two senior ministers in the cabinet, Finance Minister Pranab Mukherjee and Defence Minister A.K. Antony had not been in favour of arresting Anna.

DAY 11 – 26 AUGUST

We were therefore a little surprised on 26 August when Rahul Gandhi finally spoke in Parliament on the Lokpal Bill. Before he could say anything, the entire newsroom had inferred that, since the hero had now entered the scene at the eleventh hour, he would do something dramatic which would propel him into the big league. It really was the most opportune time for him. The whole country was discussing the Anna episode and there could not have been better timing. Journalists were even more convinced that some announcement was imminent when they saw his sister, Priyanka Wadra, in the visitors' gallery. I was at Ramlila Maidan then. My earpiece was connected to the PCR and I could hear Rahul Gandhi's voice loud and clear from the live transmission on Lok Sabha TV.

Sadly, even his very first sentence was enveloped in an unnecessarily aggressive tone. Rahul Gandhi said, 'Witnessing the events of the last few days, it would appear that the enactment of a single bill will usher in a corruption-free society. I have serious doubts about this belief.' This was an open invitation for a confrontation with the protestors. This statement was made when there was reconciliation in the air; Anna had agreed to climb down from the Jan Lokpal Bill to three demands and he had apologized to the prime minister for any unpleasantness that the movement may have caused. And the government was ready for a discussion in Parliament on the issue. Rahul went on to say, 'An effective Lokpal law is only one element in the legal framework to combat corruption. The Lokpal institution alone can't be a substitute for a comprehensive anti-corruption code. A set of effective laws is required.' There was a taunt in his tone. He threw out a suggestion that he thought was a game-changer. He said, 'Madam Speaker, why not elevate this debate and fortify the Lokpal by making it a constitutional body accountable to Parliament, like the Election Commission of India?' Then he tore apart Anna and his entire protest narrative. He said, 'However, individual dictates, no matter how well intentioned, must not weaken the democratic process . . . A tactical incursion, divorced from the machinery of an elected government that seeks to undo the checks and balances created to protect the supremacy of Parliament sets a dangerous precedent for a democracy.' He clearly accused Anna of treading a dangerous path. Well-known political scientist Yogendra Yadav criticized the speech as being badly timed. He said that a good speech had been made at a wrong time.

As in his Kalavati speech, Rahul mentioned that he had been touring India. There was no denying the fact that Rahul was the only politician who had been trying to establish direct contact with the masses to understand their concerns. Mahatma Gandhi was his ideal. He had read Gandhi extensively and he was aware of the fact that, before embarking on a journey to free India and donning the cap of a politician, Gandhi had travelled in the general compartments of Indian trains to feel India, to know India, to be one with India. Gandhi is the only Indian leader who knew the essence of India, body and soul of India, the blood and bones of India; why it laughs and why and how its tears roll down its face, why it gets angry and why it feels hurt and psyched; why it loves somebody and why it hates somebody. Gandhi did not think of India as a vast land mass only, but as a human being. He wanted to feel that human being, he wanted to be friends with him/her, he wanted to understand the mood swings of that human being, and he wanted to fall in love with India.

Rahul tried to emulate the Mahatma. He did not rush to become the prime minister of India or the party president. He ventured out to understand India, to explore India through Gandhi's eyes. This was an attempt to experiment with Gandhi but not in the twentieth century but a hundred years later. It was a political mission to prepare himself for the bigger responsibility. So, after an initial hitch, Rahul was seen on a different path which was completely disowned by modern-day politicians, barring a few. Very soon, he was seen in the company of the Shashikalas and the Kalavatis. In the beginning, he was heckled by politicians and Opposition leaders, but then everybody realized their mistake and attempts were made to politically neutralize him. But Rahul was undeterred. He was busy with his own journey. One day he was in a Dalit *basti*, and another day he was eating at a villager's house, sitting in a small *rasoi*. He slept on an ordinary *charpoy*, ate ordinary dal and roti, bathed at the *chapakal* (tube well) in an open space. He travelled in a Mumbai local train with ordinary people; he withdrew money from a public ATM; he used the Delhi Metro and hired a local taxi. He went to Bhatta Parsol, Greater Noida, to understand farmers' issues and protest police brutalities. He walked from Bhatta Parsol to Aligarh and was arrested in the process. He interacted with university students, answered tough questions. He had openly praised his opponent Nitish Kumar, chief minister of Bihar, for his good work in the state. He admitted that dynastic rule was wrong and against democratic norms and, though he was a product of that system, he said he wanted to change the system. It seemed as if he was breaking away from the traditional politics.

He stuck his neck out and decided to go it alone in the UP and Bihar elections, and did not shake hands with the likes of Mulayam Singh Yadav and Lalu Prasad Yadav. One of the reasons for his decision was allegations of corruption against them. In UP he succeeded and in Bihar he failed. He was appreciated and condemned in the same breath. Rahul was emerging as the name of a new hope in India, a new icon for the youth. He would have been the ideal candidate to lead an anti-corruption movement. Four years ago in Jhansi Rahul said that his father used to say that only fifteen paise of every rupee reached the people, but he was of the opinion that not even five paise percolated down to the people (*The Telegraph*, 17 January 2007). This statement of Rahul Gandhi's had provoked one of the finest brains among Indian editors, Vinod Mehta, editor of *Outlook*, to say that the time had come for the national debate to shift from problems to solutions (*Outlook*, 18 May 2009). But to the disappointment of thousands of people present at Ramlila Maidan, Rahul never showed up – neither in body nor in soul. This was the crowd that Rahul Gandhi had been targeting since 2007 when he became the general secretary of the party. It was a young, urban, intelligent, aspirational crowd; it was the assertive middle class; the argumentative small India, nationalistic and inclusive – it was an India that Rahul Gandhi had long wanted to explore. But he was not there. The crowd was asking, '*Desh ke yuva yahan hai, Rahul Gandhi kahan hai*'(The youth of the country are here, where is Rahul Gandhi)?

Rahul Gandhi was not at Ramlila Maidan nor at Azad Maidan, Mumbai nor at the Freedom Park, Bangalore. Rahul Gandhi was not in the Chennai bike rally, he did not sit on a hunger strike, he did not raise slogans against corruption, he did not appreciate Mumbai's dabbawalas when they decided not to deliver food. He was not seen holding the national flag to condemn corruption. And finally, when he showed up, he was condemning the Jan Lokpal Bill, condemning Anna for his anti-democratic streak. It was a huge disappointment. If he had openly supported the anti-corruption agitation and then spoken of the need for constitutionally valid procedures, people would still have accepted him. But with his speech and with his non-conduct during the agitation he had lost his connect with the *aam aadmi*. So he was hooted at in the Ramlila Maidan and elsewhere in India. He had also joined the illustrious list of P. Chidambaram, Kapil Sibal and Manish Tiwari. The problem with him was that he was reading a book when he was expected to write one.

During the agitation I had told many senior and not-so-senior Congress leaders, 'The Congress has to think out of the box to counter Anna and the anger of the people, and ideally Rahul should go and sit with Anna and declare that he is with him in this Mahabharat against corruption and see to it that Anna blesses him as an elderly father figure. Or he should take an initiative to go and request Anna to break his fast in full public glare.' I can tell you there were a few among the youth brigade who agreed with me, but the senior politicians were living in a different world. A leader close to Rahul Gandhi told me that he had advised Rahul not to go to Anna as he was not sure how Anna and his team would react. After all, Gopinath

Munde and Ananth Kumar had been mocked by Kiran Bedi and booed by the crowd when they went to the Ramlila Maidan to visit Anna. But Rahul is no Gopinath Munde. A good gesture in traditional Indian style is always appreciated. A senior Congress leader confided in me that Rahul had been wrongly advised; he was asked to maintain a distance from the movement and from any attempt to solve the crisis. I was told by another leader that except in the beginning, Rahul himself had been aloof throughout. He was not even responding to the party leaders' phone calls and messages. As *India Today* reported (5 September 2011), his party had no clue what his thinking on the problem was. *India Today* writes, 'On 20 August he presided over the Rajiv Gandhi awards and later over Praja Rajyam Party's merger with the Congress in Delhi. When he was asked to comment on Anna, he dodged the media.'

According to a report in *DNA* (4 September 2011), his advisors and spin doctors had tried to project the Anna movement as an RSS-sponsored agitation, and an attempt had been made to make it a contest between Rahul Gandhi, who would most likely lead the Congress in the 2014 parliamentary elections, and Anna Hazare, who will be the kingmaker. The report says, 'A Congress general secretary said that the party would suffer because of Hazare's anti-corruption crusade, and that this was the big RSS-BJP plan to eject the party out of power.' And then concludes, 'Rahul supporters had convinced themselves that the Anna Hazare movement was not really against corruption, it was not even against the Congress; it was aimed at undermining Rahul Gandhi's growing youth base.' This conclusion was further strengthened when Team Anna decided to campaign in the Hissar Lok Sabha bypoll, where the team worked aggressively to defeat the Congress candidate Jai Prakash. The Congressman lost his deposit and Arvind and his supporters who had camped there throughout the elections were credited with the defeat. Everybody knows that Rahul Gandhi had vowed to revive the Congress in UP. It was part of a bigger game plan. The Congress is aware of the fact that it can't form the government on its own at the Centre unless it gets a substantial number of seats in UP. Naturally, Rahul and his party don't want to be in a position where small parties and little-known individuals get to call the shots.

Anna had made a solid dent in Rahul's image. *New York Times* wrote on 28 August 2011, 'For Mr Gandhi, the crisis interrupted what was widely assumed to be his own coming out as the new leader of the Congress . . . Instead, Mr Hazare upended the political landscape and Mr Gandhi disappeared for days before his speech in Parliament.' There can't be a bigger setback for Rahul Gandhi than losing UP. He has staked a lot on his success there. I think this may well decide his chances of succeeding Manmohan Singh as PM. This also explains why every change or shift in the political landscape is carefully analysed. Every minor, even perceived, threat to his career is therefore seen with suspicion. I believe that this is what ultimately dictates his attitude and actions to the Anna stir.

As things stand, though, it is a lost opportunity. Rahul Gandhi could have seized leadership of the party, established himself as having grown out of his mother's shadow and having become a leader in his own right. The topmost leader of the party, Sonia Gandhi, was ill and away in New York, the four-member team that was assigned the job to take decisions on her behalf was dithering, the party and the government were facing the biggest challenge to their authority since 2004, the prime minister was committing one mistake after another, his senior ministers were blundering, the crisis within the Congress was waiting for a leader, but that leader did not find the issue at hand exciting enough to exert himself. *India Today* was scathing in its criticism: 'Let alone seize the initiative with civil representatives, he did not provide leadership even to his band of young MPs . . . Rahul could have choreographed these voices (young MPs) into a pressure group within the party. Instead, he led his party to the verge of a nervous breakdown' (5 September 2011). *New York Times* quoted Pratap Bhanu Mehta, president of the Centre for Policy Research, 'This could have been an opportunity for him to assert leadership, instead all it does is raise the question of how much leadership he has shown.' Chetan Bhagat, an Anna Hazare supporter and a very popular English fiction writer, was sceptical of his future. He wrote (*Times of India*, 10 September 2011), 'Seldom has the scion of the first family been criticized so much. One wonders if he will be the last major leader of the first family, much like Bahadur Shah Zafar.'

I don't want to hazard a guess about Rahul's future. I don't want to say that he developed stage fright given the enormity of the occasion. In my opinion, Rahul Gandhi is not an instinctive politician. Politics had been forced on him. He has set notions about Indian politics and over a period of time he also established certain dos and don'ts for himself. He reads books and takes guidance from them. But Indian politics is a complex beast. It is eternally evolving, and so concepts and ideas about it constantly need to be fine-tuned. Rahul Gandhi over-dissected the Anna movement and lost valuable time in weighing the pros and cons, defeat and victory. I agree with British politician David Owen that no general in the midst of a battle discusses what he is going to do if he is defeated. He should learn from his grandmother, Mrs Indira Gandhi, that if one is not adventurous, one is not victorious. Rahul Gandhi had ceased to be adventurous, so he lost the plot during the movement, and that's why I still see that small child holding his father's hand in a time of crisis. He has to learn to let go of that hand if he wants to grow up.

PS: On the eleventh day of the *anshan*, it was expected that Parliament would discuss the three demands raised by Anna through Vilas Rao Deshmukh, and Anna would announce the breaking of his fast. Nothing of that kind happened. Parliament did initiate a discussion in the Lok Sabha under Rule 193, but due to the *hungama* in Parliament proceedings had to be suspended till the next day, i.e., Saturday. This meant that Parliament had shown great respect and urgency on the issue and decided to work on a day off. Anna's health was normal. He had only lost weight.

JUDGEMENT DAY

DAY 12 – 27 AUGUST

Har sant kahe, sadho kahe
Sach aur sahas ho jiske mann mein
Anth mein jeet usi ki rahey

The song from the film *Lagaan* was in the air. People at the Ramlila Maidan were oscillating between pessimism and optimism. Judgement Day had dawned and everybody was anxiously waiting for the day to unfold. Parliament was to discuss Anna's three demands and the government had promised to incorporate them in the Lokpal Bill. But Team Anna was still not confident that the government would not resort to mischief. Team Anna had assembled to take a final call, to decide the final strategy, to finalize plan A and plan B. The core committee was sitting in a corner and the song being sung on the dais was:

Raah mein kaaten bikhre agar
Uspar toh phir bhi chalna hi hai
Shaam chhupa le suraj magar
Raat ko ek din dhalna hi hai
Rut yeh tal jaayegi
Himmat rang layegi
Subah phir aayegi

Some members in the committee were asking their leaders if Parliament would seriously pass the resolution to which the government had agreed in principle. Nobody knew for sure. So it was essential for them to have an alternative plan in place. An intense discussion took place. Various scenarios were discussed in case a resolution was not passed:

1) The government won't let Anna continue with the fast. If Anna defied that order, he would be arrested.
2) The government would instruct the doctors to put Anna on a drip.
3) Were the government to decide to abandon Anna and not care whether he lived or died, what was to be done?

There were three options, but the consensus was that nothing would be done at cost of Anna's health. His life was precious. Anna must live to fight another battle. Once there was unanimity on this, it was easier to decide the future course of action. As a matter of fact, despite its belligerence and determination, Team Anna was scared about Anna's health. They were also under tremendous pressure. Within the team, there were people who were opposed to stretching things beyond a point and wanted a respectable way out very soon. On the eighth day, one of the young team members, Swati, started crying when she saw Anna looking lacklustre. She said, 'Let him eat.' Anna's secretary, Suresh Pathare, lost his cool, he said, 'Please stop this.' In Anna's home town, Ahmednagar, and in his village, Ralegan Siddhi, people were very upset. They had been sending messages to Team Anna that the government would not listen to them and that they did not want Anna to die like this. Anna's family members were worried especially. His nephew, Ganesh Maruti Hazare, was with Anna as long as he was in Tihar but, once he was out, Anna sent him back to Ralegan Siddhi to lead the movement. Ganesh's wife, Kaushalya Ganesh Hazare, told TV channels, 'Whatever Anna is doing, he is doing for the country but the government is not listening. I don't know if the Jan Lokpal Bill will be passed, but if something happens to Anna, then? The country needs Anna.' The older village members of Ralegan Siddhi requested Popat Rao Pawar to go to Delhi and do something. Pawar is an old friend of Anna's and the sarpanch of nearby village Hebre Bazar. Popat Rao Pawar had been inspired by Anna's work and worked to change the face of Hebre Bazar, which is now considered to be even better developed than Ralegan Siddhi and is a model village for the rest of the country. Pawar was in touch with Anna and Team Anna since 22 August. He had been at Ramlila too. Pawar was the one who went to Vilas Rao Deshmukh along with other supporters of Anna from Maharashtra and put pressure on him to do something about the impasse. Meanwhile, Anna was continuously saying that he was fighting for the country and, therefore, nothing would happen to him. It was the twelfth day of the fast and doctors had expressed concerns about his health. According to Dr Trehan, 'Every hour we are checking him. His heartbeat is decreasing, his pulse is slowing. He has lost 7.5 kg in weight. The muscles are getting weak; though the vital organs are stable, I am worried' (IBN7, 9 p.m. bulletin).

The team was conscious of the fact that, God forbid, if something were to happen to Anna, no one would ever forgive them. So Team Anna was as desperate as the government for a solution. But they were also aware that the movement had gone too far and it would be suicidal to surrender without any tangible benefit. The government had been elected to rule for five years and could still bounce back, but Anna and his team had only their credibility and, unlike the government, they had just one chance. They had already been down in the dumps once before when Pranab Mukherjee had shouted at them on 24 August. That episode had shaken them. They had regrouped and moved on but another episode of that nature would be fatal. But now the sharks of the political ocean were out to kill them so they had to be extra careful. So the team discussed everything threadbare. They decided that, in case of a rejection of the resolution by the Parliament, they should let the government forcibly pick up Anna, arrest Anna, or put him on a drip. Team Anna had to ensure that they did not appear to be in cahoots with the government. If they needed to protest, they would. If they needed to obstruct, they would. If they needed to put up a fight, they would. But after an initial obstruction, they would let the police take Anna away. It was the best possible way out of the crisis.

The core committee knew that if the government decided to do nothing, it would be a very tricky situation. The team was very clear that, after the rejection, it would be stupid to still continue with the fast. If that were to happen, they decided to take the matter to the people's court, to the public, explain to them and confess before them that the movement had lost the battle, but that they had only lost the battle, not the war, and to win the war it was essential to intensify the battle for the final assault and, for that assault, they needed Anna's leadership. So with the consent of the people, the team would request Anna to break his fast and then Anna would address the public. He would say that a powerful few had won, the people had lost; the system had won, the common man had lost and that they gracefully accepted their defeat and would now live to make the people strong enough to defeat their oppressors. That would be a new beginning for a new battle.

Having reached a decision, they were relaxed, but the suspense continued. It was an extended session of the Parliament, especially called to discuss Anna's three demands and pass a resolution. At 11 a.m., Finance Minister Pranab Mukherjee, leader of the House, initiated a discussion in the Lok Sabha. He said, 'With Anna's fast entering the twelfth day, the situation is getting out of hand. Issues which have been raised by Anna are genuine and important; MPs will have to consider Anna's three key demands within the constitutional framework and preserving parliamentary supremacy.' He added, 'The question before the Parliament is whether the ambit of the Lokpal should cover all central employees? Another issue before Parliament is whether there would be Lokayuktas in all the states. And should the Lokpal have the power to punish all those who violate the proposed grievance redressal mechanism? And if the House arrives at a consensus, the standing committee will take into account the practicality, implementability and constitutionality of these issues.'

Mr Mukherjee had set the ball rolling. Sushma Swaraj, the leader of the Opposition in the Lok Sabha, said, 'On behalf of my party, I am agreeing to all the key issues raised by Anna and let this legislation not suffer the fate of the last eight Lokpal Bills.' The debate was simultaneously taking place in the Rajya Sabha. Leader of the Opposition, Arun Jaitley, was more frank. He said, 'All employees and public servants must be accountable, and an accounting mechanism could be a part of the Lokpal. We need a citizen's charter. But I decline to support Anna Hazare's demand to bring the conduct of the MPs inside Parliament and the judiciary under Lokpal.'

Jaitley's speech reminded me why the Jan Lokpal Bill had generated a fierce debate from the very beginning. It was a political issue, but it turned into a legal and technical battle. A lot of people were opposed to the Jan Lokpal Bill. Some of these opponents were a smokescreen for the government. A very powerful minister, out of personal vendetta, sponsored a section of journalists and intellectuals to kill the Jan Lokpal Bill. It was projected as the new monster that would destabilize the constitutional equilibrium of democracy. Then there were the intellectuals who had a problem with a half-educated village man, and a village patriarch, a symbol of the feudal system. People like Ramachandra Guha, out of frustration quoted C.P. Surendran to express themselves, saying how 'a retired army truck driver whose only strength really is a kind of stolid integrity and a talent for skipping meals' could challenge a powerful government. This was the description of Anna that the English-educated so-called intellectuals came up with. They were not only insulting 'rural India', but also insulting lakhs of Indians who had trooped out to fight corruption. These intellectuals decided to be blind to the mass upsurge.

Aruna Roy and Jayaprakash Narayan were another matter. They made the effort to present alternatives to the government's Lokpal Bill. Aruna Roy was empathetic with the strikers as well. She went to the Ramlila Maidan to meet Anna during the fast. It was Aruna Roy's organization, NCPRI, that had initiated the process of formulating the draft of Lokpal Bill in the month of September 2010. Arvind was the chairman of the committee that was to draft the bill. According to Arvind, when the draft was ready, Aruna did not show much interest. So Arvind drifted apart and set out on a journey that later came to be known as the Anna movement. The bill that Arvind drafted with NCPRI was later named the Jan Lokpal Bill. This bill was proposed as the most potent weapon against corruption. The Jan Lokpal Bill proposes to establish an institutional framework which will address the inadequacies of the current anti-corruption systems, and have the power and independence to investigate and prosecute cases of corruption (as per the synopsis of the bill, posted on the India against Corruption website). According to the website, 'Any ordinary citizen can approach the Lokpal or Lokayukta with any complaint of corruption. The Lokpal or Lokayukta will have to complete their inquiries or investigations within one year. After investigations, if there is evidence of corruption found against a politician or any official, the Lokpal or Lokayukta will have to file a case in the appropriate trial court. The trial court will have to complete the trial and announce punishment within a year. The Lokpal or Lokayukta will have the power to get a guilty official dismissed or suspended.'

The draft of the Jan Lokpal Bill gives overriding power to the Lokpal. As per the draft, 'The full bench of the Lokpal will give permission to file a case against any judge, including those of the high courts and the Supreme Court, and no permission will be required from the Chief Justice of India. Other than government officials of all categories, ministers and the prime minister will also come under its purview. The Lokpal will be able to recommend removal of the minister, except prime minister, if the allegations are substantiated through an inquiry or investigation. Even conduct of MPs will be under the Lokpal's scrutiny.' The bill has other powers too. According to the draft, 'Every department shall prepare a citizen's charter listing all the routine and easily definable works along with the official responsible for a particular work and the time frame in which the work is to be done, and if it does not happen so, the official concerned will be punished. And for the purpose of the investigation all the existing anti-corruption agencies – CBI, CVC and the vigilance wings of all the departments – will be merged into Lokpal. And whistle-blowers will be provided protection by the Lokpal or Lokayukta.'

Aruna Roy, a member of Sonia Gandhi-led National Advisory Council, has a problem with the Jan Lokpal Bill on two counts:

1) In her opinion, 'Lokpal was too simplistically ordained by the campaign as a solution to all varieties of corrupt practices in our lives.' The problem with Aruna Roy was that she had not followed Anna and the movement. Anna and other members of the team had said so many times from the stage and in their interaction with the press that Lokpal would not eradicate corruption hundred per cent. It would only clean up about sixty per cent of the existing corruption and, for the rest, other reforms had to follow. Right to recall is one step in that direction.

2) She also objected to it on the grounds that 'vesting jurisdiction over the length and breadth of the government machinery in one institution will concentrate too much power in the institution, while the volume of work will make it difficult to carry out its tasks.' Aruna Roy hated the idea of giving so much power to one institution. It is bad for democracy. Instead, she proposed multiple agencies to curb corruption. She wrote in her letter that, instead of one, there should be at least five institutions at different levels to tackle corruption.

i) National Anti-Corruption Lokpal: An institution to tackle corruption of all elected representatives, including the prime minister (with some safeguards), ministers and members of Parliament and Group A officials.

ii) Central Vigilance Commission (CVC): Amending the CVC Act to remove the single directive and empower the CVC to investigate and take appropriate action against mid-level bureaucracy.

iii) Judicial Standards and Accountability Lokpal: To ensure that the judiciary is also made effectively and appropriately accountable, without compromising its independence.

iv) Public Grievance Lokpal: To set up an effective time-bound decentralized system for grievance redressal for common citizens to make the government answerable in terms of its function, duties, commitments and obligations towards citizens.

v) Whistle-blower Protection Lokpal: To ensure appropriate protection to whistle-blowers.

Aruna Roy also recommends that these institutions should also be created in the states where it is relevant. There is no denying the fact that Roy has structured a multi-agency Lokpal beautifully and that she was right in her understanding that no single institution should be given so much power as to defeat the checks and balances enshrined in the constitution. But her problem was that she failed to understand the nature of the movement and the grammar of agitational politics. Agitation by nature starts at a much higher pitch and, at the bargaining table, it comes down to the main issues. This happened with the Anna movement too. It started with the Jan Lokpal Bill and finally ended with the three demands which were fundamental in dealing with the corruption that affects the common man the most. The common man is not most affected by the big-ticket corruption of big men, but by the daily harassment of a clerk or a patwari in a government department demanding a bribe of a few rupees.

Like Aruna Roy, Dr Jayaprakash Narayan also drafted a Lokpal Bill and at present it is with the standing committee of the Parliament. He asks, 'Should it be an omniscient, omnipotent body that will slay the demons of corruption everywhere? Or should it be a focused body that alters the reward–risk perception of corrupt behaviour and helps reverse the tide of corruption' (*Economic Times*, 31 August 2011)? The salient features of Jayaprakash Narayan's draft of the Lokpal Bill are:

1) The PM should be brought under the purview of Lokpal, but he could be exempt from any enquiry on matters relating to security of State, foreign relations and public order, and in other matters, the prior sanction of enquiry by a Parliamentary committee comprising the vice-president, the Speaker and the leader of the Opposition should be obtained.

2) Judiciary needs accountability but Lokpal is not the right forum to ensure this because that would violate the concept of the basic features of the constitution.

3) There cannot be a monolithic institution for the whole country, instead there should be Lokayuktas in the states and local ombudsmen in districts and major cities.

4) There is a need to integrate the CVC with the Lokpal, make the CVC as the ex-officio member of Lokpal with specific jurisdiction over local bureaucracy (*Economic Times*, 31 August).

The government had also formulated its own Lokpal Bill, which had been introduced in Parliament. Anna and his team opined that the government Bill was very weak. Union Minister for Law and Justice Salman Khurshid later said that the government was committed to a stronger Lokpal. He wrote (*Times of India*, 13 September 2011) that the standing committee had a bigger challenge of drafting a Lokpal Bill that had the backing of the Parliament and the people of India alike. He also hinted that the Lokpal Bill would be elevated to the level of a constitutional body as suggested by Rahul Gandhi.

The former chief justice of India, J.S. Verma, hit the nail on the head when he said that Anna Hazare had provided an opportunity for an intensive search for the best method to combat rampant corruption. 'The churning process to find the best solution has begun' (*Indian Express*, 28August 2011). Yes, a part of that churning process was on in Parliament and everybody was glued to the TV to know the end result. But outside Parliament the suspense was deepening.

On the morning of 27 August, when I spoke to Prashant Bhushan, he told me that he was drafting a resolution as requested by the government. He had sounded quite confident and, when Prashant Bhushan reached Parliament at 1.34 p.m. to meet Pranab Mukherjee, good news was expected any minute. At 2.07 p.m. Salman Khurshid went to discuss something with the prime minister. They were joined by Pranab Mukherjee, Kapil Sibal, Pawan Bansal, Rajiv Shukla and the principal secretary to the PM, T.K.A. Nair. Meanwhile, Arvind, Medha Patkar, Prashant Bhushan and Manish reached Salman Khurshid's residence, but he was not there. Khurshid later called up Team Anna and at 3.10 p.m. Prashant came out and addressed reporters. He said, 'Last night we were told that a resolution would be passed and voting on the resolution would also take place. And now we are told that nothing of that kind will happen.' Was there a crisis brewing again?

Arvind's statement further accentuated the apprehension that was palpable at Ramlila Maidan. He said, 'It is a clear case of betrayal. In the last four days the government has changed its stand thrice.' Anna supporters in Maharashtra were losing patience. The Pune–Aurangabad Highway had been jammed since morning by residents of Ralegan Siddhi. More than 250 Anna followers were arrested by 2.30 p.m. In Mumbai, washermen at the famous Dhobi Ghat, Mahalaxmi, did not work that day in support of Anna – for the first time in post-Independence India. Rahul Gandhi's house in Delhi and Pranab Mukherjee's in Kolkata were also gheraoed by young protestors.

Through the day though, at the Ramlila Maidan, there was a

new wait along with the one for the result of the debate: for Aamir Khan. He reached the ground at 3.25 p.m. Raju Hirani, the director of *Three Idiots*, was also with him. Aamir had been one of the most enthusiastic supporters of the anti-corruption movement and was constantly in touch with the team with his suggestions. It was rumoured that the public demonstration at the residences of ministers and MPs was his idea. Aamir sat through the evening. He sang a song from his film *Lagaan*, '*Mitwa – ye dharti apni hai aur apna ambar hai . . .*' with Kumar Vishwas and Nitin Dabar. It was also rumoured that the government had tried to persuade Aamir not to go to the Ramlila Maidan, but Aamir came, he sat, and extended his full support to Anna and the Jan Lokpal Bill. He also requested Anna to break his fast as his message had now reached every nook and corner of the country.

Meanwhile, the debate in Parliament was still on. After the statements from Team Anna, deadlock looked like a possibility again. By now it was 3.56 p.m. Another meeting had just begun. Pranab Mukherjee was leading the pack. L.K. Advani, Arun Jaitley, Kapil Sibal and Sharad Pawar were there. News doing the rounds was that the BJP was opposed to voting on the resolution. At 4.05 p.m. Sushma Swaraj clarified on behalf of the BJP that this was a lie and a rumour, and that the BJP was for voting on the resolution. Finally, the PM met with Advani and Jaitley and all confusion was cleared up. Kapil Sibal was once again very active throughout the day. One senior minister told me that, since he was the prime minister's blue-eyed boy, he was being patiently tolerated. On the other hand the Congress's young brigade actively tried to scuttle any efforts at sabotage and openly supported the efforts of Pranab Mukherjee. Jyotiraditya Scindia, Jitin Prasad, Sachin Pilot and Milind Deora had been canvassing for a meaningful resolution. They believed that the Congress should not be seen to be opposing the anti-corruption campaign as that would be detrimental in the long run. But Rahul Gandhi, who had only the other day made an appeal for making the Lokpal a constitutional body, was absconding throughout the saga. When Kapil Sibal's objection on the wording of the resolution stretched to the point of derailing the entire process, the PM stepped in and overruled him. Finally, by 5.30 p.m., a draft was agreed upon. So after nine hours, the debate was stopped and a few lines were read in the form of a resolution and, with the thumping of desks, the resolution was unanimously passed. It was sent to the standing committee and the Lok Sabha was adjourned till Monday. With this, the suspense was over.

But the message was yet to be communicated officially to Anna. The onus fell on Vilas Rao again. When he reached Ramlila Maidan, Anna was resting in a small room behind the stage. It was pitch dark. There was no light in the room. Vilas Rao went in. He sat down on the cot and handed over the PM's letter to Anna. It was the most important moment for Anna, it was his moment of light, a light he could see even in his dark room. He immediately called Arvind, Prashant and Kiran. They were there within seconds. Anna told them, 'The PM's letter has come. I have decided to break my fast tomorrow at 10 a.m. What do you think?' They said, 'As you decide.' Anna again said, 'I will go to the stage, Vilas Rao will accompany me there. Arvind, first you will brief the people.' Vilas Rao was scared to go on stage. He knew how Gopinath Munde and Ananth Kumar had been hooted. But he could not say no to Anna. People were already delirious with expectation. The ground was charged. Volunteers were having a tough time controlling the crowd. Patience was running out. At 9.03 p.m. Anna was on the stage. I was wired to the studio and getting constant feedback from the PCR. Suddenly, the line got disconnected. The channel was going live on air. There was no need for any anchor. It was one of those moments in history when anchors are redundant. I was there only as fill-in, in case there is a technical failure. So I stood still. Anna made a short but crisp statement and announced that he would end his fast the next day. Democracy had triumphed. People had won. The supremacy of the Parliament and the dignity of the movement had both been upheld. Nobody had lost, everybody had won. People were rejoicing in the ground and outside too; people were rejoicing in Delhi and in other parts of the country too. They were rejoicing because they had realized that democracy was not about a chosen few, but about the citizens.

ANNA BREAKS HIS FAST

DAY 13 – 28 AUGUST

I was running towards the stage through a maze of TV cameras.
There was chaos all around. Every camera crew wanted to
capture the best pictures and did not want to miss a single
moment. They were battling it out with the print photographers.
'Don't come into my frame'; '*Oye* hero, *baith ja, abe tu mera*
frame *kyon kharab kar raha hai*' (Hello, please sit down; don't
spoil my frame). Everybody was shouting at everybody. The
media enclosure was filled to capacity. Rarely had I seen so
many cameras and print journalists, national and international
channels and newspapers, together. I could see a few senior
journalists too. They were there to witness Anna breaking his
fast. Anna was sitting on the dais. He seemed normal. There
were kids around him. His team was also there. Everybody was
waiting for Anna to end his 288-hour-long fast. They all
looked relaxed. The tension had disappeared. One could see
smiles on their faces and a sense of victory. Even Gandhiji in
the backdrop seemed to have a satisfied look.

After receiving a letter from the prime minister, Anna had
announced in the presence of Vilas Rao Deshmukh that he
would end his fast the next day. Anna never breaks a fast after
sunset. By 5.30 p.m., we learnt that Anna would break his fast
only on 28 August. He had done the same at Jantar Mantar
and at Ramlila Maidan too he would follow that self-imposed
rule. Anna follows a very strict diet schedule. He eats a very

light breakfast in the morning, followed by lunch around noon and a glass of juice before sunset. He does not eat anything after sunset. He had been following this schedule for more than three decades.

This was the thirteenth day of his *anshan*; he had not eaten since 16 August. But Anna looked fine. His blood pressure was 110/70, pulse rate 94. All his vital organs were functioning normally. According to Dr Trehan, who was looking after him during the fast, he was all right except for losing seven-and-a-half kilograms and a deficiency of water and glucose in his body. I had crossed the barrier that separated the media enclosure from the one meant for the members of the core committee and other volunteers. I was close to a makeshift gate that was manned by a volunteer who happened to know me. He did not stop me. I was trying to convey through gestures to Kumar Vishwas that they should wind up fast. Before running all the way here, I had tried calling Team Anna, but nobody seemed to be free to attend phone calls. Vikrant and Prabhanjan had also tried to call them, but in vain. I had been at the Ramlila Maidan for more than a week now and knew how disciplined the crowd had been, but on this day the atmosphere was different. The Maidan was full and there was no place to sit or stand. It was very hot and extremely humid. I was sweating profusely. The sun was very strong and I could barely open my eyes, though it was just 10.15 a.m. There must have been nearly a lakh people there. The roads outside the ground were also jam-packed. With tricolours in their hands and an Anna cap on their heads, people were shouting slogans and slowly the crowd had started getting restless, and that was my main worry. Meanwhile, Anna broke his fast. Two young girls helped him have honey and coconut water. One girl was a Dalit and the other was a Muslim. This was his way of replying to the handful of Muslim and Dalit leaders who had criticized the movement as anti-Dalit and anti-Muslim. I have reasons to believe that, like during the second Gulf War, when a section of the American press and civil society had volunteered to be part of embedded journalism and embedded civil society, the same had happened in India as well. During the Anna movement, all of them had one goal, which was to rubbish the Anna movement at the government's prompting. Of course, I am by no means suggesting that all those who criticized Anna were government stooges.

There was no need for Anna and his team to get into this symbolism. They did not need to prove that the movement had no disconnect with Dalits and Muslims. A social movement does not need to prove whether it is inclusive or exclusive. A movement is defined by the issue and the programme, not by the subjective understanding of a few individuals. Corruption is value-neutral, gender-neutral, religion-neutral and also caste-neutral.

I was finding it impossible to ignore the restlessness and impatience of the crowd, which seemed to be attaining serious dimensions. After breaking his fast, Anna was addressing the people and all the TV cameras were airing it live, reaching millions of homes. Anna had just announced that he had broken his fast but he had not ended his *anshan*, had only postponed the movement and he would wait to see what action the government took, and if the government did not fulfil its promise, he would resume his movement with much renewed vigour.

He also appealed to his supporters to follow a certain lifestyle. He said anybody who was wearing an Anna cap should observe five principles:

1) Impeccable conduct
2) Purity of thought
3) Spotless life
4) Sacrifice
5) Courage to bear insult.

Later, on 2 September, he had repeated the same thing in his speech in Ralegan Siddhi. He said, 'Just saying "I am Anna and you are also Anna" will not make everyone Anna. One has to improve his or her conduct and one has to lead a different life. Sacrifice has been an integral part of the Indian civilization for thousands of years. And especially the youth has to sacrifice, because they are the torch-bearers of the society.' Anna had been repeating the same thing almost on a daily basis from the stage and that was part of the training and education that he wanted to ingrain in his followers; and until then, people had been religiously following his instructions. But now my concern was that people had forgotten his call for peaceful conduct and just wanted to get as close to Anna as possible. This had created a stampede-like situation, which is why I was running to the dais. I reached the steps of the stage and shouted at Kumar and Manish to announce from the platform for the public to maintain discipline. I was really scared that if a stampede broke out, dozens of people would lose their lives, including a few media persons, and the situation would be unmanageable even for the police. The media enclosure barrier was gone and the crowd had jumped in. They were pushing towards the stage. Team Anna had realized the danger, an announcement had been made, long speeches had been cut short and the function came to an abrupt end.

On 28 August, along with the fast, discipline too had been broken. A discipline that I had admired all through and never had any hesitation in saying that the crowd at the Ramlila Maidan was the most disciplined I had ever seen in a public rally. I was not privileged to witness any of the JP rallies as I was too young then, but I had seen VP Singh's rallies during the Bofors scam and later during the Ram Mandir movement, the anti-Mandal agitation and also a few Mahendra Singh Tikait rallies at the Boat Club and many other rallies. I must say if the Sarvodaya leader and staunch Gandhi follower Vinobha Bhave had been alive he would have called it 'Anushasan Parv', i.e., the era of discipline, a term that Bhave had used wrongly for the early days of the Emergency when he had seen a noticeable improvement in social discipline, for example, people stood in queues at bus stops and ration shops, cities bore a cleaner look, traffic in cities moved in an orderly fashion. Bhave was not appreciating the Emergency, but criticizing the JP movement, with which Anna movement had been compared during his *anshan*. Bhave had had serious differences with JP on the nature and method employed in the movement and also the purpose of the movement. He had a fundamental difference over the use of violence in the agitation. Vinobha Bhave had asked JP in June 1974, 'How did the agitation begin?' And then he answered, 'With looting and arson. Do you have the capacity to check that?' Vinobha Bhave was very critical of the 'non-violent means of the movement as manifested in the coercive methods of dharna and gherao, often leading to violence' (Bipan Chandra, *In the Name of Democracy: JP Movement and the Emergency*, p. 52).

Vinobha Bhave was right. A mass movement, which had started from Gujarat with students of an engineering college protesting against the mess bill hike, spread to other parts of the country, especially Bihar, and was popularly called the JP movement. It was this movement that was credited for the defeat of Mrs Indira Gandhi, the third prime minister of India, in 1977. It was to quell the onslaught of the JP movement that Mrs Gandhi imposed Emergency in the country on 25 June 1975, which continued for nineteen months. The Congress at the time was too powerful and the Opposition too weak to stand against the Indira government and it was through the efforts of the JP movement that, as the Emergency was lifted, all the Opposition parties except the Left merged into one political party within two days. It was named Janata Party and managed to defeat the Congress government to form the first-ever non-Congress government at the Centre. This movement was led by JP, a veteran of the freedom struggle and a one-time colleague and admirer of Jawaharlal Nehru.

JP, like Anna Hazare, was not the initiator of the anti-corruption movement. It was primarily started by the students of Gujarat, but later political parties and leaders hijacked the movement for their political ends. In the LD Engineering College,

Gujarat, when the mess bill had been hiked by forty per cent in the month of December, the students could not control their anger, and on 20 December 1973, they set the college canteen on fire and attacked the rector's office. The students' agitation did not calm down, but intensified in the month of January and, when they gave a call for Ahmedabad bandh on 10 January 1974, the Opposition parties latched onto the issue and supported the movement. Large-scale violence ensued and the agitation spread to other cities of Gujarat, and finally a movement which began against a hike in the canteen mess bill was now demanding the resignation of the chief minister and the dissolution of the Gujarat assembly. The movement got a major boost on 9 February, when the central government, under tremendous pressure, asked Chimanbhai Patel, the then chief minister of Gujarat, to resign and suspended the assembly. The movement then demanded that the assembly be dissolved and fresh elections held. It was at this stage that JP visited Ahmedabad. As recounted by Bipan Chandra, 'Lauding the students, he said, he was inspired by the movement and it should be an example for the youth in other parts of the country.' Bipan Chandra quoted JP: 'For years I was groping to find a way out . . . then I saw students in Gujarat bring about a big political change . . . And I knew it was the way out' (Chandra, ibid., p. 36). JP termed this a youth revolution. He did not criticize the violence unleashed by the movement in the land of Gujarat where Gandhi was born. Bipan Chandra in his book quotes the foremost sociologist of Gujarat, Ghanshyam Shah: 'The riots continued in many cities and towns. Attempts were made to loot banks and cooperative societies. Stone-throwing incidents and looting and burning of public and private property continued on a large scale, violence became widespread. Terror prevailed in the state and nobody could oppose the agitators.' By a rough estimate, more than 100 people were killed and more than 3,000 were injured in the Gujarat movement alone. JP at that time was not part of the movement; he could have condemned the violence as non-

Gandhian. But JP did not do that. He was in fact getting inspired. I must mention here that JP had formally dissociated himself from active politics since 1953 and had been advocating non-violence and party-less democracy. He was contemptuous of the parliamentary system of governance. If he had been practising the Gandhian method, violence would not have attracted him, but it did.

When students from Bihar formally invited JP to lead the movement, he told them, 'I won't agree to be a leader in name only. I will take the advice of all . . . but the decisions will be mine and you will have to accept them' (Chandra, ibid., p. 44). When the Chhatra Sangharsha Samiti asked him to lead, he put forth two conditions: that it should be scrupulously non-violent and that it should not be restricted to Bihar (Ramachandra Guha, *India after Gandhi: The History of the World's Largest Democracy*, p. 479). But within six days of JP's taking over of the reins of the movement, eight people were killed in a police firing in Gaya, a district of Bihar, during the 'paralyse the government demonstration'. After a lull of two decades, the hero of the Quit India movement was enjoying public life and public attention. Although he had told students that the agitation would be non-violent, JP remained ambivalent all through, and his fellow protestors used violent means. JP was not like Gandhi who had withdrawn the agitation after the Chauri Chaura violence by his supporters. Bipan Chandra found an opportunistic streak in JP's personality, 'There are numerous examples of JP's irresponsible rhetoric and provocative statements, even while asserting that his movement was peaceful and non-violent. For one, his attitude towards violence was ambivalent.' Chandra quotes a newspaper report, 'He (JP) said that though he believed in non-violence, he would follow the violent method if any Opposition party was capable of toppling the government.'

Unlike the JP movement, the Anna movement in its genesis and in its DNA was non-violent to the core. Except for one instance where a few ruffians had beaten up unarmed policemen in a drunken stupor, there was no complaint from anywhere in India. No stone-throwing, no bus-burning or train-burning, not a glass was broken, no public property was looted, no attempt was made to block traffic or trains or disrupt schools, colleges or universities; and therefore, there was no police firing. Even the policemen at Ramlila Maidan were instructed to carry no arms. They were not even allowed lathis. No tear-gassing took place and nor was there any pitched battle with protesters. Anna had been very particular about the practice of non-violence. He would say, 'If we indulge in violence, the government will crush the movement as the government is very powerful and we can't hold out against it.' He openly condemned the incident of the policemen being beaten up and warned everyone present in Ramlila Maidan and elsewhere that it was not acceptable. I distinctly remember that when he had come out of Tihar Jail, he had instructed the people assembled there to not stop traffic as that would inconvenience the public – it is another matter that people did not mind being stuck in traffic jams that day, as several TV channels reported. On the other hand, my first recollection of a political movement was the repeated ringing of the school bells and me, then a little boy, running out of the class. This had been done forcibly at the behest of the agitationists. I remember another time walking through the bylanes of Mirzapur with my father, and suddenly seeing people running out of shops with things in their hands. Later, when I grew up, I realized this was looting during a political bandh. This was around the same time when the JP movement was at its peak and a small-town local leader Arun Kumar Dubey alias Muhatedwa was leading such an agitation. But here I have a different recollection: of auto drivers in Daryaganj ferrying people to the Ramlila Maidan for free. If violence had been the dominant feature of this movement, women, often with their kids would not have participated in such large numbers.

There is no denying the fact that anti-corruption was one of the pillars around which the building of the entire JP movement was built. Ramachandra Guha quoted JP: 'It is not for this I had fought for freedom.' He had now 'decided to fight corruption and misgovernment and black-marketing, profiteering and hoarding' (ibid.). Bipan Chandra writes (*India after Independence 1947–2000*, p. 250), 'the main justification of the JP movement was that it arose to end corruption in Indian life and politics.' Katherine Frank had no doubt in saying, 'Corruption thrived. That of course was not new. Both Nehru's and Shastri's governments were tainted by it, but it was only under Indira that corruption became endemic to the working of government at every level' (*Indira: The Life of Indira Nehru Gandhi*, p. 349). In his book, *An Eye to India*, David Selbourne quotes C. Subramaniam, the health minister under Indira Gandhi, 'The political system is becoming more corrupt, undisciplined, devoid of character and immoral.' Katherine Frank was more direct, 'Corruption also permeated Congress party fundraising, now directly controlled from the Prime Minister's office. Party contributions were collected in the untraceable and unaccountable form of cash which was delivered to Indira's offices at 1 Akbar Road. After Sanjay Gandhi began dabbling in politics, cash donations went directly to Indira's home at 1 Safdarjung Road.' The Maruti car scandal, Rustam Suhrab Nagarwal's death and Railway Minister L.N. Mishra's assassination were already issues of public debate. So the mood of the nation at that time was quite reminiscent of the post-2009 parliamentary elections, when one scam after another tarred the image of the Manmohan Singh government. Both movements had a very strong raison d'être, the difference was in their approach and scope. The JP movement had very soon acquired a political colour. In Gujarat, the mess bill movement ended with the resignation of Chief Minister Chimanbhai Patel, dissolution of the state assembly and, finally, assembly elections. In Bihar, the energy of the stir was directed towards seeking the resignation of the chief minister and dissolution of the state assembly. Mrs Gandhi did not oblige, as she had become wiser after the Gujarat episode.

Once JP was at the helm of the movement, he directed the movement towards unseating Mrs Gandhi. In his opinion, Indira Gandhi was the fountainhead of all types of problems in India and her removal was the only cure. And when the Allahabad High Court declared her election invalid due to illegal election practices, he became very desperate to get rid of her as prime minister. On 25 June 1975, at a rally in Delhi, JP declared that 'Mrs Gandhi had no legal, moral and constitutional right to govern and she should resign in four days.' He appealed to 'military, police and government servants to not take orders from a disqualified government'. This was a declaration of rebellion against a democratically elected government. In contrast, the Anna movement has been majorly focused on corruption and is looking for systemic changes to deal with corruption. Demand for the Jan Lokpal Bill is projected as one of the remedies along with electoral reforms. The Anna movement is yet to completely reveal its gameplan, but as of now it does not look ambitious enough to delve into politics, despite its anti-Congress campaign in Hissar and its threat that if the Manmohan Singh government does not bring the Jan Lokpal Bill in the winter session of the Parliament, Team Anna will campaign aggressively against the Congress in the forthcoming UP elections. It did not show any interest in demanding the resignation of any particular government. Despite the stubborn and obstructionist attitude of the Manmohan Singh government, Anna and his team did not demand the replacement of the government by some other political party or coalition because, in their opinion, 'no party can claim to be untouched by corruption'. Many a time, I heard Anna saying from the dais at the Ramlila Maidan, 'If one party is an MA in corruption, the other is a PhD in corruption. So there is no gain in regime change, system change is the final solution.'

I have no reason not to believe Team Anna when they say that they were not interested in playing at destabilizing the government. I know for a fact that, during the Ramlila Maidan *anshan*, an attempt was made to topple the government. There was a definite plan to use Anna and his team and their indefinite fast to organize a group of small political parties. A very senior member of the movement received hints that a good number of disgruntled members of the Congress Parliamentary Party were ready to cross over and support them if the plan for an alternative government succeeded. According to a very senior member of the movement, this proposal was mooted through a go-between whose name never came up in the media. This 'mystery man' suggested that he could talk to senior members of the BJP and wanted to be authorized by Anna to meet BJP leaders as a negotiator. When one senior member of the movement got wind of the conspiracy, he revolted and shouted at the 'mystery man'. The 'mystery man' was upset as he had apparently already spoken to the BJP leaders projecting himself as an informal mediator on behalf of the movement. My source in the movement confided to me that other senior members of the movement also strongly opposed this proposal and finally the move was scuttled. I investigated the matter further and this story was reconfirmed. I was told that a very senior member of one of the coalition partners of the UPA was also very active behind the scenes, along with a very senior member of an ideological affiliate of BJP. The game was simple. Team Anna had to openly show displeasure with the response of the Manmohan Singh government and appeal to other political parties to come together. Other political parties would then scramble to support their cause and then an attempt would be made to repeat the experiment of the National Front government of 1989, which was supported by the right and the left from the outside. It was not known how many smaller parties had shown an inclination to be a part of this and what basis there was to believe that a good chunk of Congressmen would defect. It all depended on a 'yes' from the BJP. But when two very senior members of the movement rejected such a plan, the conspiracy could not gain momentum and died prematurely; though I am not sure that this plot is still not continuing in some other form outside the ambit of the movement.

Like Team Anna, JP too used to say that 'he was not interested in changing governments and advised his followers not to indulge in toppling governments . . . but in the end the movement's mainstay became Indira Gandhi's removal from the office' (Bipan Chandra, *In the Name of Democracy*, p. 106). He even propagated the installation of the Janata sarkar at local levels. It is another matter that nobody took him seriously, except his die-hard followers. So it is difficult at the moment to say what shape the Anna movement will take in the future, except to trust Anna and his team. Arvind has declared, 'The movement will always remain outside of political parties and outside of electoral politics.' When he was asked if he would float a political party, he said, 'No, never' (*The Hindu*, 31 August 2011). Anna also declared on 13 September in Ralegan Siddhi in an interview to Rajdeep Sardesai for CNN-IBN, 'In politics people would like to get benefited by me but I won't join any political party.' He said that he believed in the Parliament, but that he did not trust parliamentarians. So if the MPs decide to oppose the Jan Lokpal Bill, he will campaign against them and see to it that they don't get elected again (CNN-IBN, 13 September 2011).

It is also true that the Anna movement had been labelled by the Congress and a few intellectuals as being sponsored by the RSS. Anna had vehemently denied this, but JP never had any problems in accepting open support from the RSS and its political affiliate, i.e., Jan Sangh. Bipan Chandra writes, 'JP did not oppose the RSS–Jan Sangh penetration and domination of the JP movement and, instead, gladly accepted their active participation, even though he had been all his life a staunch opponent of communalism and a sharp critic of RSS–Jan Sangh.' Bipan Chandra argues that JP was aware of the communal character of RSS. He quotes JP, 'Those who attempt to equate India with Hindus and Indian history with Hindu history . . . are in reality the enemies of Hinduism itself and of the Hindus.' JP was also reported to have demanded a ban on the RSS in a meeting of the National Integration Council in 1962. But during the movement when the Jana Sangh was labelled a fascist organization, JP had reacted very strongly. He said, 'If Jana Sangh is fascist, I am also fascist.' K.N. Govindacharya, ex-general secretary of the BJP and architect of the JP movement in Bihar told me, 'Due to his open defence of RSS and Jana Sangh, socialists and Sarvodaya leaders were very unhappy with him but they could not do anything because of his towering personality.' According to Govindacharya, JP used to say that they were following his policies, there was nothing to worry about. JP needed the RSS to overthrow Indira Gandhi, so he had no qualms utilizing the organizational energy of the RSS for the bigger goal. But Anna and his team had no such objective. They had no need for the overt support of the RSS. And when RSS Sarsanghchalak Mohan Bhagwat said that swayamsewaks of the RSS participated in the Anna movement in a big way, Arvind took offence and shot back that Bhagwat should stop taking credit for the anti-corruption campaign, rather he should take credit for Gujarat. Arvind, in fact, in an interview to *The Hindu* was even more categorical. He said, 'We have been very clear that no BJP leader or leader of any communal organization will share the stage with us. This is the decision of the core committee.'

At the moment, one can say that the Anna movement is political in nature as their goal is to correct the political system through a constitutionally approved method, but unlike the JP movement, they don't want to overtly align with any political party. Team Anna never allowed any political leader to use the anti-corruption platform in its political capacity. The JP movement not only used the organizational structure and leadership of political parties like the Congress (O), Bharatiya Lok Dal (BLD), Jana Sangha, Socialist Party and Akali Dal, but also convinced them to fight elections under one banner, the Janata Party, to defeat the Congress. This they did successfully in 1977. In this sense, the Anna movement is remarkable and bigger than the JP movement as it did not use any political party to spread its message nor did it take their help for mobilization. It had no organizational support to boost its muscle power. It was totally dependent on the NGO network and modern means of communications – TV, social media and the mobile network. It is easy for a political formation to hold a rally or spread its message because it has a ready-made support structure in terms of party cadre to hold the people's attention without such a structure for thirteen days was a miracle. Political parties are notorious for their ways of mobilizing people. Most of these rallies are dependent on borrowed crowds which are paid handsomely or compensated in kind to be there. Modern means of transportation are used to ferry people. Crores of rupees are spent to make such events successful.

But at the Ramlila Maidan and in other cities no such method was used to organize people against corruption. In the words of Yogendra Yadav 'people were self-organized' and came on their own, as in Anna they had a basic trust because of his moral authority. During the JP movement people had faith in JP, but they did not have the same trust in other leaders who were part of the movement. The JP movement also had a very limited footprint. South India and Maharashtra were almost untouched by the magic of JP. The Anna movement was equally strong in Bangalore, Chennai and Hyderabad. Mumbai was its hub after Delhi. Guwahati, Kolkata, Patna, Bhopal, Lucknow, Chandigarh, Jaipur, Bhubaneswar and Ahmedabad responded with the same vigour as Delhi and Mumbai. Candlelight processions in the north-eastern states made good visuals on TV channels regularly. In this context I will take the risk of inviting the wrath of JP supporters and say without hesitation that the Anna movement was bigger in terms of its reach and spontaneity. It was a revolt against the status quo of the political establishment and if I can borrow the words of Nicholas Kulish in the *New York Times*, 'Increasingly, citizens of all ages, but particularly the young, are rejecting conventional structures, such as parties and trade unions, in favour of a less hierarchical, more participatory system modelled in many ways on the culture of the web.'

It can be argued that the social base which is rejecting traditional structures of society and polity all over the world is the robust middle class. It was the same middle class that formed the backbone of the JP movement as well. According to Bipan Chandra, 'The hostility of the middle classes was a major political blow to the Congress and Mrs Gandhi . . . the urban lower middle class and middle classes whose living standards were being rapidly eroded because of soaring prices and shortage of goods, virtual freeze of salaries in July 1974 in a period of rampant inflation and growing unemployment among the educated youth were getting alienated from the ruling party.' (p. 26) He wrote, 'The activists of the JP movement or its mobilized segments comprised mainly students and youth coming from the traditional middle classes and newly emerging rich and middle peasants.' (p. 274) So I was not surprised when I saw the same growing middle class hungry and annoyed at Ramlila Maidan. Surprisingly, this middle class had mostly prospered under the economic liberalization of Manmohan Singh, but in the context of the unimaginable corruption and uncontrolled price rise it had turned against him. Their number is not insignificant. They are more than 250 million strong and growing at a very fast pace and sixty per cent of the India's population is below the age of twenty-five years, the most voluminous young crowd in the world. They are young, well educated, have newly earned money, and most of them are first-time owners of cars, big cars and other luxuries of life, including TV, refrigerators, ACs, computers, cellphones and a house or a flat for their families. Most of them have for the first time driven a Honda City, travelled by air, operated a bank account online, used an ATM, visited a mall and a multiplex, been to the McDonald's and KFC, tasted Chinese and Italian cuisine, worn Reebok and Adidas shoes and gone to a pub with their girlfriends. Money and opportunity have given them confidence and they are desperate to leave a mark; they want to be noticed, recognized. In your arrogance you may call them upstarts but they are powerful and you can't ignore them even if you want to, because they are all over, they are all-pervasive with their loud laughter and giggles and now they are in the mainstream. They are the new Indians. Some call them 'children of liberalization' or 'butterfly generation' or 'midnight's grandchildren' (*Outlook*, 31 October 2011).

I had seen them and interacted with them in abundance at the Ramlila Maidan and outside as well. They have a dream, they think differently, they don't suffer from complexes like their parents or grandparents do. They are not in awe of anybody. They are not scared of anybody and want to compete with the best in the world. They don't have any colonial hangover and they don't have low self-esteem like their parents either. They want to question the brightest, and don't want to take things for granted. They want their own space and respect others too. They are confident Indians.

My generation was not that privileged. Unlike them, we had too many inhibitions and restrictions. We had a life ordained and controlled by elders. Our fathers were not friends but heads of the families. We were lovers, not boyfriends. We had more don'ts than dos. We were not born with ACs and refrigerators, a very few had cars and phones and those were not flashy either. We did not have the luxury of instant communication with our loved ones. We did not send SMSs, instead we used to write letters, wait for hours for the trunk calls to talk to outstations. We did not grow up with pizzas and pastas; masala dosa was our fast food. Mineral water was a dream, tap water was a reality. We had no money for branded clothes; father would buy cloth in bulk for our shirts. We had canvass shoes to play cricket. But my generation is the privileged one, because we saw a nation changing fundamentally, and these are not normal generational changes but civilizational ones. India has transformed beyond recognition in the last two decades. Why then does the political class think that our value system will not change and why will the new generation keep quiet and remain politically neutral?

Even more so than during the JP movement, the middle class

is better equipped and better connected. Now they can easily relate to the frustration and angers of their brothers and sisters in Tunisia, Egypt, Libya, Saudi Arabia, Syria, Jordan and Yemen. 'They can connect with the protesting youth of the Middle East, and this new generation has formed a new kind of transnational identity, one that cannot be contained by ethnic, national or sectarian borders. It is an identity founded on young people's shared ambitions to free themselves from the grip of their corrupt and inept political, religious and economic institutions and thus to return their culture and society to the days of glory it achieved in Ibn Batuta's time' (*Time*, 1–8 August 2011). They are breaking with the past and reinventing themselves. This generation of India also gets excited when it reads that people in 800 cities of eighty countries are protesting simultaneously in the streets, on the lines of the Occupy Wall Street movement in New York, and is trying to understand the biggest crisis of capitalism in the last eight decades. It sympathizes with the protestors of Israel and also of Moscow when they converge on the streets for the largest demonstration in the country's history. They are also conscious of the fact that it is extremely difficult to raise one's voice in China despite its unprecedented growth. Therefore, they admire the courage of the unknown Chinese when they get to know that 180,000 mass incidents of protests had been reported in 2010, a huge increase from 74,000 in 2004. The new Indian is a global citizen with local moorings; therefore he hears his own voice when he listens to twenty-six-year-old Yonatan Levi of Israel saying, 'Political system has abandoned its citizens,' and also to twenty-seven-year-old Marta Solanas from Spain saying, 'The biggest crisis is the crisis of legitimacy; we don't think they are doing anything for us'(*Mint*, 29 September 2011). Anybody who had gone to the Ramlila Maidan knows that the young middle class in India was saying the same things; they felt that the Indian political class had abandoned them. Yet they had gone there because, like Li Chengpeng who contested elections to local People's Congress in China knowing full well that he would never win, they too wanted to tell the world, 'I am eager to tell everyone that we are all shareholders of our country' (*Time*, 31 October 2011). That is why I was running to the dais, because I knew any accident would grant the enemies of these voices an opportunity to turn their own defeat into victory and the voices of a new generation would be buried.

AFTER THE ANSHAN

When the Empire is pushed to a corner it does fight back, and fight back with a vengeance. Team Anna had been audacious in its attempts to bring the Empire to its knees and force it to enact the Lokpal Bill, and the Empire was trying to take it head on. From the very beginning of the movement, Team Anna was attacked and one after the other issues were raised to demonstrate to the world that they were not fit to fight corruption as they themselves were not clean. The whole country had been watching this game. This had happened after the fast at Jantar Mantar and continued after the Ramlila Maidan movement as well. So I was not surprised when Kiran Bedi was confronted with the alleged misappropriation of funds. Delhi police on 27 November 2011 registered a case against Kiran Bedi. According to a PTI report, 'A local court had ordered registration of an FIR against her after taking note of a complaint of a Delhi based lawyer Devinder Singh Chauhan who alleged that she looted various paramilitary forces and police organizations in the name of imparting free computer training under the banner of her NGOs.' The court order had come the day before and on the next day the police did their job. She had been booked under sections 420 (cheating), 406 (criminal breach of trust) and 120B (criminal conspiracy) of CrPC.

In his petition to the court, Mr Chauhan alleged, 'Kiran Bedi received a donation of over Rs 50 lakh from Microsoft for teaching, without charging, the children and families of personnel belonging to the BPRD, BSF, ITBP, CRPF and other police organizations under the *Meri Police* project; but instead of imparting free training or distributing free computers, Bedi in collusion with some unknown persons, cheated the Vedanta Foundation and made a plan to cheat the children of various paramilitary and civil police personnel. For the purpose she planned to collect Rs 20,000 per month per training centre (*Mail Today*, 27 November 2011).' The petition further alleged that, 'To siphon off the money for herself, she entered into a donation agreement with Vedanta Foundation. And according to the pact, Rs 6,000 of the total Rs 20,000 were to be paid by Vedanta to her two trusts on the false ground that Bedi had arranged for the land and electricity at the training centres for their day-to-day activity whereas both the facilities were arranged by the police organizations and Kiran had nothing to do with that' (*Mail Today*, 27 November 2011). The complaint went on to state that the facts clearly demonstrated that there was an on-going criminal conspiracy between Kiran Bedi and others to cheat the government of India and common and innocent persons by siphoning off funds from trusts for her personal gain and to dupe various tax authorities (*Mail Today*, 27 November 2011).

Before this episode, allegations had been levelled against Bedi that she had used her gallantry medal to get a discount of seventy-five per cent on Air India tickets and then submitted inflated invoices to claim the full fare from organisers who had invited her to their functions. It was also alleged that she had claimed business class fare even when she had travelled in the economy class. Such reports appeared in the third week of October. Bedi told newspersons that it was not for personal gain but that the money she thus saved went to the NGO that she ran (*Livemint*, 20 October 2011.).

Kiran Bedi is not new to controversy. She had always been in the news, even during her tenure as a senior police officer but the FIR controversy is by far the most damaging of them all.

And if proved guilty she can be behind bars for up to seven years. During the Anna agitation at the Ramlila Grounds she had infuriated parliamentarians by mocking them from the podium. MPs had been very upset with her conduct and had wanted her to apologize.

Those who know Kiran Bedi can vouch for the fact that she is not corrupt and if corruption had been in her DNA she would have amassed wealth when she was an IPS officer. And I can say with confidence that she had never been accused of corrupt practices when she was a government servant. But yes, she was always in the news due to her no-nonsense temperament and outspoken ways. If she had not rubbed people the wrong way, she would have retired as Commissioner of Police, Delhi, something which she wanted desperately. But she was denied that opportunity. So, despite the court orders, I would like to give her the benefit of doubt and at the risk of being misunderstood suggest that this was part of a conspiracy to malign her and through her the entire anti-corruption movement, of which Kiran Bedi is an integral part. Don't forget that she is an iconic figure for millions of women, particularly the aspirational young ones in the country. She has the distinction of being the first woman IPS officer in the country and had been very bold in her entire career and is famous for the jail reforms she initiated at Tihar. Kiran, unlike Arvind, is not very organized in her financial matters. So I won't be surprised if she lands up in jail one day and then is proved innocent later, but by then the trick would have worked for the Empire. It is too powerful and there are far too many who want to oblige the Empire for future gains. This was exactly what I was telling Arvind, Kiran, and Prashant when they visited our studio for a TV talk show in mid-November, before the FIR controversy became public. Kiran was very agitated. She was apprehensive that something of this nature might happen and complained about how a particular TV channel had been going to her NGO and was trying to do an undercover operation with the kids there with a view to 'prove' how she and her NGO had been exploiting them. Arvind too had complaints about a few TV channels especially one particular channel that he felt twisted his words and tried to prove that he had criticized Kiran for inflating her Air India bills. I argued with them that every journalist has a different perspective on things and not all of them were partners in the crime to malign them. I don't know if they got my message but the registration of FIR against Kiran Bedi immediately got them into an attack mode. They declared that Anna would launch an agitation from 27 December 2011 at the Ramlila Grounds and before that, to put pressure on the government and the parliamentary committee, would sit on dharna on 4 December at Rajghat and on 11 December at Jantar Mantar. At the outset it might have looked like a pressure tactic but it was a way of telling the government that the Team would not be a mute spectator if their members were targeted randomly.

If Team Anna had thought that once the Ramlila Maidan agitation was over they could sit back and relax, they were highly mistaken. They had no idea how things would unfold. They were busy in their own world, a dream world. Other than the Kiran mischief, problems had been brewing on other fronts since Anna went on the *anshan*. During the fast also, a very serious attempt was made by the powers that be to convince Anna that he had been used by his so–called followers and that in fact he was nothing but a hostage to their ambitions. In the beginning Anna ignored it but with the entry of the wily Vilas Rao Deshmukh, two times the chief minister of Maharashtra and, at the time of writing, a Union cabinet minister, the game had completely changed and acquired a different dimension. Deshmukh who, it was rumoured, felt sidelined with a minor portfolio, found in the Anna movement an opportunity to make himself relevant and to get back to Maharashtra as its CM again. He was the one who brokered the deal with Anna and got him to end his Ramlila Maidan *anshan*. There were also whispers that he wanted to convey to the party high command, i.e., Sonia Gandhi, that it was only he who could handle Anna. He is rumoured to have stressed the fact that Anna would continue to be a headache for the Congress and that Vilas Rao Deshmukh needed to be the Maharashtra CM to manage Anna. Many senior Congressmen were also party to his machinations.

I was told in confidence by many senior Congressmen and journalists from Maharashtra that post the Ramlila *anshan*, with the exception of a few, all of Anna's staff members at his village had been swayed by a very senior Maharashtra politician and that they would do what they were asked to do by their political master. The game was to cut Anna off from his team in Delhi and control and manipulate him. Then, there was also the Marathi versus non-Marathi angle. There was a feeling among sections of the intelligentsia in Maharashtra that when Anna became a national icon, Marathis had no role to play and north Indians were controlling him. So once Anna went back to Ralegan Siddhi, attempts were made to poison his ears against Arvind, Kiran, Prashant and Manish. And the time-tested trick used was to involve local newspapers in this conspiracy and get two kinds of reports printed regularly – how all four had become too ambitious and how they were using Anna for their personal goals, and that all of them were not clean. Controversies like how Arvind had not paid Rs 9.27 lakh due from him to the income tax department, the allegation by Swami Agnivesh on 22 October 2011 that Rs 80 lakh donated by the public during the Ramlila Grounds agitation had been diverted to Arvind's Trust, and Kiran's inflated airfare bills were grossly exaggerated and magnified before Anna. Slowly, the conspiracy started showing results. Suddenly from nowhere a blogger appeared on the scene and he became Anna's mouthpiece. When Team Anna in Delhi was facing its worst crisis and personal attacks, Anna was on a *maunvrat* (vow of silence) from 17 October 2011 and the blogger was articulating Anna's mind. The Team was highly confused and demoralized. I remember a chance meeting I had with Arvind and Manish in the last week of October. This was the time when two members of Team Anna's core committee, waterman Rajendra Singh and P.V. Rajgopal of Ekta Parishad, had resigned and had attacked them; Rajendra Singh was especially very bitter. Later in interviews to the press he minced no words. He said, 'There is no place for decent people in Team Anna. There is no inner democracy there . . . I quit the group because I could not have been party to the kind of power brokering they did in the Hissar by-elections'. He was particularly harsh on Arvind. He said, 'Kejriwal did the maximum damage to the movement' (*The Hindu*, 27 October).

On 13 October 2011, assembly by-election was to be held in Hissar, Haryana. Team Anna had decided to campaign against the Congress candidate, arguing that since the Congress was in power it could, if it wanted, bring a strong Lokpal Bill but wasn't keen to do so and therefore Team Anna wanted to put pressure on the party by ensuring its defeat in the by-election. Arvind and Manish held more than half a dozen meetings in Hissar. They had advised voters not to vote for the Congress candidate. This was construed as a backdoor entry into politics. This was also severely criticized as candidates who were seen to be benefiting out of this campaign were as corrupt as the Congress candidate. So the question was that if Anna was fighting corruption, then how could he help those who were seen to be corrupt. How could he differentiate between two corrupt persons?

It was true that Team Anna's move to campaign in Hissar against the Congress candidate was not received well by a section of the media or even some of Anna's supporters. Rajendra Singh was not the only one who disagreed with this step. Even I was not convinced with Team Anna's logic. This was a dangerous game. The fundamental reason for the success of the movement was the fact that it was equally scathing in its criticism of all the political parties. It spared none. In the eyes of the public all the politicians are the same and they don't expect any good from them. So how could Team Anna justify targeting the Congress as a pressure tactic because it was only the Congress who was capable of bringing and enacting a strong Lokpal Bill? The Team had also planned to repeat the same exercise during the UP elections if their demand for a strong Lokpal was not met in the winter session of the Parliament. In fact, members of Team Anna had already started moving in the hinterlands of UP even before Prime Minister Manmohan Singh wrote a letter to Anna on 10 October promising a strong Lokpal Bill in the winter session. Mission UP, however, was put on hold even as the present looked very bleak.

While talking to them during that chance meeting, I could sense that Arvind and Manish were extremely worried about themselves and also about the movement. Arvind told me that attacks were so vicious that for days they had no idea what was happening to them and what was the way out. They were plagued by self-doubt. They were badly shaken. When they had launched the movement, they had dreams and now just two months after the Ramlila *anshan* they had only nightmares. They were drained to the core. I could see long shadows of disappointments on their face. They were not the same energetic young men with big ideas and idealism. Their biggest worry was that in this time of crisis they did not know if their leader was with them and trusted them or not. According to them, at times it took them days to talk to Anna. Whenever they contacted Anna for any advice or suggestions or clarity they were simply told by Anna's staff that he was busy and would call them later and these calls never came. They had no other way of contacting Anna as he did not carry a cell phone. Arvind and his other colleagues were convinced that it was not the same Anna they knew, something was amiss; doubts were getting stronger and confidence was weakening. They needed their leader and he was not there.

Manish and Prashant were sent to talk to Anna. He was on *maunvrat* then. There they found themselves amongst strangers. Anna handed over a copy of a survey which was said to have been done in the cyber world and had attracted 54 lakh hits. This was a phenomenal number, unheard of, but surprisingly nobody seemed to know about such a survey. At a time when each and every action of Anna and his Team was under the scanner, a survey of such magnitude was done and did not attract anybody's attention! At first, the duo did not realize the importance of the survey but when they read it carefully they did not know how to react. The survey allegedly reflected the public opinion about Anna and each of his team members. There were positive things about Anna and only negative comments about members – Arvind, Kiran, Prashant and Manish. Apparently Anna had been briefed that this survey had been done and it was found that the public loved him but hated his team members who lived in Delhi. They had all the reasons to believe that it was part of a conspiracy to finish them off and hijack the movement which they built with their blood and sweat.

It so happened that during the last week of October 2011, Anna's blogger appeared on IBN7 and dropped the bombshell that Anna was going to reconstitute the core committee and would admit a few retired army men and judges. This was the time that Team Anna in Delhi was getting sick and tired of allegations and desertions one after the other. The Team was slowly coming to the conclusion that it was better to dissolve the core committee to avoid further embarrassment and to write to Anna that he was their leader and they were his soldiers and would do whatever job he assigned to them. This was also the time when the Team was trying to get over the shock of the beating meted out to Prashant Bhushan, the legal brain of the movement. Prashant was beaten up in his chamber on 12 October by a few lunatics who had problems with his statement on Kashmir. A few days ago, on the issue of Kashmir, Prashant had stated in Varanasi that a referendum should take place and if the people so desire Kashmir should be freed. (*Times of India*, web site, 12 October 2011, 4 p.m.). In an earlier interview Prashant had reportedly said that the 'Kashmiri people should be given Azadi if they don't want to live with India.' His statements infuriated members of Bhagat Singh

Kranti Sena who sought an appointment with him ostensibly for some legal consultations, entered his chamber and unleashed their fury on him. He was not seriously injured but it shocked the whole nation. The idea of individual freedom and freedom of speech was at stake. Within a few days innocent sympathizers of the Anna movement were also thrashed in the presence of police at Patiala House courts. During this time Arvind and his team members were touring UP for a mass contact and everywhere they were asked by angry mobs what their stand was on Prashant's statement on Kashmir.

Anna's anti-corruption movement became synonymous with the new found nationalism of many Indians. It was no coincidence that patriotic songs and the national tricolour were in vogue with Anna supporters in and outside Ramlila Grounds and in the interiors of small towns. Prashant Bhushan's stand on Kashmir had pitted nationalism against individual freedom. Prashant was not willing to apologize. He preferred to be away from the movement than sacrifice his principle. The movement needed both nationalism and Prashant. But traditional supporters were not willing to listen to Prashant or for that matter Arvind. During the UP tour, wherever Arvind. Manish, Kumar Vishwas and Kiran Bedi went they faced angry reactions and people wanted them to clarify the movement's stand on Kashmir. The think-tank was of the opinion that Prashant's statement was damaging the movement and very soon a solution had to be found to wriggle out of this crisis. This was a bigger challenge than the allegations against Arvind and Kiran. This was a direct attack on the core of the ideology of the movement. This would in the long run unsettle the social base of the anti-corruption campaign. But Prashant was equally valuable and a middle path had to be found. A few members were of the opinion that the core committee should be dissolved and all the powers should be given to Anna. This would have saved them from the embarrassment of throwing out Prashant and also lessen the chances of any further resignation from the likes of Rajendra Singh and targeted attacks on Team Members as nobody would then be a member; everybody would be a supporter like rest of the population. It was in this context that Kumar Vishwas wrote an open letter to Anna on 28 October demanding that the core committee should be dissolved.

In the core committee meeting at Kaushambi, Ghaziabad, on 29 October 2011, there was a possibility of this proposal being adopted but the night before the think-tank received information from Ralegan Siddhi which was very disturbing. A coup d'état of sorts was a real possibility. They were told by their well-wishers that Anna had been completely brainwashed and he had little faith in them and there was the real possibility of them being marginalized in the newly constituted core committee. If the present committee was dissolved, decision-making powers would pass from them to those who had nothing to do with the movement. This seemed to be to the liking of the government as well. Most unexpectedly the proposal for the dissolution of the committee was shelved at the last minute and Kumar's letter was declared as his personal opinion. The committee tried to send out a very strong signal that in the hour of serious crisis they were united and were willing to fight together. Prashant, Arvind and Kiran went to Ralegan Siddhi to brief Anna about the outcome of the meeting. Here it must be stated that Anna had been defending Arvind and Kiran and had been saying that a malicious campaign was on to discredit them and this was an attempt to weaken the movement. About Prashant's statement on Kashmir, he had been very forthright. The *India Today* web site on 14 October 2011, at 06.20 a.m. reported Anna saying, 'Prashant's statement is not right and it is his personal opinion, and not of the movement. And in my view Kashmir is an integral part of India and I am ready to sacrifice my life anytime for Kashmir as it belongs to India and will remain with India.'

So, in the month of October, a trust deficit and serious communication gap between the general and his army could easily be felt. I cannot forget those demoralized faces when I met them three days before the core committee meet. They were very apprehensive and I overheard one very senior member saying, 'Everything is over'. They decided to talk straight with Anna. They wrote two letters. One was signed by Arvind, Kiran, Prashant and Shanti Bhushan stating that since Anna no longer had trust in them they were willing to quit and the other was written by Arvind. He had written an emotional letter telling Anna how much respect and love he had for him, and that for him Anna was greater than his father but of late he had felt that Anna had developed some kind of distrust towards him. He also explained in the letter, in the context of the allegations of financial mismanagement, that he had been an income-tax commissioner who was respected by his peers in the department for his honesty and if Anna felt that Arvind needed to further prove himself he would not leave any stone unturned to live up to Anna's expectations.

Manish was given the responsibility of handing over the letters to Anna. Anna was to come to Delhi on 3 November 2011 to attend a meeting with the standing committee of Parliament on law and justice for the Lokpal Bill. Manish was to accompany him. Manish went to Ralegan Siddhi and met him and gave him both the letters. Anna saw them and asked a few things in writing. He had still not broken his *maunvrat*. He was expected to do that in Delhi. Those were testing times. Anna came to Delhi and all of them met Anna. They discussed issues threadbare, clarified misgivings, apprehensions and doubts and decided to work together as one again. Anna made his intentions clear when he was asked by reporters if he was disbanding the team as was hinted at by his blogger. He said, 'I have not told him anything. If he has written anything like that then I will take action.' But he also confessed to the press that he had developed some doubts when he heard the allegations of corruption against Arvind and Kiran during his stay in Ralegan Siddhi but he hastened to clarify that his doubts have been cleared after talking to them and that he had full faith in his team. With this statement Anna had made it clear as to which side he was on and Team Anna finally felt relieved after weeks of nervousness and confusion. The coup was averted and the conspiracy thwarted and the Empire disappointed. I did not have the time and opportunity to check as to who were the real brains behind this attempted coup, and what they must be feeling now. But yes, the blogger was still crying hoarse and was threatening that he would expose the 'gang of four' sometime in the future.

So with the latest FIR controversy about Kiran Bedi, one had reasons to believe that Team Anna had again been targeted and Kiran being the most vulnerable may have to suffer if she had done something wrong. But if history is anything to go by, who knows it may turn out to be another St Kitts for the Congress. On 20 August 1989, *Arab Times* had published a report that Janata Dal leader and the main anti-Bofors crusader V.P. Singh was a beneficiary of a secret bank account with deposits amounting to $21 million in the Caribbean Island of St. Kitts, which ultimately turned out to be false and those who had allegedly conspired, including former Prime Minister Narasimha Rao, had to bear the brunt of law and V.P. Singh went on to become the Prime Minister. It's a different matter that he had to resign within a few months due to the withdrawal of support to the government by the BJP. But that is a different story. So one can say that if in the 1980s V.P. Singh had been the target, then in 2011 it is Team Anna. Who says times have changed? Only years have gone by.

But let me also take the liberty to state that whether the Empire likes it or not, the movement had forced the Empire to change itself and these changes are quite visible. The fundamental change is the perception that corruption is evil which was earlier considered an accepted fact of life. Efficiency with corruption was the motto. In the last one year, however, the anti-corruption campaign has been blamed for administrative paralysis, as ministers and top bureaucrats have been scared to take decisions, lest they land up in jail. Of course, to that I can only say that an honest person has nothing to fear except one's own conscience.

Secondly, despite so much noise and opposition against the Lokpal, the Uttarakhand government has passed a very strong Lokayukta Act on the lines of Jan Lok Pal bill to fight corruption. The Chief Minister of Uttarakhand, Mr B.C. Khanduri, in an interview told me that he was not scared of a parallel structure as he is honest and others should also not worry about a strong Lokpal or Lokayukta. The Bihar government too has moved fast and got a Lokayukta Bill passed. Though Team Anna was not happy with the Bihar Bill, there was a sense of satisfaction in that at least some state governments have woken up to the anti-corruption movement's demand. There are many states including Delhi which have passed laws for setting up Citizens' Charters in their states and are carefully monitoring their functioning. So things are looking bright and I would like to humbly submit that those thirteen days changed India for the better, whether one admits it or not. The New India has arrived and one should celebrate that.

EPILOGUE

He was a frail-looking person whom nobody seemed to know. He was 'painted' white from top to bottom. His hair was white; he was wearing white kurta-pajama and a white sweater. And the only body part which was visible was his face. Throughout the day nobody noticed him but on 29 December just before 11 p.m. he was making a speech in the Rajya Sabha. He was vehemently critical of the Lokpal Bill which was to be put to vote to become law. The chairman of the house, Mr Hamid Ansari, wanted to stop him from continuing to speak as his time was up but this man paid no heed. He was getting very emotional. He was trying to underline the point that he was an honest man but he was scared of the Lokpal Bill as any MP could be put behind bars for corruption even seven years after retiring from the Rajya Sabha. The chair somehow managed to stop him. Finally, the minister of state in the prime minister's office, Mr V. Narayanasami, stood up to reply on behalf of the government and wind up the entire debate which had been going on for more than eleven hours. As Mr Narayanasami was reading from a paper, that frail-looking 'white' man walked up to him, snatched the copy of the Lokpal Bill from him and tried to tear it up. Another minister, Ashwini Kumar, did intervene but in vain. That gentleman had already torn the copy of the bill and had thrown it in the well of the house. Suddenly, all the TV channels scrambled to capture that moment, and that man's picture was all over TV. The whole world came to know his name. He was Rajneeti Prasad, a member of the Rashtriya Janata Dal.

It's not the first time that a copy of a bill was snatched from a minister and torn in the house. It had happened earlier and may also happen in the future. But that day it came as a shock to the majority of the viewers. The whole nation was watching the debate in the Parliament. Excitement was running high. Everybody was wondering if the bill would get passed in the Rajya Sabha. If passed by the Rajya Sabha, the Lokpal Bill, with the assent of the President, would finally become law after forty-four years. The Lokpal Bill had already been passed in the Lok Sabha on 27 December 2011 with a few amendments. However the government failed to give the Lokpal a constitutional status as had been desired by Congress general secretary Rahul Gandhi. It did not have the requisite numbers. It was a major embarrassment for the Manmohan Singh government and the Opposition immediately demanded the resignation of the government. Manmohan Singh said that such things did happen in politics. Finance Minister Pranab Mukherji was very upset at the turn of events. He described this as a sad day for democracy. But the government could still say that they had fulfilled their promise to Anna and his team and had got the bill passed in the Lok Sabha. In this context, 29 December was an important day in India's parliamentary democracy. Everything went smoothly throughout the day. But with Rajneeti Prasad the complexion of the house changed dramatically. The Opposition smelt a conspiracy. It was past 11 p.m. and Opposition members wanted to know when voting would take place and if the house would sit beyond midnight. The chair was in no position to give a straight answer. Members became restless, there was chaos and finally around 11.30 p.m. the house was adjourned for 15 minutes. As it resumed again around 11.45 p.m. chaos ensued yet again. The Opposition stuck to its demand wanting to know if voting would take place. The Parliamentary Affairs Minister, Pawan Kumar Bansal, stood up to reply. He said that 'the government did not want to pass a hodgepodge legislation and needed time to sift through amendments' (*The Times of India*, 30 December 2011). There were in all 187 amendments pressed by the Opposition and Congress allies. Despite the leader of the Opposition Arun Jaitley and other members saying that they were willing to sit through the night, Chairman Ansari rose to address the house: 'An unprecedented situation has arisen. There seems to be a desire to outshout each other. It is a total impasse. Proceedings cannot be conducted in this noise. There is no option . . . most reluctantly . . . (but adjourn the house sine die)' (*The Times of India*, 30 December 2011).

So voting did not take place. It was later announced that the government would bring the bill again during the budget session and would try to pass with appropriate amendments. But the Opposition was furious. It immediately alleged that the whole episode had been well rehearsed and nicely choreographed at the behest of the government. The government did not have the required numbers to pass the bill. It was in a minority. And unfortunately for the government, the Trinamool Congress, its ally, developed cold feet and decided not to support the bill in the Rajya Sabha. It was rather strange. Two days earlier it had voted in favour of the Lokpal Bill in the Lok Sabha. The government tried its best to convince the Trinamool Congress but to no avail. It had a problem with the Lokayukta chapter in the Lokpal Bill. The Trinamool Congress wanted to scrap this part of the bill as they thought it was an infringement of the states' rights to legislate an anti-graft institution. Surprisingly, the Trinamool Congress did not notice this in the Lok Sabha and had gone along with the majority opinion and had supported the bill. Along with the Trinamool Congress, the Samajwadi Party (SP), the Rashtriya Janata Dal (RJD) and the Bahujan Samaj Party (BSP) also had problems with the bill. The three of them had not participated in the voting in the Lok Sabha but in the Rajya Sabha they insisted on opposing the bill. So with the non-cooperation of these four parties the government knew in advance the fate of the bill. The government's trouble-shooters tried the whole day to persuade its allies and win them over but by the evening it was clear that it would be impossible to get a majority of votes for the bill. By late evening the whispers in the corridors of power became very strong that the bill would not pass muster and voting would not take place. In the central hall of the Parliament it was also strongly rumoured that the government, with the help of a few friendly parties, would create a situation in which voting would be difficult. A few news channels ran this sabotage story much before it actually happened. The Opposition therefore had strong reasons to believe that the whole episode was pre-planned and executed to perfection and that Rajneeti Prasad was just a player in the drama.

Team Anna was also convinced that the government was never interested in bringing the Lokpal Bill but the people's pressure had got them going. Even Law and Justice Minister Salman Khurshid had obliquely referred to this basic mistrust. He wrote in the *Times of India* on 27 December 2011, 'A premise on which some people have criticised the bill is basic mistrust of government . . . the obsessive suspicion of elected representatives is the beginning of the end of democracy and freedom.' After the Jantar Mantar movement a very intense debate had engulfed the country about the need for and the nature of the Lokpal. In the charged atmosphere, Team Anna and its supporters were of the opinion that corruption could not be eradicated without a strong Lokpal whereas another section which included the government was of the firm view that a Lokpal was needed but it should not be another administrative colossus which would disturb the equilibrium of democracy. So after a lot of deliberation three drafts of the Lokpal Bill had so far seen the light of the day. The first draft was the result of the nine sittings of the joint drafting committee, which was immediately rejected by the Team Anna. According to Prashant Bhushan, 'This government bill fell short of what was required to even set up an independent and comprehensive anti-corruption investigative organisation' (*The Hindu*, 2 January 2012). As a mark of protest, Anna sat on an indefinite hunger strike at the Ramlila grounds in the month of August for thirteen days and forced the government to adopt the three minimal demands – all government servants and the Citizen's Charter should be brought under the Lokpal and, within Lokpal, Lokayuktas must be established in the states – by a unanimous 'sense of the house' resolution. The government bill was referred to the standing committee of the Parliament which gave its report in the month of December with 17 dissenting notes. Team Anna was furious with the draft report. According to Prashant Bhushan, the legal brain of the movement, the standing committee bill was even inferior to the earlier government bill. The earlier bill had provided its own anti-corruption investigative body to the Lokpal which was removed by the standing committee.

Towards the end of the winter session of the Parliament, on the basis of the standing committee report, a new Lokpal Bill was introduced in the Parliament. This bill was drafted in the light of the three guiding principles. In the words of the Salman Khurshid: 'No single institution can overcome corruption, the need for the separation of powers calls for keeping investigation, prosecution and adjudication at arm's length and finally a Lokpal can't be a policeman and must be a quasi-judicial body that can't delegate its powers' (*The Times of India*, 27 December 2011). In this bill, the prime minister was kept under the purview of the Lokpal with certain conditions. The judiciary was kept out; all government servants – groups A, B and C – were covered, except group C which was to be held accountable to the Lokpal through the CVC, and Lokayuktas were to be set up in the states. The Citizen's Charter was not part of the bill as it was to be brought under a separate bill. Team Anna had serious problems with this bill. In their opinion this was a toothless structure which had no powers to nail corrupt officials and ministers as it did not have investigative powers and was a government-appointed body. Prashant Bhushan wrote in *The Hindu* (2 January 2012) that 'in order to make the Lokpal workable, selection and removal procedure should be made independent of the government; CBI should be brought under the Lokpal's administrative control or Lokpal should have its own investigative body; all government servants should be brought under the Lokpal's investigative ambit and the procedure for investigation should be in line with the normal criminal investigation procedure.'

This bill was also severely criticized by BJP and other Opposition parties. The BJP had serious objections to the provision of reservation for minorities – which Congress dubbed as representation, not reservation – in the appointment of Lokpal. Secondly, the BJP felt that creation of Lokayuktas for the states under the same Lokpal, in the words of chief spokesperson of the party, Ravi Shankar Prasad, 'was a serious assault on the principles of federalism' (*The Times of India*, 27 December 2011). During the debate in Parliament, BJP's leaders of the Opposition in the Lok Sabha and Rajya Sabha, Sushma Swaraj and Arun Jaitley, very strongly put forth their views on these lines and called the bill 'constitutionally vulnerable' and the Lokpal 'ineffective' in the absence of an independent investigative agency. Despite the 'pessimism' of the Team Anna and 'obduracy' of the Opposition parties Salman Khurshid argued, 'We are persuaded, it is an idea whose time has come and let us not hesitate to take the first step just because it does not seem to be a giant leap' (*The Times of India*, 27 December 2011). But the incident in the Rajya Sabha on 29 December was indicative of the fact that Salman's words fell on deaf ears either by design or by conviction.

This incident proved a boon in disguise for Team Anna. The day before, Team Anna had had to pack up from the Mumbai MMRDA grounds. They had initially planned a three-day *anshan*, followed by three days of *Jail Bharo Andolan* (Fill the jails agitation). They were to sit on dharna from 27 to 29 December and from 30 December 2011 to 1 January 2012 they were to court arrest and go to jail to protest the government's Lokpal Bill which they argued was too weak and ineffective to fight corruption. But to their utter dismay, the crowds which till then were the hallmark of their agitation were missing from the grounds. It was dubbed a flop show. Anna was also not well. Three days before the *anshan* he had had fever and had not eaten, still he sat on dharna. On the evening of 27 December his temperature and blood pressure shot up to alarming levels. By 10 p.m. on the same day his temperature touched 102 and blood pressure was 170/104. The Team was worried. It requested Anna to end his *anshan* and depute somebody else in his place but he did not listen. Doctors were worried too as Anna had not eaten anything for the past four days and, without food, doctors could not recommend any antibiotic medicines. Anna refused to eat. The next day, doctors warned that if Anna continued with his stubbornness it might affect his kidneys. The Team finally convinced him to end his *anshan*. Anna announced from the podium late on 28 December that he was suspending all agitation including the *Jail Bharo Andolan*. Undoubtedly, the main reason was Anna's health but it could also be construed that they were looking for a face saver, particularly since the crowds were missing. Anna's ill-health, therefore, came as a godsend.

This was their first agitation in Mumbai. Before this, Anna and his team had had two at Jantar Mantar, one at the Rajghat and one at the Ramlila grounds in Delhi and all of them were overwhelmingly successful, having attracted unprecedented crowds especially at the Ramlila grounds. Though the team blamed bad management by the local Mumbai team and wrong choice of MMRDA as the venue for the agitation for the failure to attract the crowds, somewhere they also must have known that something was amiss. The youth was missing as also the spontaneity and enthusiasm. The global 'Protester' who became the person of the year for *Time* magazine and whom it defined 'as maker of history' (*Time*, 26 December 2011) was absent in Mumbai. It was a matter of great concern for the Team. In my opinion three things went wrong. First, it was bad timing. On those very days the Parliament was discussing the Lokpal Bill. All eyes were glued to the TV screens. Since 5 April 2011,

Team Anna had been demanding a Lokpal Bill from the government and now when the bill had reached the Parliament, the famed 'protester' wanted to wait for a minute and test the honesty of the government. This was the first opportunity when the initiative was not with Anna but with the government. And Anna and his team too should have waited for the outcome of the parliamentary proceedings but they did not.

Second, Team Anna's campaign in the month of December became shriller and shriller and also political. They seemed to be in a great hurry and were not willing to wait. In the public's eye they were putting undue pressure on the Parliament and its institutions. On 30 November 2011, Anna had declared at a press conference at Ralegan Siddhi that he would wait till 23 December and if the Lokpal did not become a reality, he would launch an agitation from 27 December. On 1 December 2011, the standing committee of the Parliament in an emergency meeting overturned its day-old decision of keeping Group C and D government servants under the Lokpal and instead decided to put them directly under the chief vigilance commissioner's office. Anna responded with vengeance. He thundered, 'This was done at the behest of Rahul Gandhi' (9 p.m. bulletin of IBN7, 2 December 2011). Anna did not stop here. In the days to follow, his attack on Rahul Gandhi became more vitriolic. He said, 'It appears Rahul does not want to fight corruption and a man with such thinking will be dangerous as prime minister.' Anna's team thought that in the context of the impending Uttar Pradesh assembly elections, attacking Rahul Gandhi would unsettle the Congress and its strategists. As a matter of fact, it did. The government hastened the process and declared that the Lokpal Bill would be brought in the winter session of the Parliament and if need be the session would also be extended. But sometimes, in our strategic thinking we tend to ignore the perception of the people. From the beginning Rahul deliberately avoided being closely associated with the Lokpal issue except for his speech on 26 August when he advocated a constitutional status for the Lokpal. Though Rahul had been heckled for his speech by the crowd on the Ramlila grounds, he was never the principal villain in the government versus Team Anna game. So to link Rahul with the decision of the standing committee did not go down well with the people. Besides, Rahul is too young a person for Anna to take on. It did not behove his stature to attack somebody who was like a child to him. The Team also forgot that on 11 December, when it had provided its platform to Opposition leaders to articulate their stand on the Lokpal (the Congress party did not accept Team Anna's invitation to be there and clarify its stand on the Lokpal), it broke the very premise of its movement that it was an anti-political platform where traditional politicians were not welcome as they did not carry the confidence of the people whom they claimed to represent. With the second *anshan* at Jantar Mantar the Anna Movement tried to change flavour and became political by trying to buy respectability for the movement from the same individuals that it had rejected earlier.

Third, the Anna movement had lost its novelty factor. When he sat on a dharna at Jantar Mantar in the month of April, the world had looked at him with nostalgia: he was perceived both as Gandhi and JP. He was non-violent in his method but militant in his attitude. Here was a man who was talking about non-violence in a violent world, in the age of Al Qaida he was resorting to Satyagraha. In a complex world his simplicity caught the imagination of the people. So in the month of August when he refused to come out of Tihar Jail, the common man could not believe that there could be a leader like him who was not scared. Over a period of time, however, his familiar rhetoric and regularity of appearance on television killed the sense of novelty about him. Let's not forget that we live in the age of television and ours is a neo-consumerist society which, every minute, redefines itself. Anna at the beginning of the 2011 was a new product but by the end of the year, consumer fatigue was setting in and he needed to reinvent himself, as also the movement, to make him and the movement durable for the long term.

Mumbai's 'flop show' got them thinking hard and introspecting. Team Anna was vertically divided on the issue of campaigning against the Congress in the Uttar Pradesh assembly elections. Finally, after eight hours of a marathon meeting in Ghaziabad on 9 January 2012, the Team decided to intervene in the elections but not to target any political party. This was an indication that Team Anna would not repeat the mistake of Hissar by-election where they campaigned against the Congress candidate. The Congress must have heaved a sigh of relief. But for the movement this was a landmark decision and also indicative of great churning within the movement. It was also indicative of the fact that the movement was at the crossroads and the journey from this point needed new energy and a fresh approach to consolidate the gains and to move forward for the future Yatra. Can Anna and his Team do it, is the challenge.

ACKNOWLEDGEMENTS

It was 4.30 in the morning of 28 August 2011. I had woken up for no apparent reason. Anna had broken his fast during the day and the agitation at Ramlila Grounds was over. I was very tired and had slept quite late. So I was a little surprised about waking up so early in the morning. I was thinking about the anti-corruption movement and suddenly it struck me that I could write a book about my experiences. I had never written anything resembling a book except for my M.Phil dissertation. Normally, I would have taken time to think and decide but at that early hour I instantly made up my mind to go ahead. I woke up my wife and told her. I was expecting her to be irritated as this was no time to talk about it but to my surprise Maneesha immediately liked the idea and promised to help me out. She was a great help and took time out to painstakingly read my manuscript many times and gave valuable suggestions that have made the book better.

Dr Pushpesh Pant, Professor in JNU, was equally excited about the idea when I discussed the concept with him. He also went through the manuscript. He helped me concretize my thoughts. He has been a pillar of strength throughout my career, a pillar around which my identity and individuality gained confidence and took shape.

Rajdeep Sardesai, my Editor-in-chief, was more excited than I was when I told him about my plan. No boss could have been more indulgent than he has been and he readily granted me leave for one month without which it would have been next to impossible to finish this book in such a short time.

My friends and colleagues in IBN7 have been a great support throughout and bore my absence without any fuss. I am especially indebted to Prabhanjan Verma and Vikrant Yadav with whom I discussed the minutest details and every nuance of the movement as they were the ones who covered the Anna movement from day one and spent more than 14–15 hours every day in the field in the most trying circumstances. Kiran Deep, Anurag Singh, Anant Vijay, Neeraj Gupta, Sukesh Ranjan, Ashutosh Singh, Brij Duggal, Mausami Singh and Sakshi Khanna, my colleagues in the newsroom, helped me in their own way. Sanjay Sinha, research head of IBN7, readily agreed to dig out material for my research. Sanjeev Paliwal, M.K. Jha and Prabal Pratap Singh read the initial few chapters and gave me the confidence that I was on the right track. Puneet Shukla helped me with phone numbers of those that I needed to get in touch with.

There are many people and individuals who were part of Team Anna who went out of their way to discuss things and who provided insights and clarified many doubts. Similarly, there were many senior leaders in the Congress and other political parties and ministers in the UPA government who were very patient with me when I demanded their time for the book. Many of them were gracious enough to request not to be quoted which I duly obliged though I would have preferred them to be on record but then the flow of information would have been a casualty. Without their support this book would not have been possible.

Professor Ashis Nandy was very gracious in accepting to write the foreword.

Professor Yogendra Yadav didn't take a minute to agree to write the introduction for the book at a very short notice.

Karthika, at HarperCollins, was most supportive and helpful all along the way.

I just want to say a BIG THANK YOU to all of them and apologize to anyone whose name I may have missed out. And also thanks to Mogu and Chhotu who didn't disturb me with their barking even once while I was writing.